CRIME AND COMMUNITY IN CICERONIAN ROME

CRIME AND COMMUNITY IN CICERONIAN ROME

by Andrew M. Riggsby

University of Texas Press ◆ Austin

Requests for permission to reproduce material from this work should be sent to
Permissions, University of Texas Press, P.O. Box 7819, Austin, TX 78713-7819.

⊗ The paper used in this book meets the minimum requirements of
ANSI/NISO Z39.48-1992 (R1997) (Permanence of Paper).

Library of Congress Cataloging-in-Publication Data

Riggsby, Andrew M.
    Crime and community in Ciceronian Rome / by Andrew M. Riggsby. — 1st ed.
        p.   cm.
    Includes bibliographical references and index.
    ISBN 0-292-77098-7 (alk. paper). —ISBN 0-292-77099-5 (pbk. : alk. paper)
    1. Criminal law (Roman law)   2. Criminal justice, Administration of—Rome.
3. Cicero, Marcus Tullius.   4. Rome—History—Republic, 265–30 B.C.
I. Title.
KJA3340.R54   1999
345.45'632—dc21   99-13718

D. M.
Claude E. Buxton

Contents

Preface

Like most complex societies, ancient Romans had mechanisms to suppress what we would regard as crime. But what exactly is suppressed and how that suppression is accomplished can vary widely with the structures of the individual societies. "Crime" may be seen, for instance, as the violation of divine will (often in the form of kingly will), a breach of the social contract, or a social pathology. Directed against crime, however defined, are an equally broad variety of responses: divine sanction, formal trials, lynchings, shunning, gossip in the streets, and so forth. This book examines the role of the Republican (roughly 150–50 B.C.) *iudicia publica*, "public courts," often taken as analogous to modern American criminal courts. I ask what the distinctive functions of these courts were, and in particular, I am interested in examining the various discursive practices that cluster around the *iudicia publica*, in order to analyze the conceptual categories that are only crudely represented by the modern terms "crime" and "criminal court."

The bulk of this work is devoted to the analysis of four individual charges that fall under the jurisdiction of the *iudicia publica* (chapters 2–5). I have chosen these four "crimes" because they are far and away the best documented. They are as follows (I append the conventional but potentially misleading translations): *ambitus* (electoral bribery), *de sicariis et veneficiis* (murder), *vis* (assault, riot), and *repetundae* (extortion by provincial administrators). The evidence examined comes largely from legal and oratorical texts, and the first chapter is devoted to the various methodological issues that arise from this choice of material. The former class is, perhaps surprisingly, less important to the immediate study; advocates' speeches will be the primary evidence used here, and there are several reasons for this. Our records of the legal texts of the time are highly fragmentary and do not necessarily derive from reliable sources. The fragments that do survive have been studied fairly thoroughly by previous scholars. The most important reason, however, is that it would be a methodological error to focus too narrowly on formal legal definitions. Other forms of discourse can reveal just as much about relevant conceptual categories, because they do just as much (at least potentially) to create those categories. This is a particularly compelling consideration for the evaluation of Roman courtroom oratory. Since Roman advocates are not subject to any significant rules of procedure, and because there is no charge to the jury in a Roman court, there is little to give legal definitions the privileged position that some feel they hold in other societies. If the orator is externally constrained, it is by the preconceptions of the audience (the jurors), which had in turn been formed by previous speeches and other, less specialized discourses.

Given this evidentiary base, I analyze the concerns and categories that underlie *ambitus, vis*, and the rest. We are at a special advantage in approaching *ambitus* (illegal electoral practices) because we have a surviving "how-to" manual of electioneering, probably written by Cicero's brother, Quintus. The core notion of *ambitus* is a *quid pro quo* exchange of cash for votes, but many practices which deviate somewhat from this prototype are also understood to constitute *ambitus*. These include the giving of nonmonetary goods (e.g., food or public games) and the indirect use of cash to win votes (e.g., by hiring campaign staff). However, the "exchange" can be defended if it is not a strict *quid pro quo*. Thus patrons might direct favors and goods to clients, and their clients would be expected to vote for them; obligation in these cases does not derive from any particular transaction but from generalized, ongoing roles. It was acceptable to pay off the voters, so long as one did so on a continuing basis. This is a typical pattern among (economically) primitive societies. They attempt to establish a firm distinction between interactions within a community (characterized by the "free" exchange of "gifts") and those between separate communities (characterized by exchange of commodities, and particularly the supercommodity—money). Even in societies that are largely dominated by commodity exchange, gift-exchange often retains an ideologically privileged position. Thus *ambitus* law attempts to enforce gift-exchange in the politically sensitive area of electioneering.

Earlier Roman homicide law was highly fragmented. Separate courts considered killing of a near-relative and murder by poison, as well as crimes of violence (including homicide) by professional criminals. There is no recorded legislation in this period concerning simple homicide. But early in Cicero's career the various courts were consolidated, and, most important, the professional crime law was expanded to include all intentional homicides. The common element of homicide was extracted from the bases of its various components (religious pollution, racketeering). This common element, in generalized form, becomes the basis of all prosecutions before the court *de sicariis et veneficiis* (a composite name which continued to reflect the history of the court). Courtroom argumentation in these cases confirms that the crime being tried is fairly simply a matter of intentional killing: arguments are directed at motive and opportunity rather than social context (as in cases of *ambitus*). Even in the absence of direct evidence arguing in either direction (as is usually the case in ancient societies), the language of sight and perspicuity is used to describe the advocate's conclusions. The crime is thus made out to be a fact of the physical, not the social, world. This language is not broadly used in trials on other charges (again, contrast *ambitus*). Here the intuitions we derive from a modern popular understanding of murder or homicide are less likely to lead us astray. In both cases the question is largely just "Did X kill Y?"

Vis is the ordinary Latin word for "force" or "violence," but we now recognize that it was applied in criminal cases only if they had political overtones. My additional claim, however, is that *vis* was reconceptualized during Cicero's lifetime, and that this was because of a change in the underlying notion of how broadly the "political" was to be defined. Even before the advent of Caesar's dictatorship and the subsequent establishment of the imperial system, there was a growing centralization of authority in the Roman state apparatus. Two aspects of this centralization are an increase in force used by the state to enforce public order and a parallel suppression of the use of force by private individuals. This reconfiguration of the public/private distinction, eventually aligning violence nearly completely with the former term, produces a corresponding change in *vis*. As a result of this change Cicero and other advocates are eventually deprived of arguments which had earlier been used to good effect. In particular, it was no longer possible to claim that acts of violence had no political significance. They automatically constituted usurpation of state authority. Particularly interesting is a case in which Cicero eschews a political line of argument in court (in attempting to secure an acquittal) but then uses it in a published version of the same defense, in an apparent attempt to reverse the change that was going on at the time.

The last of the four charges, *repetundae*, was to be laid against provincial governors (or other officials) who took too much money from their subjects. We may reject two proposed views of the true nature of this charge. The first is that *repetundae* consists of undue exploitation of office to extract any amount of money from provincials. Yet a quasi-public letter of advice from Cicero to his brother Quintus suggests that avoiding such exploitation represents an unusual and voluntary level of morality. Nor is mutual consent or goodwill ever offered as a defense. An opposing view holds that in reality *repetundae* courts were a sham staged to mollify provincials; this view is superficially supported by a reading of the defenses, which often stress the untrustworthiness of the provincials. However, a more careful reading of these texts shows that these attacks are narrow and (in the ancient scientific context) reasonable attacks on one of the two generally available sources of evidence—local witnesses. The credibility of the other source (written records) is also attacked, and by the same methods as are used in other types of cases. Instead of either of these views, courtroom practice seems to support a narrowly statutory definition. The law apparently forbids the extraction (by whatever means) of more than a certain amount of money (fixed by law) from a province by a governor (or other official). Such a charge could very well have been handled as *ambitus* in reverse, with the crime resting in the social circumstances of the exchange, but, as noted above, the precise circumstances do not seem to matter. As with murder the central issue is seen as a matter of fact (and here there is the possibility of direct evidence) and is discussed accordingly.

These individual studies allow us to address in the final chapter more general questions: If these individual offenses are all prosecuted by the same mechanism, what is the supercategory? Why are these diverse problems addressed by largely the same solution? Realizing then that "criminality" is a category at least potentially specific to the contemporary world, I want to consider the objects of the Roman *iudicia publica*. There does not seem to have been any academic discourse on "crime" in ancient Rome nor any political (in the conventional sense) talk which spoke of "crime" or "law and order" as objects in the Roman field of view. On the one hand, this forces us to rely primarily on induction from the individual subjects of the *iudicia publica* to draw our conclusions. On the other, this lack of a specifically criminological discourse can itself serve as a marker of the character, and particularly the alien character, of the Roman courts. The *iudicia publica* were courts in which the public as a whole could seek redress for wrongs done to it (i.e., the whole community); by contrast, the private courts *(iudicia privata)* were places where the individual sought redress for individual wrongs. But while this means that the public courts tried people for crimes, they do not reflect a more abstract category of crime.

Acknowledgments

This book is a revised version of a 1993 University of California, Berkeley dissertation. First and foremost I must thank Tom Habinek (my chair) and Charles Murgia for their comments on the original work and particularly for the different perspectives they brought to it.

Several others have read various intermediate versions. I received useful comments on the work in its entirety from Michael Alexander, Shadi Bartsch, Tim Moore, Gwyn Morgan, Matt Roller, and the anonymous readers for the University of Texas Press. Bob Cape, Karl Galinsky, Eric Orlin, and James Zetzel also commented helpfully on substantial portions of the manuscript. I have profited as well from more informal discussion on various points with (at least) Jerise Fogel, Judy Gaughan, Erich Gruen, Beth Severy, and Peter Wyetzner. None of the above should, of course, be held responsible for any view I express in what follows.

Most of the original dissertation was written during the tenure of fellowships awarded by the Department of Classics at UC Berkeley and funded by the Mellon Foundation. Substantial revisions were funded by a Summer Research Award of the University Research Institute of the University of Texas at Austin. My thanks to all the granting institutions. Section 2 of chapter 1 is taken from my article "Did the Romans Believe in Their Verdicts?," *Rhetorica* 15.3 (summer 1997), pp. 235–51, © 1997, by the International Society for the Study of Rhetoric, and that material is reprinted here by kind permission of the Society and of the University of California Press.

Finally I must thank two groups of people who made all this possible in a more general way. First, my original Latin mentors: Pat Allen, Alex Maxwell, the Warrens, and Chris Craig. Second, and most important, several members of my family: mom and dad, grandmom, and the dedicatee of this book, my grandfather, professor of psychology at Yale University, who did not live quite long enough to see his first grandchild enter the family business.

Abbreviations

The speeches of Cicero primarily under discussion will be referred to by the following abbreviations:

I Verr.	*In Verrem, actio prima*
II Verr.	*In Verrem, actio secunda*
Cael.	*Pro Caelio*
Clu.	*Pro Cluentio*
Flacc.	*Pro Flacco*
Font.	*Pro Fonteio*
Mil.	*Pro Milone*
Mur.	*Pro Murena*
Planc.	*Pro Plancio*
Rab.	*Pro Rabirio Postumo*
Rosc.	*Pro Roscio Amerino*
Scaur.	*Pro Scauro*
Sest.	*Pro Sestio*
Sull.	*Pro Sulla*

Other abbreviations include:

FIRA	*Fontes Iuris Romani Anteiustiniani* = Riccobono et al. 1940
Her.	[Cicero], *Rhetorica ad Herennium*
IO	Quintilian, *Institutio Oratoria*
MEFRA	*Mélanges d'Archéologie et d'Histoire de l'École Française de Rome: Antiquité*
MRR	*The Magistrates of the Roman Republic* = Broughton 1951–60
SB	*Scholia Bobiensia* (ed. Stangel)

TLRR   *Trials in the Late Roman Republic, 149 B.C. to 50 B.C.* = Alexander
            1990
ZSS   *Zeitschrift der Savigny-Stiftung für Rechtsgeschichte*, römanistiche
            Abteilung

Works of Cicero, Quintilian, and the Bobbio scholia are cited without author's
name. For abbreviations of other ancient titles, see the *Oxford Latin Dictio-
nary*. For abbreviations of other modern works, see *American Journal of Ar-
chaeology* 95 (1991), pp. 4–16. All dates are B.C. unless otherwise specified.

CRIME AND COMMUNITY IN CICERONIAN ROME

CHAPTER 1

What Can We Know and How Can We Know It?

1. THE QUESTION AND SOURCES

The topic of this book is the Roman *iudicia publica*, literally "public" (usually described as "criminal") courts. In particular I want to consider the various rubrics under which cases were tried during the Late Republic, ca. 150–50 B.C. (henceforth all dates will be B.C. unless noted). Andrew Lintott (1990: 10) has said of the offense of *ambitus* (usually translated as "electoral bribery") that the Romans took it as a serious threat to the political order and that therefore we must ask, "What was precisely understood by *ambitus* and why, in their view, had it to be suppressed?" This question of definition is of central importance and deserves to be extended to the other criminal offenses studied in this book as well. The difficulty here is that we have virtually no direct evidence for what Roman jurors thought about what they were doing in particular cases. We do, however, have evidence in a more general sense for what went on in the courtroom—Cicero's speeches in a number of criminal cases. We must use these speeches, in combination with evidence from outside the courtroom, to attempt to triangulate the position of the jurors and to try to estimate what their concerns were in judging criminal cases. In so doing we can only produce an approximation of the criteria by which defendants were in practice acquitted or convicted. Nonetheless, what evidence we do have has not been fully exploited because of concentration, on the one hand, on technical legal investigations, and, on the other, on historical studies that generally ignore the substance of individual trials. John Crook (1995:196) has described advocacy as "the point of input into the law of the values from outside, the perceptions of the community at large." Rather than following that input into the law, this study will attempt to trace it back to its source in "the community at large."

In coming to these questions, I take a somewhat different approach from most current Anglo-American work on Roman legal institutions.[1] The conventional (and quite successful) approach has been to pick an interesting area of social practice and then ask what the law governing that area tells us about it. I take the reverse approach. My objects of study are all creations of the law — *ambitus, vis* ("violence"), *repetundae* (conventionally "extortion"), homicide, and the *iudicia publica* themselves. What I wish to study about these courts is less their formal legal structure than their practical functioning as a part of the broader political and social life of the community. In particular I will be interested primarily in speeches Cicero gave in court in actual cases. The *iudicia publica* operated not on the basis of briefs, written motions, or private deliberations but through public speaking. Hence, these speeches get us to the heart of the institution. Obviously I have exaggerated the methodological contrast here for the sake of clarity. Responsible historians have always been aware of nonlegal evidence and integrated it into their studies. Likewise, this work will not ignore important technical issues of the criminal law. Nonetheless, I think the different interests and emphases are clear and significant.

This method is meant not as an advance on, but as a complement to, other approaches. While I have chosen it partly as a matter of individual taste as to what constitutes an interesting scholarly question, there are also specific reasons that this approach is appropriate to a study of the *iudicia publica*. First, the strictly legal evidence for the Republican criminal courts is extremely limited and fragmented.[2] Insofar as they can be separated, we are in a better position to examine the practice of the courts than their legal framework. Second, the *iudicia publica* were in substance a less "legal" institution than, for instance, the "civil" (i.e., private) courts. This claim will be argued in detail below, but a few brief observations can be made here. In criminal cases no magistrate charged the jury or made evidentiary or other legal rulings. (And even if they had had this function, the presiding officers did not necessarily have any legal expertise.) Lay jurors tried both law and fact.[3] Prosecution and defense were ordinarily conducted by orators rather than jurists. Third, to the extent that the meaning of any social practice is constructed by the discourses in which it is embedded, all of those discourses should be taken seriously. For instance, Leps (1992) has shown the importance of journalism and detective fiction to nineteenth-century constructions of criminality.[4] Similarly, the principles of oratory in the Roman criminal courts are, in themselves, important facts about those courts. These facts are doubtless related to the law but cannot even in principle be refuted or superseded by legal facts.[5] Nor, to be sure, can they themselves refute or supersede "legal" facts (in the narrow sense). They are simply of different orders.

This method brings with it new opportunities but also certain limitations.

First of all, only certain offenses can be dealt with. Chapters will be devoted to each of the four charges on which we have at least two surviving speeches. Thus other charges such as *peculatus* (theft of public funds),[6] *perduellio* (apparently an archaic form of treason), and *maiestas* (the more modern treason-like charge) will be dealt with only peripherally. A major problem is that virtually all the evidence comes from the speeches of Cicero. Here we are limited both to the work of a single individual and (with one notable exception) to defense speeches alone. Comparison of different speeches may help cancel out factors peculiar to individual cases, but it might still leave us with personal Ciceronian biases. However, while Cicero was an extraordinary advocate in many ways, here that may work to our advantage. As it is one of the central tenets of modern rhetoric that the persuasive speaker must recognize and work with the expectations of his audience, Cicero's success indicates that he understood the jurors' preconceptions very well indeed.[7]

Even Cicero once pointed out that a successful advocate (such as himself) must have a firm grasp of his audience's presuppositions and prejudices: "I would not, jurors, be competent to plead any case, if I, who am involved in fending off men's dangers, could not see what is fixed in the common sense and in the very nature of all" (*Clu.* 17).[8] That is, Cicero's genius in this respect should not be seen as a matter of unfettered creativity and originality in the Romantic fashion. Rather, it is a matter of being able to articulate and/or exploit broadly held prejudices. As Anthony Corbeill (1996 : 8) has noted in his recent study of Roman political humor, "[Cicero's] success virtually ensures that the humorous appeals found in these oratorical texts articulate values and presuppositions present in the majority of his Roman audience." Of course, it will also be useful to parallel any conclusions drawn from the Ciceronian material with other evidence, where possible. It must be kept in mind, however, that most of this other material was produced under different circumstances and for different ends than courtroom oratory and so is suspect evidence for that courtroom practice. For instance, even if we have an account of a trial recorded by a historian such as Livy, we do not know whether that version was originally intended to convict, exonerate, or make some entirely different moral or political point. When dealing with Cicero we have the enormous advantage of knowing exactly what his main bias was: he wanted to win the case at hand. In the end we will simply have to (as so often in ancient history) admit the limitations of the evidence; for this aspect of the *iudicia publica* we are largely dependent on a single voice. While this is unfortunate, we should remember that that is one more voice than we often hear.

The matter of having largely defense speeches seems to be easier to control.

Naturally, the prosecution will ordinarily try to construe any offense as broadly as possible, while the defense will try to narrow it. Nonetheless, there is reason to hope they were not simply talking past each other. When we compare the strategies of Cicero's *repetundae* defenses with those found in his prosecution of Verres on the same charge, they mirror each other closely. That is, he uses roughly the same set of categories to structure both prosecution and defense.[9] We are helped here by dealing with those charges on which several different cases each were tried. In individual cases Cicero may try to avoid this or that aspect of an offense, but from several different speeches we have some hope of piecing together the whole. Thus, while it can be dangerous to try to reconstruct any specific prosecution claim from Cicero's corresponding defense, we can expect a generic resemblance between prosecution and defense.[10] It must also be kept in mind that the present task rarely requires us to decide whether Cicero was telling the truth. We ask rather, "What is it that he wished the jurors to believe?"

Treatments of the laws themselves (the first section of each chapter) serve two purposes in this context. First, laws naturally offer definitions much more explicitly and concisely than oratory. Hence they are useful in establishing quickly the general area with which each offense is concerned. Second, examination of the laws can alert us to potential substantive issues that we should consider in the oratory surrounding each charge. Tracing the history of legislation, not just the details of the formally applicable statute, will be particularly important for establishing points of potential conflict. These treatments of the law, however, will be deliberately partial; they will be restricted almost entirely to issues that will arise again in the main discussion of each chapter. As a result, certain issues of genuine legal significance will be omitted, particularly those involving general principles of criminal liability. For instance, Roman law ordinarily requires a culpable mental state, in addition to the criminal act, to establish liability.[11] Lack of this culpable mental state is only once and obliquely offered as a defense in surviving speeches, so it will not be treated in much detail. Roman law also has a notion of vicarious liability (as for, e.g., aiding and abetting), though not one as elaborately articulated as in Anglo-American law.[12] Again, no defense turns on these issues, so I will largely pass over them.

All these methodological questions notwithstanding, there is not, in any case, a great deal of evidence either for Republican criminal law or for the detailed conduct of trials in other sources. In the last chapter I will argue that this lacuna is significant and not merely an accident of transmission. Here let me just be more specific about the nature of the evidentiary situation. For texts of the statutes we have a fragmentary inscription of the text of one law and scattered quotations from Cicero of a few others. The *Digest*, the sixth century A.D. compilation of legal commentary, treats criminal law in only one of its fifty books. Its immediate sources are all imperial. Nor are juristic comments on Republican criminal law preserved in other sources. Some of Cicero's rhetorical treatises and works of political philosophy touch on crime, but only briefly and generally intermingled with other matters. Other rhetorical writings (e.g., Seneca the Elder, Quintilian) mention criminal cases fairly often but generally use them as examples in treating other kinds of technical issues. While there are references to individual crimes or criminal acts, there is little evidence of an overarching Roman category of "crime."

2. TAKING THE ROMAN COURTS SERIOUSLY [13]

The reputation of a Roman orator/politician could depend in large part on his performance in the criminal courts. Cicero himself said that he owed his start in political life to his defense of Sextus Roscius on a murder charge in 80 (*Brut.* 312; *Off.* 2.51) and his special prominence on the Roman scene to his prosecution of Verres for *repetundae* in 70 (*Brut.* 318–19). Yet the courts did not exist purely to give aspiring statesmen opportunity for oratorical display, or did they? A central problem in the interpretation of Cicero's forensic speeches is their tendency to avoid (so it is said) substantive discussion of the charges. Alleged tactics of avoidance include flamboyant use of certain rhetorical figures, extensive self-reference, and invoking the ambiance of the arena or the comic theater.[14] This disappointment of our expectation that criminal accusations are to be countered by denial might well lead us to suspect a fundamental cultural mismatch; what we casually call the Roman "criminal courts" (the *iudicia publica*) are perhaps in some respects fundamentally different from the institutions of that name in our own society. This mismatch can be (and has been) exaggerated, but if we take it seriously, there are at least two responsible approaches to the problem. One set of theories argues that "discussing the charges" is not what the Roman *iudicia publica* were for—that we have improperly imposed our concept of "court" across cultures. One theory of this sort has been expressed in the claim that "truth itself, the guilt or innocence of Cicero's client, was rarely very important. . . . [Instead,] what won the juries over was not the validity of Cicero's case, but the amazing boldness of his argument; not truth, but sheer, unmitigated effrontery."[15] This account requires a certain collusion between the parties, and in fact the whole society, to speak of the courts in terms of crime and guilt. Another collusion theory claims that the official charges were merely a pretext for a contest of another sort. On this account, though, the competition is not one of eloquence but of very generalized social standing. "The trial in all three cases examined [*pro Roscio Amerino, pro Cluentio, pro Caelio*] was not of evidence and documented reports about the crimes, or legally definable versions of the truth, but of reputations and of place within the community. . . . What we witness in these events is less a judicial and more a social occasion."[16]

The other approach, and the one for which I wish to argue here, is to suggest that the problem is not with the concept of "court." Instead, there has been a tendency to drastically underestimate the "relevance to the case" of many of Cicero's arguments. The bulk of this book will, *inter alia*, outline a more adequate notion of relevance, which depends primarily on accepting the evidentiary value of claims about character and on reexamining the definitions of the various offenses tried by the courts.[17] First, however, I want to address the external arguments: what is the evidence for the Romans' understanding of their own courts? I hope to show that Roman courts were understood primarily to establish whether defendants had or had not committed certain reasonably well defined crimes. I begin with a brief look at Roman prescriptive accounts of the *iudicia publica* and at the history of those courts. Following this will be a more extended consideration of descriptive accounts of various trials, drawn mostly from Cicero's letters. All these types of evidence will show that an account of the courts must center on the role of truth in their proceedings.

Roman prescriptive accounts of the function of the courts are not very different from our own. Cicero restricts the partisanship of a man serving as judge in a friend's trial to "preferring that the friend's case be true *(veram)*" and, within the limits of the law, to arranging the schedule to the friend's liking (*Off.* 2.43). Cicero's weighting of the importance of obligation to a friend versus duty to state may perhaps be idiosyncratic, but the passage would not usefully assert his position if it mischaracterized the nature of the duty (i.e., a true verdict).[18] We know jurors swore to judge by the laws, so presumably the verdict is supposed to be about the subject of those laws — a crime or crimes (*Inv.* 1.70, 2.131–33, *Verr.* 1.46, *Clu.* 164, and especially *Verr.* 1.3; cf. *Cael.* 21, *Rosc.* 152, *Clu.* 27). For instance, *Inv.* 1.48 reports, "A court judgment is a matter of religion because those who made the judgment have sworn an oath according to the laws."[19] "Truth" seems to have been the goal of the witnesses' oaths as well (*Rosc.* 101, 104; *Rab. Perd.* 7; *Flacc.* 11, 12, 18; *Cael.* 20, 25).[20] Thus these prescriptive accounts (both legal and theoretical) give no hint that defense advocates would, as it is claimed, avoid the notional charges.

The history of the *iudicia publica* also makes unlikely the collusion theories, according to which the overt charge had nothing to do with the "real" reason for the trial. The Romans were willing to hand over a great deal of power to these courts, and the allotment of senators and/or *equites* to the juries was a strongly contested issue from the creation of the courts until 70.[21] Furthermore, since there was no state prosecutor, ambitious politicians could and did bring their opponents before the bar on their own. Despite all this, we do not hear of aggrieved convicts or demagogues or (most significantly) desperate defense advocates calling for the restriction of courts and prosecutions in general.[22] Rather, they must have been seen as serving some necessary societal function by restricting the behavior of individual citizens (for moral, pragmatic, religious, or other reasons). This argues against the entertainment-oriented theory, but it still allows for the possibility of a test of status, after the fashion of Athenian ostracism. But neither collusion theory accounts for the proliferation of criminal courts. In the Roman system the jurisdictions of the *iudicia publica* were not divided geographically or hierarchically, but by offense (i.e., one for murder, one for treason, and so forth). The number of these courts grew from one to seven in the period from 149 to 81 as more and more offenses were subjected to this kind of jurisdiction. The penalties of these courts are also distinctive: virtual exile for many, but also fines (for provincial extortion), a ban on office-holding (for electoral malpractice), and an exotic form of execution (for parricide, killing a near relative, at most periods). Under either collusion theory there would be no motive for the proliferation of distinct charges. Any one of them (or a more generalized offense) would always suffice, as with ostracism.

We also have a more specific reason to believe that for at least one Republican politician—Cicero—trials were about murder, electoral malpractice, *vis*, and the like. Cicero often refers to the outcome of trials in his letters, and the consequences are frequently described as if judgment had been passed or was understood to have been passed on the respective crimes.[23] For instance, he says of his own defense of Sestius on a charge of *vis* (seditious violence):

> *Our Sestius was acquitted March 14 by a unanimous vote, and indeed it was most beneficial to the state that no disagreement appear in a case of this sort* (in eius modi causa).

> (*Q. fr.* 2.4.1)

Sestius, Cicero had argued in his preserved speech, was a patriot rather than a thug. His motivation supposedly justified his use of violence. Hence Cicero sees the acquittal as a vindication of this alleged legal principle. The issue as described here is not Cicero's performance, nor even Sestius' character or standing, but the informal precedent established. Note that Cicero here says *causa*, "case," not *viro* or *homine*, "person."

Verdicts of individual trials might well be affected by politics (e.g., *Att.* 2.3.1, 4.18.3,4; *Fam.* 3.12.1, 7.2.2–3), bribery (e.g., *Att.* 4.17.4), the performance of the speakers, or all of the above (*Att.* 4.18.1; cf. *Q. fr.* 3.3.3, 3.4.1). However, these influences are all seen as deflecting the jurors from their normal, proper task.[24] Thus in 56 Cicero lamented that the *iniquitas* of the conditions under which one Sittius was tried was stronger than *veritas* (*Fam.* 5.17.2). Moreover, the impropriety of these factors is not merely a matter of Cicero's personal moral evaluation, as the following example illustrates nicely. In 54 he complained about the leniency of the courts:

> *Sufenas and Cato were acquitted on the fourth of July; Procilius was convicted. From this it's clear that the jurors do not care a bit about electoral malpractice, the assemblies, the failure of the elections, treason, and not even the republic as a whole; at least they do not want to see a* pater familias *killed in his own house, though even this was a close call, for 22 voted to acquit, 28 to convict. Publius, in tears, did move the minds of the judges with his eloquent conclusion.*
>
> (*Att.* 4.15.4)[25]

The jurors' verdicts are taken as reflecting their judgment on criminal acts, not on the performance of advocates. (There is rhetorical slippage here between specific criminal acts and general categories of crime, but that slippage, still common today, presupposes a factual judgment on the defendant.[26] The rhetorical trick works precisely because the criminality of homicide is never really at issue.) It is important that Cicero claims the public impact of the judgment is weakened by the close vote, even though he personally attributes votes for acquittal to an effective defense performance. This illustrates the work of a widespread presumption that jurors judge crimes.[27] Without Cicero's specific insight into this particular jury, the observer would assume that they were genuinely divided on the issues. Conversely, Cicero can claim that the conviction of Rutilius Rufus was unjust, despite an admittedly inadequate defense, precisely because he was innocent (*de Or.* 1.229–30; *Brut.* 115–16). Cicero's commitment to Rufus' innocence may well be personally or ideologically motivated, but he can expect that, if accepted, the fact of innocence justifies his outrage.[28] In this case a judgment allegedly based on performance can be used to exculpate the defendant in the eyes of later audiences.

If, on the other hand, we see trials as centered on questions of social standing, it is difficult to explain a passage such as the following. At *Att.* 4.17.5 Cicero complains that he does not know what to say in three apparently routine defenses in cases of electoral malpractice. "I don't for the life of me know what I'll say; I can't find a thing in those three books[29] you praise so much." That Cicero would have such a problem is compatible with a performance-oriented theory (though no more so than a crime-oriented one). What it cannot support is the notion that the jurors are primarily interested in the defendant's general position within the community. If this were the case, then there would be little need for arguments specific to each case. Knowing what kind of persona would be acceptable to a broad spectrum of jurors, Cicero could simply construct it without regard for specific accusations demanding specific refutation.

Even Cicero's jokes presuppose the notion that juries should (and ordinarily do) judge crimes. During the campaign for the consulship of 65 Catiline was being hindered by an accusation of electoral malpractice. Cicero's evaluation of the situation in a letter to Atticus is that "Catiline will certainly be a candidate if it is judged that the sun does not shine at mid-day" (*Att.* 1.1.1).[30] This might simply mean that Cicero thought Catiline's acquittal unlikely, but in that case the expression "it is judged that" is rather wordy. One might also wonder why Cicero would have considered undertaking the defense himself (*Att.* 1.2.1) if he had thought the case a hopeless one. What Cicero seems to mean is that Catiline is, to Cicero, clearly guilty and needs to get the jury to miss (or ignore) that fact. Nonetheless, the jurors are presented as passing a judgment, whether or not the correct one, on a crime, not a performance or general social standing. A similar interpretation attaches to Cicero's famous remark (preserved in Quintilian) about his defense of Cluentius:[31]

> *Nor did Cicero himself lose his sight [of the truth], when he boasted that he had covered the jurors in shadow in Cluentius' case.*

> (2.17.20–21)

We are not likely ever to know precisely what strategy Cicero referred to by "covered the jurors in shadow."[32] But what is clear is that the general sense of the phrase must be like that of the English "pulled the wool over their eyes" (cf. Val. Max. 3.8.3). This is precisely not what one would need to do according to the "collusion" scenarios described above. It would, however, be appropriate if jurors were, in principle, fact-finders.

But even if the theoretical goal of the courts was discovery of the truth, we cannot, of course, count on orators automatically to provide it. One of the advances in our reading of Cicero over recent decades is the recognition that his version of events does not consist of "the facts" or even a favorable selection of the facts.[33] He presents a construct which is neither historical nor antihistorical, but rhetorical (in the sense of "aimed at persuasion"). As Harold Gotoff remarks:

> *The only thing Cicero needs to create in his listeners is a disposition to acquit. Whether they should so vote because the charges against his client are dismissed as irrelevant, disproved as false, or despised as a cover for the character assassination of his client is a secondary matter.*[34]

In observing this sound principle, however, we must be careful not to adopt a point of view too focused on the performer. Obviously not all arguments are equally effective, and the difference lies in the local context. We cannot meaningfully ask what jurors find persuasive without asking more specifically what they find persuasive under these particular circumstances, i.e., sitting as jurors.[35] Today we would attribute different persuasive value to an identical anecdote about a car's reliability, if that anecdote were recounted by a used-car salesman, a boasting neighbor, the secretary of transportation, or *Consumer Reports*. Similarly, we must not assume that Roman jurors could simply be bullied into accepting anything as grounds for acquittal. If, then, orators were constrained by the audience's dispositions and expectations, we must ask what those were.

The discussion above has hinted at one of the central factors in influencing a criminal jury—"truth" (*veritas, Fam.* 5.17.2; *veram . . . causam, Off.* 3.43). This should perhaps not be surprising in an institution whose other official description was *quaestio* ("inquiry"), rather than *certamen* ("contest") or *ludi* ("games"); contrast here the common Greek use of ἀγών ("contest") of lawsuits. Now of course this cannot mean truth in an absolute sense. Even if the speakers had intended to be informative (which, *ex hypoth|esi*, they did not), and even if the jurors had the benefit of rumor now lost to us, neither had any more direct access to absolute truth than we do. Rather, "truth," as Gotoff (1993:297) remarks in a later article, "is just a ploy." What Gotoff means by this remark is that truth (as understood by the orator) is deployed only if doing so happens to coincide with what would have been the most effective strategy anyway; an orator might, for instance, eschew a factual defense, even a truthful one, in favor of a more exciting counterattack.[36] We can, however, give another interpretation to Gotoff's claim. Truth, that is to say the production of a truth, a plausible account of reality, is a trope or strategy.[37] Hence Cicero claims (*Off.* 2.51), "In trials it is always a juror's duty to pursue the truth *(verum)*; the defense advocate's is sometimes to protect his client by means of the plausible *(verisimili)*, even if it is less true." But what we have seen above suggests that in forensic oratory truth was not just any trope, but a distinctive and obligatory one. The orator's case must appear true.

We see a further illustration of the status of truth in oratory in Quintilian's repeated warnings about bringing the habits of scholastic declamation to court. Some of these warnings could be seen in purely formal terms, referring to the danger of being rhetorically one-upped. Yet others must refer to confrontation with (some version of) the facts (*IO* 2.10.8, 5.13.36, 7.2.54–55), and even the attempt to one-up the opponent is always based on producing a "truer" account (*IO* 5.13.6, 6.1.43). Cicero provides a concrete example in his anecdote about a pleader named Caepasius (*Clu.* 58–59). Caepasius was humiliated in court one day not because his client left the courtroom while he was still arguing his case (for that had happened some time before the disaster), but because the advocate gestured in what he thought was his client's direction after the latter had fled. The contradiction, the mismatch with reality, was the source of the humor and so of the rhetorical failure.

3. POLITICS AND THE COURTS

Before leaving these issues, we should consider two complications: one dealing with external political power, the other with power relationships internal to the courtroom. We noted briefly above cases in which Cicero suggests a political motive for some jurors. It might be objected that, whatever the "official" function of the courts, these political interventions rendered that function irrelevant for the orator and even rendered the orator himself irrelevant. This fails to account for the evidence noted in the preceding section, but even on its own terms the argument fails. In none of the cases cited above does the outcome seem to be known in advance (bribery is likely to have been similarly unpredictable, especially when used by both sides). Hence it would have behooved the orator to make the best available argument, to produce an acceptable truth.[38]

It may, however, be worth considering a little longer the question of how political the Roman courts were, as most aspects of the question have received surprisingly little direct attention. The largest-scale recent works focusing on the Republican criminal courts are Erich Gruen's (1968) *Roman Politics and the Criminal Courts, 149–78 B.C.*, along with the relevant sections of his later *The Last Generation of the Roman Republic* (1974:260–357), and J.-M. David's (1992) *Le patronat judiciaire au dernier siècle de la république ro-*

maine. Gruen's interest in the courts is primarily instrumental; he uses patterns of prosecution along with more traditional prosopographical methods to trace patterns of political alliance and factional strife in the Late Republic. David's opus is more sociological in its focus, but it takes a similarly procedural view of the courts: who played the various formal roles and under which circumstances? The trial itself remains something of a "black box." The questions about individual crimes raised at the beginning of this chapter require that we look inside the box. But in asking the question "How political were individual Roman criminal trials?" we must first consider the sense to be attached to the term "political."[39]

One sense this notion has been given is the idea that the motivation for prosecutions was normally factional[40] or personal[41] enmity. Since there was no state prosecutor's office, this will necessarily have been true to some extent. The defendants we know of are largely men of affairs; it would not have been hard to find someone with a grudge to prosecute when a prominent person did something that could be taken as a violation of the law. Or, in the absence of long-standing enemies, there was the possibility of aspiring young prosecutors (like Cicero himself against Verres) who would benefit both from the exposure of a public trial and even more from the various rewards for most successful prosecutions (Taylor 1949:113–15; Alexander 1985). We in fact know of cases where the primary motivation was political, such as Caelius' second prosecution of Dollabella (*Fam.* 3.10.5). Gruen also points out that cases in which there is a long gap between offense and prosecution are likely to have been significantly motivated by politics (1974:266), as are *ambitus* cases prosecuted only after the defendant had held office or even lost the election (1974:301). We also know of a few cases, such of those of Q. Servilius Caepio (*TLRR* 97) and M. Tuccius (*TLRR* 335), where prosecutions were apparently mounted for the tactical motive of delaying another trial. Cicero even suggests in *pro Roscio* (§55, cf. §30) that a prosecutor needed to show personal enmity to show that his accusation was in earnest.

None of this suggests, however, that jurors or the creators of the courts had similarly political motives. And we also know of cases where the original motivation of the prosecution seems to have been seeking justice, not political advantage. The Sicilians apparently approached Cicero in regard to Verres' prosecution, rather than the other way around (*Scaur.* 24), and Cato famously promised to prosecute the winners of the consular elections of 63, whoever they might be (*Mur.* 62).[42] We will see in the next chapter that Cicero often ends up opposing personal friends and political allies in the courts without, apparently, damaging his relationship with them. This may indicate that personal loyalty was not the primary issue. Personal anger may be more important, especially in cases (such as *pro Milone* or most *ambitus* trials) where the prosecutor was the victim (or a close relative of the victim) of the crime. There is, however, little reason to doubt that a coincidence of opportunity (in the form of some action by the defendant) and personal animosity motivated most criminal prosecutions. But the motives of individual prosecutors do not bear on the issue of the motivations for the creation of the system, nor for the votes of jurors. That Roman nobles won political prominence by military victories does not imply that the army was (solely) a "political" institution in the sense usually attached to that word. So it was with the courts, as well.

Another interpretation that has been attached to the notion of the "politicality" of Roman criminal trials is that, whatever the motive for prosecution, conviction or acquittal was a test of factional or personal strength. This is relevant to the present work since, if all the parties know that the trial is an irrelevant formality, the evidentiary value of the speeches can be called into question. It is impossible to trace jurors' motivations directly, but we do have some circumstantial evidence that trials were not political in this sense (in addition to the general arguments of the previous section). Consider first the class of trials mentioned above, in which the alleged offense significantly predates the trial. These defendants are regularly acquitted.[43] We may also look at trials which seem to form part of a series of accusations and counteraccusations between political enemies (see Gruen 1968:196, 206).[44] Again the ready inference is that these trials were motivated primarily by political or personal hostility. The fact that such defendants are also normally acquitted suggests that the juries did really want to be convinced that some wrong had been done.[45] Also important in this context is Cicero's remark at *Brut.* 106 that, since the introduction of the secret ballot in 137, jurors had to be persuaded.[46] That is, presumably, the secret ballot neutralized the force of predictable political ties. Thus participants at least expected that cases would be won in court, rather than by preexisting alliances. This is not surprising. No doubt some jurors in particular cases went in with a personal commitment to vote for (or against) the defendant. However, the bulk of the jurors (especially among the two lower and larger orders) will have had weak and/or ambivalent political interests in the parties in a given case.[47] Hence it behooved the advocates to try to convince at least part of the jury that the defendant did (or did not) commit the crime in question, and Cicero knew this. To the extent that other jurors came to the trial strongly committed on personal grounds to a particular verdict, they would not affect his rhetoric; they were a lost cause.

A third sense of "political" might be that the outcome of trials was determined (at least in part) by differences in policy or ideology. One case that is described in these terms in our sources is that of P. Rutilius Rufus (*TLRR* 94). He was allegedly convicted partly because of his refusal to mount an emotionally effective defense (*de Or.* 1.229) and partly because of the anger of the *equites* at his handling of tax collections in Asia (Vel. Pat. 2.13.2; Dio fr. 97). Here there is a division between the senate and the *equites,* for tax-collection was largely in the hands of the latter. The current tendency (reasonable in my opinion) is to minimize the difference of interests between the two orders, but the question of the tax contracts seems to have been one of the genuine sticking points (Brunt 1988:148–50). Doubtless, at this level of abstraction some Roman trials were political; in fact, we will show just that in some of the studies that follow. However, to anticipate the general argument somewhat, this need not conflict with the assertion that Roman courts ideally existed to judge and punish the criminal acts of individual citizens. We will see not only that several of the individual offenses tried in the *iudicia publica* are, on their face, political in character, but that on further examination the same can be said for all the acts that were in their purview. There are no crimes at Rome which are not political crimes.[48] But if crimes are *defined* in political terms, this still leaves it to the jury to determine whether that definition has been met in particular cases. Politics and truth are not contradictory but complementary.

So much for politics outside the courts, but what about the politics—that is, power relations—inside the courtroom? It was claimed above that, looking in from the outside, Romans expected jurors to pass "true" judgments on the basis of the law and fact in each case. But how far could the advocates go inside the courtroom in shaping the jurors' understanding of the substance of that law and fact? To some small extent reshaping of presuppositions presumably goes on in any argument (or even conversation). But more to the point, advocates could potentially have imposed certain assumptions by virtue of the specialized, restricted world of the courtroom. Compare the imposition on a modern jury of terms of art like "murder" (as distinct from homicide), "possession" (which might not include items in one's hand), or even "not guilty" (meaning merely "not demonstrably guilty," rather than "innocent").[49] Of course, this imposition is facilitated by a judge who is authorized to give definitive judgments on such matters and, less obtrusively, by the formal training and licensing the advocates (as well as the judge) are known by jurors to have undergone. What of the Roman situation? The following sketch of Roman legal procedure will address these questions. (It will also serve to clarify procedural references that will come up in the course of the study as a whole.) This examination will result in a conclusion that is at first sight paradoxical. Compared to their modern counterparts, Roman trial advocates were relatively unconstrained in formal terms; they seem to have been particularly free from detailed intervention in matters of law on the part of the presiding magistrate. Yet it may be argued that the overall effect of this procedural system, combined with the limited range of jury selection, creates considerable informal constraints on the advocates. Roman jurors were major actors in their own right, and knowledge of their prejudices and preconceptions about the law and the case would have been even more important than it is in a modern court. These preconceptions may not have been absolutely fixed points, but altering them significantly would have been prohibitively difficult.

The Roman system of criminal courts *(quaestiones)* was strongly adversarial. The defendant, usually represented by one or more counsel, squared off against a private person (or persons) who served as prosecutor. The prosecutor might also be assisted by one or more so-called *subscriptores*. Neither side's speakers were (normally) legal professionals, though these will have been consulted. The state (in the person of the praetor or lesser presiding officer) only participated to the extent of allowing or rejecting the prosecution, then arranging to pick the "best" prosecutor when several had made themselves available. The jurors technically had three options: acquit *(absolvo)*, condemn *(condemno)*, or not proven *(non liquet)*.[50] However, as the prosecution needed an outright majority of the votes cast to win, the trial could have one of only two official outcomes.[51] The social distinction between votes of *absolvo* and *non liquet* is less clear; for an example of the exploitation of this voting possibility see below. The penalties for most crimes were clearly fixed by law. In cases where variable damages were assessed, they were determined in a separate proceeding before the same jury *(litis aestimatio)*.[52] Nor were there clear guidelines for what we would call burden of proof.[53] This fact by itself might indicate either that the issue had not even been clearly formulated or that it was so well resolved that it could "go without saying." The way Cicero manipulates the point suggests that the former may have been the case.

The individual courts were presided over by one of the praetors or a subordinate or *iudex quaestionis*— either is called a *quaesitor*.[54] Once the case had been accepted by the praetor and the prosecutor had been chosen, there was little official interference in the conduct of the case; the quaesitor kept time and counted the votes.[55] Nearly anything within the time limits seems to have been allowed.[56] Most important for the present topic is the lack of a formal charge to the jury instructing them on what issues they were to decide or what the applicable law might be.[57] This, at any rate, is the orthodox view. Bauman (1996: 25–26) has recently offered a challenge which, while not ultimately successful, deserves notice. The central figure here is Lucius Cassius Longinus Ravilla, known for two things in antiquity: his judicial severity and his admonition to jurors "whenever he was the quaesitor in some homicide case" to ask "who benefited *(cui bono)?*"[58] This certainly looks like influence by the presiding officer, but what exactly is being influenced? The one trial under Cassius about which we have detailed information was a *quaestio extraordinaria*—an *ad hoc* investigation by a magistrate, usually at the direction of the senate or assembly.[59] The other references to his severity all refer to him acting in the capacity of a judge.[60] This description makes more sense for a *quaestio extraordinaria*, in which the investigating magistrate probably himself had a hand in the judgment, than for a standing court, in which the official verdict at least was decided by the jurors.[61] We do not know much about Cassius' judicial career, but he was tribune in 137, consul in 127, and censor in 125 and presided over the trial of the Vestals (the trial cited above) in 113. The chronology of the various standing courts (and especially for those of the different kinds of homicide) is highly uncertain, but they are not clearly attested for the period in which Cassius was active. It is quite likely, then, that his instructions were addressed not to the jurors of a standing court but to his own *consilium*, or circle of advisors. This is certainly the case for the Marcus Scaurus criticized by Sallust for his conduct of hearings against Mamilius *(BJ* 40.4–5).

Given this freedom during the course of the trial, a particular point of pretrial procedure becomes important: the indictment *(inscriptio).*[62] How does it restrict the advocate's freedom in advance? Criminal procedure at Rome was never as highly developed as was civil procedure, and the system was not regularized until the *lex Iulia iudiciorum publicorum,* probably of Augustus (conceivably of Julius Caesar).[63] Thus in our period procedure may have varied somewhat from court to court. What then can we tell about the *inscriptio* (often, but slightly less formally, the *subscriptio*) in the time of Cicero? The only preserved specimen (Paulus, *D.* 48.2.3) is for an adultery charge, not a criminal offense until Augustus and so presumably postdating the procedural reforms. In addition to charge, accuser, and defendant, this passage gives the barest details of the crime: time, place, and the person with whom the adultery was committed. Passing references in Cicero (*Inv.* 2.58; *Clu.* 86) indicate only name of prosecutor, defendant, and the law under which the case was to be tried, but there is no way to be sure that these remarks are comprehensive. Distinctions were made within the jurisdiction of individual courts: *Inv.* 2.58 discusses a homicide case where parricide is specified in the *inscriptio.* However, this need not imply that the details of a crime were normally included. Parricide had different legal consequences, certainly in procedure and perhaps in penalty, from other forms of homicide, so its inclusion may well have been exceptional.[64] The direct evidence suggests that details of the crime were sketchy or nonexistent in the Republican *inscriptio*.[65] There is also an *argumentum ex silentio*. Even when claiming the irrelevancy of opposing arguments (e.g., in the opening sections of *pro Cluentio*), Cicero never makes a procedural argument based on the *inscriptio*; he relies only on general notions of duty.[66] More positively, we should recall that the main purpose of the pretrial proceedings was to ensure an energetic prosecution (cf. *Divinatio in Caecilium*). We must keep in mind that such a procedure would give the defendant only minimal protection; he was not even present most of the time.

The form of the indictment raises a methodological issue that will be relevant to several points in the body of this study. It may thus be best to deal with it immediately. It is a well-established fact that some actions exposed the actor to criminal liability under more than one statute. For instance, a provincial governor who exceeded his authority in various ways might be tried under the *maiestas* or *repetundae* laws; though apparently rare in practice, independent prosecutions under all applicable statutes were possible.[67] Most examples are imperial or slightly earlier (involving especially Julius Caesar's *repetundae* law of 59). Under the empire the law of *maiestas* seems to have absorbed virtually the entire Republican law of *vis*. Nonetheless, the phenomenon does originate earlier; presumably Milo could have been tried for homicide as well as *vis* in the killing of Clodius. Despite these overlapping jurisdictions, however, the one thing we know certainly that the prosecutor had to be clear about in his indictment was the formal charge, so that the case could be handled by the "proper" court. Jurors were not asked whether, on the one hand, a given act looked more like *maiestas* or *repetundae* or whether, on the other, it was offensive regardless of legal grounds; they were asked whether it was *repetundae*. Even if the boundaries of the various offenses were sometimes unclear or overlapping as a matter of statute, the structure of the court system guaranteed that specific trials continued to be about specific offenses. Whether those same offenses (defined operationally) also overlapped is an empirical question. Thus when we turn to actual cases which might in theory have been tried under different statutes, we may for the most part ignore that fact. The prosecution presumably felt they could show the offense charged, and in any case the defense would certainly have denied that offense.

We have considered the judge, the indictment, and the parties to the suit. Now we must look at the composition of the jury. A jury panel was fairly large, often containing more than fifty members. One-third of the total was drawn from each of three orders (the top three legal statuses): senators, *equites*, and *tribuni aerarii* (*Att.* 1.16.3; *Q. fr.* 2.4.6).[68] The juries were highly uniform with respect to sex (all male) and class. We may also expect considerable similarity of education (rhetoric and literary classics and exposure to political oratory in courts and *contiones*)[69] and of occupation (simultaneous interests in land, business, and often politics). We should note that these similarities are all in areas which might potentially have produced differences in conceptions of the legal system or in the weight given different evaluative criteria, and thus there is a strong potential for a uniformity of judging expectations for Cicero (or any other advocate) to target.[70] Also important for this topic is the simple fact that these jurors can be expected to have had relatively clear and fixed expectations going into a trial. The groups subject to jury duty were relatively small (especially the senators).[71] The upper classes were also the special target of much of the criminal legislation (*ambitus, repetundae*). A rhetorical education aimed precisely at forensic speaking was the central form of formal education for the upper class. Finally, the penalties for many of the crimes to be considered were severe: loss of all civil rights, normally resulting in exile. Hence the jurors as a group would have both motivation and opportunity to form opinions about the proper functioning of the legal system prior to their actual appearance on a panel, and these beliefs would likely have had deep ideological and/or philosophical grounding.

The situation in the *iudicia publica* was in many respects similar to that in the *iudicia privata* as described by Frier (1985:197–234).[72] The major differences are the much larger criminal juries, the apparent absence of jurists as advisors to the jurors or even as authorities to be cited by advocates, and the absence of a formula given by the praetor to specify the issue(s) at stake for the jurors. (Advocates in criminal, as well as civil, cases were not normally themselves lawyers.[73]) The latter two points, the absence of jurists and *formulae*, might be thought to increase the advocates' power to shape each case in the absence of an "impartial" central authority such as the judge in a modern American court. Up to a point this must be true. However, the Roman system is structurally so different that this kind of proportional argument no longer makes sense. To the lack of legal formalities corresponds the absence of expectation of legal formalism. That is, this system (unlike the American one) does nothing to suggest that the legal world is a realm of specialized discourse, understood only by initiates. After the speeches and witnesses, the advocates engaged in *altercatio*, a more informal, back-and-forth argument, which would have brought them closer to the realm of normal discourse.[74] The Roman system does not concentrate expert status (as a source of authority) in the advocates; it undercuts the pretensions to special authority of any supposed experts. Frier (1985:228–29) rightly points out that the giving of a formula does not in fact settle all issues of law for civil jurors; the interpretation of *formulae* can be quite complex and technical. However, the giving of formulae in their characteristically technical language does signal to the jurors that they have entered a marked area and that the issue they are to decide is outside their normal competence. This is not the case in the public courts. There the jurors are free to assume that their ordinary understanding of the case is (broadly speaking) the proper understanding.[75]

A courtroom is an example of an "immediate truth-determination forum."[76] That is, the judges, whether jurors or the presiding officer(s), must convert a whole trial's worth of evidence, testimony, and argumentation into a single judgment. This book will address the rules (or principles or procedures) which the jurors in a Late Republican Roman criminal court used to convert such a mass of information into their simple verdict. While it is impossible to make direct observations of jurors' thinking, we can see how an effective advocate (Cicero) would address himself to their concerns. As discussed above, oratorical success is almost by definition dependent on the speaker's ability to satisfy the audience's expectations (though this may involve some clarification or modification of the details of those expectations). I will examine the paradigms for judging which Cicero offers the jurors in his various criminal trials. These will be surprisingly limited, given the normal assumption that Cicero will say whatever will promote victory. I would maintain these few patterns represent values and concepts broadly and deeply shared among the Roman elite. Cicero exploits this "common sense" to produce a persuasive account of how his client did not commit a crime.[77] (Readers not already familiar with the individual cases may wish to consult Appendix A, which gives a brief account of the argument and *dramatis personae* of the various trials.)

Finally, I should say a few words here about the term "paradigm," which will be used frequently in subsequent chapters. For decades now this word has been used heavily in the humanities, particularly in the contexts of Thomas Kuhn's analysis of scientific revolutions as "paradigm shifts" and of various postmodern appropriations of Kuhn's work. I have in mind something rather different and more limited. Much of the present study will be concerned with "judging paradigms," that is (as the previous paragraph suggested), paradigms offered to jurors as models for how they should make their decisions.[78] After all, there must be some procedure for reducing hours of speeches, testimony, and other evidence to one of three, preexisting verdicts. It is, of course, in the absence of an authoritative paradigm in the form of a judge's charge that the jurors' and advocates' paradigms become most important. Sometimes the paradigms we can recover from Cicero are only partial models, e.g., suggestions that a specific piece of information is (ir)relevant or about burden of proof. Often they are more holistic. The entire case, Cicero will sometimes suggest to the jurors, comes to this or that single question or problem.[79] In any case, when the word "paradigm" appears in what follows, it should be understood as "judging paradigm" as defined here.

CHAPTER 2

Ambitus *and the*
Varieties of Economy

1. THE *CRIMEN AMBITUS*[1]

Let us begin by considering the crime of *ambitus* ("electoral bribery"?) and related charges such as *sodalicia* ("electoral conspiracy"?), apparently tried by the same court. Although Cicero argued two cases on the subject (Murena's in 63 and Plancius' in 54), we will start with a brief examination of other sources: rhetorical handbooks, a campaign manual, and the fragmentary sources for the laws involved. Though limited, this evidence will give us a working model of *ambitus*, which we can compare to the modes of argument employed in Cicero's two speeches. Those speeches will be examined first for "paradigms" explicitly offered to the jurors to instruct them how to vote; then we will examine other aspects of the argumentation which complement those paradigms.

These crimes make sense only in the context of the Roman state apparatus. Such crimes could be committed by only a very small fraction of this society, other members of that small elite were the most obvious victims, and the offense could occur only in the context of a small, well-defined civic institution—the magisterial elections. The character of these crimes is also political in a more involved sense. In *de Oratore* (2.105) Cicero at first suggests that defense speakers should meet charges of *ambitus* with flat denial. Only rarely, he says, is it practical to argue that "liberality" *(liberalitas)* and generosity have been mistaken for *ambitus* and largesse. Yet of the several crimes for which he recommends this flat denial (a form known as the *constitutio coniecturalis*), *ambitus* is the only one for which any alternative defense is even suggested.[2] Cicero's recognition of a natural correlation between the criminal and non-criminal descriptions of similar actions suggests that there is an inherent similarity between permissible electoral liberality and proscribed *ambitus*.[3] *Ambitus* is not just an illegal supplement to "normal" legal campaigning, but something very much of a piece with that campaigning.

This suggestion is confirmed by inspection of the history of the relevant laws. This history is somewhat opaque but contains some intriguing traces. Livy (40.19.11; *Per.* 47) records the passage of laws on the subject in 181 and 159, but we know nothing of their content.[4] The first permanent *ambitus* court seems to have been established between 149 and 115, by a law whose authorship and substance are otherwise unknown.[5] There appears also to have been a Sullan law, presumably dating from 81, whose penalty was a bar on seeking office for ten years (*SB* 78St.). The definition of the offense is still unknown. The primary law in force at the end of the Republic was the *lex Calpurnia de ambitu* of 67.[6] We have a number of references to the penalty imposed by the law, and several to the circumstances under which it was passed, but only one clear piece of testimony about the exact offenses covered.[7] In *pro Murena* Cicero concedes the prosecutor's assertion that, by decree of the senate, the following actions would have been illegal:

> *If [a crowd of followers] had been paid to greet the candidate, if they were hired to follow him around, if the tribes were freely* (volgo) *given places at the gladiatorial games, and if feasts were given indiscriminately* (volgo), *then the* lex Calpurnia *has been violated.*

(*Mur.* 67)[8]

Note the critical word *volgo* in two clauses, a term derived from *vulgus*, "crowd, masses." The criminality of such largesse (feasts, games) is a matter of targeting and (consequently) scale, not the simple fact of the giving. The *lex Licinia de sodaliciis* (of 55) under which Plancius was tried, shows us more of the same. Once again, the only real evidence for the scope of the crime itself is from Cicero's own speech: "Show that Plancius held the money, that he gave bribes, that he enrolled *(conscripsisse)* tribesmen and divided them into teams *(decuriavisse)*" (§47, cf. §45). To appreciate the significance of this law we need to look at a guide to contemporary electoral practice (or at least theory)— the *Commentariolum Petitionis* of Cicero's brother Quintus. This work is a long letter purporting to advise Marcus on his run for the consulship in 64.[9]

In discussing how to win popular favor Quintus lists several necessary ingredients, among them "generosity" *(benignitas)*: "Generosity lies in feasts which you should give and you should have your friends give everywhere and for all the tribes." The giving of dinner parties *(convivia)* "everywhere" suggested in this text is nearly indistinguishable from the giving of meals *(prandia)* "indiscriminately" (*Mur.* 67).[10] Other parts of the criminal statutes are also paralleled. In previous passages Quintus had urged the creation of networks of associates to get out the vote:

> *You have attached the leading men among these groups to you by friendship; through them you will easily control the rest of the mob. . . . So when, in addition, you have made partisans of those who have ambitiously ingratiated themselves with their fellow-tribesmen, as well as making those who have local or professional connections fond of you, then you should have the highest hopes.*

> (*CP* 30, 32)

This all looks suspiciously similar to the enrollment and division *(conscriptio and decuratio)* attacked by the *lex Licinia*. And before this Marcus was reminded of the support that he had secured from "four associations *(sodalitates)* of men obligated to your political advancement" (*CP* 19). From 56 these associations would have been in direct violation of a decree of the senate that they *(sodalitates)* and other teams of organized men *(decuriati)* be disbanded (*Q. fr.* 2.3.5). Arguably, when the *lex Licinia* spoke of *conscriptio*, it was directed at more formally organized groups than the *senatus consultum* and than are alluded to in *CP*. However, given the apparent wording of the law, it is an argument that would have to have been made case-by-case in court. We will encounter this potential ambiguity later in other areas of *ambitus*.

Of course the *Commentariolum* (or at least its dramatic date) precedes the decree of the senate and the *lex Licinia* by eight and nine years, respectively, but this does not in itself explain its advocacy of acts that would soon be illegal. The extensive rhetorical attacks on Cicero's opponents contained in the *Commentariolum* (§§7–10, 27, 55) indicate that it is intended as a public document. In antiquity "letters" were a common form for such political broadsides and other public discourse.[11] Indeed, the very text of the work confirms its own public character in Quintus' request for Marcus' editorial hand in polishing it up for publication (*CP* 58). The open discussion of *sodalitates* and the like indicates that they were not merely legal but expected.[12] Nor need attitudes have changed significantly over the following decade. It has been argued that many of the restrictions on the activity of the *sodalitates* and *decuriati* were established not out of general principle but in response to the domination of these groups by a single individual—P. Clodius Pulcher, "populist" politician and long time enemy of Cicero.[13] Hence, the boundaries between legal and illegal, moral and immoral campaigning are not clear.

Another comparison between extant law and the *Commentariolum* may reveal an underlying social anxiety. The first two clauses of the decree of the senate on the *lex Calpurnia* (as reproduced by Cicero) address the problem of paying people to be attendants of the candidate. Yet *pro Murena* 68–69 and *CP* 34–38 indicate that under some circumstances crowds of attendants were normal and proper. In particular Quintus suggests that Cicero's former legal clients should be present because "some retained their property, some their honor, others their safety and entire fortunes at no cost because of [him]" (*CP* 38). This is one of the clearest examples of the obsession of this text with the value of ties of *beneficium*—free gifts to friends (§§14, 16, 18, 19, 21, and *passim*). This is set in contrast to its harsh denunciation of largesse (§§55–57).[14]

To explain the difference in acceptability (as objects of exchange) between money and *beneficia*, it will be helpful to introduce a distinction between market-exchange economies (e.g., modern capitalist systems) and gift-exchange economies (especially as observed by anthropologists in many "primitive" societies).[15] By "gift" I mean a unilateral, disinterested transfer of goods (including money) or services (including labor and votes). The salient characteristics of gifts are not, of course, inherent in the items themselves; any object could conceivably be given or sold. Nor are they primarily a matter of the legal or physical circumstances of the gift. Gifts are gifts by virtue of being described and understood as such, of the rhetoric of disinterestedness that accompanies them.[16] Thus, while we may judge individual gifts to be in bad faith (e.g., *Off.* 1.43–44; Sen. *Ben.* 1.2.3; Plin. 1.8.15), the philosophical argument that there can be no such a thing as a truly unilateral or disinterested gift is not relevant (*pace* Derrida [1992:6–33]). It is the stance of disinterestedness that makes a gift a gift. In fact, it is this very instability of perspective that makes gift-giving an interesting (and politically interested) activity. The giver is constrained by his pose of disinterestedness so long as he wants to maintain the benefits (whatever they might be) of his gift, but the constraint is rhetorical and therefore partial. Different views of a gift may be offered to different people (with varying degrees of success). For instance, in addressing the recipient one might minimize the value of the gift so as to buttress one's own rhetorical claim to disinterestedness; the recipient is likely to know the value anyway. Of course, the giver is then in some danger of being taken too literally (whether out of malice or ignorance), and he may want to represent the debt more extravagantly to third parties (despite weakening thereby his claim to disinterestedness) so as to create a broader social compulsion for "adequate" repayment.

Economies (or sectors thereof) can be structured around the exchange of gifts or market-exchange. While the precise configuration varies from society to society, it is possible to make typological generalizations. The economy of electoral *beneficia* shows most of the characteristics of a typical gift-exchange economy. I will consider here three of these characteristics: incommensurability, social embeddedness, and temporal separability of exchanges. (1) Gifts are often regarded as incommensurable, or at least are divided into distinct "spheres," the elements of which are of value comparable to each other but which cannot be equated to a particular number of items from another sphere. By contrast, in markets items are all exchangeable for precise amounts of cash and so can all be valued in terms of each other. This principle would explain why Cicero could remain indebted to anyone who voted for him, no matter what *beneficium* that voter was repaying (*CP* 21, 37: "Take care that they understand that you are forever bound to them by the greatest obligation"). (2) Gift-exchange takes place in the context of an ongoing social relationship (or is designed to establish such relationships). In a market environment you can and do buy and sell from total strangers. This feature of the gift economy finds expression in Taylor's (1949:66) observation that Roman campaign advertisements are normally phrased as endorsements rather than as assertions of character or policy.[17] The value of the candidate is personally (or corporately in the case of *collegia*) guaranteed for persons who know the endorser but not the candidate. The *Commentariolum* also emphasizes the creations of "friendships," at least as a collusive fiction, as the basis of campaigning (*CP* 16, 25). (3) Although the giving of gifts creates an obligation to reciprocate, there is great flexibility in the timing of the return gift. Sales, by contrast, are completed immediately or at a contractually fixed time. Thus Cicero is repeatedly told that he must point out to potential supporters that external conditions (the nature of elections) require that favors be repaid to him *now* (*CP* 4, 6, 19, 20, 21, 26, 37, 38; eight instances in eighteen OCT pages!). That is, his debtors are not otherwise constrained by any particular timetable.[18] This is also (indirectly) another example of incommensurability. There was apparently no original *quid pro quo* on which Cicero could rely at election time. Furthermore, the emphasis on open-ended reciprocity and on the role of "friends" suggests that the voters themselves may have enforced behavioral norms like to those officially restrained by *ambitus* legislation. They encourage sharing the wealth with "friends" while discouraging indiscriminate giving.[19] The outlines of a fairly typical gift-exchange economy are visible in Roman electoral practice.

Let us consider next typical reactions when market-exchange encroaches on gift-exchange. The Romans had been using coined money, the prototypical marker of a market-exchange system,[20] for at least two centuries before this time. However, gift-exchange can retain considerable ideological importance long after it has been largely displaced as the mode of day-to-day exchange (Morris [1986:6-7] on archaic Greece). Significant anxiety can be brought about by conflict between the two systems, since market-exchange threatens the social relations within which gift-exchange is embedded and which it engenders. Hence, counterfeiting (then a recent invention) is an important metaphor in the work of Alcaeus and other archaic Greek authors. It marks an anxiety over slippages in aristocratic hegemony, a process to which the rise of a monetary economy contributed (L. Kurke 1990, also 1989:539, 1991:7, 252–54). One response to this anxiety is an exaggeration of the characteristics (particularly incommensurability) of gift-exchange in the restricted areas in which it remains important. An example of this phenomenon might include the careful calculation of the monetary value of gifts so as to *avoid* reciprocation of that exact value—a practice of both French tradesmen and the Omaha tribe of Nebraska (Bourdieu 1977:195, note 21; Welsch 1991:63). The latter take this as a mark of self-definition by contrast to mainstream white society. Much of Roman electoral legislation can be seen as ongoing resistance to the encroachment of market-exchange into an area of particular ideological sensitivity—the election of public officials.

The very act of campaigning is essentially one of market-exchange.[21] The candidate offers to carry out programs that will produce various benefits for the voters.[22] Today these benefits can be quite direct: targeted tax cuts, subsidized education, direct employment. In the Roman world the benefits were usually more indirect, such as imperial expansion or good bread, but the principle remains the same. The price is the vote of the individual elector, whom the candidate normally does not even know. *Ambitus* regulations not only attack bribery *per se*, but other forms of market-exchange in an electoral context. Recall that the *lex Calpurnia* forbade the paying and even formal enrollment of a campaign staff. The earliest history of this legislation points to this broad scope as well. The first recorded electoral law is recorded by the historian Livy (4.25.13–4); he notes a law of 432 banning the wearing of the *toga candida*—the whitened toga which was the standard method of advertising one's candidacy to a general audience.[23] The first law specifically styled *de ambitu* is not about bribery at all (358).[24] Again, Livy (7.5.12) tells the story:

> *And, with the approval of the senate, the tribune Gaius Poetelius first brought legislation about* ambitus *before the people; and they believed that this measure would deter in particular the ambition of "new men" who were wont to canvass the markets and local councils.*

What is forbidden here is *ambitus* in its concrete, etymological sense of "going about," that is, campaigning. The motive attributed to the legislation by Livy is the maintenance of aristocratic privilege. What we have seen above suggests that all *ambitus* legislation is essentially of this type. Retaining the gift-exchange structure allowed the aristocracy to retain their individual and collective electoral primacy by preserving the value of their generations-old networks of patronage. Laws against *ambitus* made it harder for new men to break in or even for older nobles to dominate without broad support among those already in power.[25] More precisely, it would not have been so much a question of stopping social-climbing but of controlling the percolation up into the elite that we know occurred at all periods (Hopkins 1983:31–119). This control could be exercised by selective endorsement, loan of resources (particularly of patronage networks in the loosest sense), and selective prosecution.

In short, then, the crime of *ambitus* is intimately connected with the practices of Roman political culture. This does not mean simply that the charge can only be defined in a political context (though that fact is not trivial). Rather, *ambitus* in most of its manifestations represents an exaggeration of normal forms of electoral behavior, not their rejection.[26] But campaigning is necessary in any society large enough that voters must choose between candidates they do not know well.[27] Given this ambiguity between offense and necessity, the question is where to draw the line. That line will vary with, among other things, the social status of the observer. We might well expect, and will in fact find, that this inextricable weaving of the legal and the social affects the way in which an advocate will handle such cases.

2. EXPLICIT PARADIGMS FOR JUDGING *AMBITUS*

Although the presiding officer in a Roman criminal trial did not charge the jurors, this did not keep the advocates from doing so unofficially. It probably even encouraged them to do so. In the third section of *pro Plancio*, Cicero makes a clear and explicit charge to the jury:

> *Unless I show in my client the purest life, the most restrained character, and the deepest faith, continence, piety, and innocence, I shall not complain at all about his punishment. But if I show you all the things expected of good men, I shall ask and pray that you, jurors, give your pity to the man whose own pity guarded my well-being [while I was in exile].*

(*Planc.* 3)

We should note two features of this charge. The first is its great breadth. Absolutely any aspect of the defendant's life or character, past or present, is fair game for the prosecution. There is no mention of the particular charge, not even as a focus for consideration of the broader issues that Cicero has raised (though this is no more ruled out than any other argument). Second, the burden of proof rests entirely on the defense: "Unless I shall have shown . . . , I will not complain at all about his punishment." The advocate must prove the moral worth of his client against a potentially infinite set of alternative hypotheses. Such a paradigm produces the greatest possible asymmetry between the two disputing parties. By adopting this model of adjudication and then taking the "wrong" side, Cicero puts himself in the worst possible argumentative position and hence gains sympathy for the beleaguered defendant. Even then he does not ask literally for acquittal but for pity *(misericordia)*. If such a charge really represented the jurors' expectations of the role of the parties, then it would hardly be advantageous to remind them of this burden; thus we should not take this concession at face value, but rather the reverse. That is, Cicero's immediate aim is probably to make the jurors "well-wishing" *(benivolos, Inv.* 1.20) by this display of submission *(obsecratione . . . supplici, Inv.* 1.22)[28]—a clever *captatio benevolentiae* ("winning of goodwill") from the person of the defense advocate *(Inv.* 1.22; *IO* 4.1.5). The normal expectation of the jurors, then, was probably not "guilty until clearly proven innocent" but could have been almost anything else.

In his speech *pro Murena*, Cicero makes a similar rhetorical move, though in more fragmented form. There he answers (reasonably) the prosecutor's charge that he, the mover of a law on *ambitus*, could not honorably defend someone accused of this very crime:

> *If I should confess that largess* (largitionem) *was given and offer as a defense that it was rightly done, I would be in the wrong, even if someone else had proposed the law. But since my defense is that nothing was done illegally, why should my proposal of the law impede my conduct of the defense?*

> (*Mur.* 5)

In rejecting the so-called *constitutio qualitatis* (the defense that a technically criminal act was, in fact, for the good) Cicero suggests that he must show that his client did not commit various actions; otherwise he himself is to be criticized, and (by ethical implication) Murena is to be convicted. In addition to refuting the prosecutor's attack on Cicero's character, this charge to the jurors serves a local rhetorical function similar to that found at the beginning of *pro Plancio*: submission as a means of *captatio benevolentiae*. Cicero then extends the scope of the trial in the textbook division at the end of the exordium:

> *As I understand it, jurors, there were three parts to the accusation: one was criticism of the defendant's life, second was a comparison of the worthiness of the candidates* (contentio dignitatis), *and the third consisted of the actual accusations of* ambitus.

> (*Mur.* 11)

The first part is clearly a question of general character, the third of the specific accusation; the second, as it turns out, is a combination. It is a replaying both of the candidates' careers and of the election itself. He immediately goes on to make clear that he takes the argument about character to be a legitimate topic for the trial but claims that the prosecution offered their (weak) arguments on this score only because custom demanded it (*Mur.* 11).

Cicero has changed the rules slightly here. As in *pro Plancio* he admits some responsibility for a fairly broad scope of argument, but this responsibility here does not extend to complete acceptance of the burden of proof by the defense. The merely partial responsibility allows the defense advocate some room for maneuvering in discussing the defendant's past life and the *contentio dignitatis*; we will see later that Cicero takes advantage of this argumentative space. This advantage depends on the relationship between what I call his "local" and his "global" strategies. Almost anything Cicero (or anyone else) says will have some immediate function: a step in a narrative or proof, the answer to an objection, *captatio benevolentiae* (as in exordia), and so forth. Connections at this level are a matter of "local" strategy. Many utterances, however, also affect the force of more distant passages or even the speech as a whole. This is "global" strategy. The simplest example of global strategy is the phenomenon of "resonance" (see note 43). This is the repetition of a proposition, image, or argument, which makes each individual occurrence more credible by virtue of familiarity. A more complex case we will see is the use of a historical example *(exemplum)* which directs jurors to subject all the arguments in a given trial to a given rule of interpretation. One would expect that in the work of a highly skilled orator (or poet) any part of the text might participate in one or more global strategies.

The different categories of the charge in *pro Plancio* and *pro Murena* can also provide us with further suggestions about the jurors' expectations of the advocate's duties. The partition of material in *pro Murena* serves to emphasize the strengths of Cicero's case (especially the issue of general character) by making them integral components of the accusation. Such a division would be easier to maintain if the categories advanced were basically traditional. Cicero's own phrase "a virtual rule of accusation" (11: *lex . . . quaedam accusatoria*) claims that they are. *Pro Plancio* also covers all three topics extensively, even though it does not use them as an organizing principle: past life, §§27–28, 30, 33–35, 61; *contentio dignitatis*, §§17–18, 51, 58–60; crime, §§45–48, 53–55. It also seems to use the word *contentio* several times in a quasi-technical sense (§§5, 16, 18), referring to the *contentio dignitatis* or comparison of candidates ("[In this trial] it seems that some test of worth [*contentio*] has to be made," *Planc.* 5; cf. 16, 18). This evidence, both from practice and from technical vocabulary, supports the notion that all these categories (character, *contentio*, and crime) and hence a considerable breadth of topic were conventionally discussed in *ambitus* cases. The assumption of the full burden of proof, however, is essentially a bluff (to which topic we will return in a later chapter).[29]

Later in *pro Plancio*, Cicero offers the prosecutor (Laterensis) another possible means of deciding the case:

> *If I defend the people's action, Laterensis, and show that Gnaeus Plancius did not sneak up on the office, but came to it by the same path which has always been open to men of the equestrian order, can I then preempt the comparison* (contentio), *a part which cannot be handled politely, of your speech and bring you at last to the charge proper?*

(*Planc.* 17)

In the middle of the speech he gives more content to this new approach, and in particular he describes the "path which has always been open":

> *These men [supporters from the lower cases] are full of a sense of duty, and of obedience, and of old-time values. . . . Organization* (decuratio) *of tribesmen, enrollment* (descriptio) *of the people, and votes bought up with cash — all these things provoke the outrage of the senate and of all good men. Show these things, bring them forth; prove, Laterensis, that Plancius organized and enrolled men, and that he held and distributed money.*

(*Planc.* 45)[30]

In these two passages, Cicero has pulled a double switch relative to the judging paradigm previously introduced in section three: in the first passage he starts to change the substantive issues at stake. The scope of the speech is now largely restricted to the specifics of Plancius' electoral behavior. Additionally, it is made clear that his campaign is to be judged in relation to a historical context. Or rather, the formal (legal) definition and the basic (political) rationale of the defense are made nearly indistinguishable. The form of judging, however, remains essentially the same. Cicero still offers to provide positive proof of his side of the case, albeit in reduced form. In the second passage the content of the paradigm is made a little more specific, but the form is reversed. It is now said to be Laterensis' responsibility as prosecutor to prove Plancius' guilt, to show that his actions fit certain categories held antithetical to ancestral custom. Cicero effects this double transition by means of two important devices. One is the simple separation discussed above: Cicero weakens two different aspects of his original extreme position in different places, and their separation in the text (more than twenty-five sections apart) mirrors their logical distinction. The other is a change of addressee. In the introduction Cicero exhibited a conventionally submissive attitude toward the jury. In the body of the speech, and particularly where the opposing advocate is the nominal addressee, a more confrontational approach is employed.

In *pro Murena* there is a similar retreat from the high standard of proof announced at the beginning of the speech. As quoted above, Cicero starts to make specific charges the key to the trial (*Mur.* 67). Then the case is again made to rest only on the commission (or not) of specific acts:

> *There is real doubt whether the event took place or not, but if it did, no one could doubt it was against the law. Thus it is ridiculous to leave uncertain what is in doubt and to adjudicate what no one doubts. . . . Show that Lucius Murena did those things in the first place; then I will concede that they were done against the law.*

> (*Mur.* 67–68)[31]

Here the subject matter is given the narrow interpretation of section 5 ("did he or did he not"), not the broad, tripartite scope of section 11. Simultaneously, the burden of proof is reversed as it is in the third step of *pro Plancio*. There are even certain similarities of language: *doce . . . tum*, "show, teach" (*Planc.* 45), *sic tu doce* (*Planc.* 47), *qua re doce . . . tum* (*Mur.* 68). Cicero goes on to enhance the authority of this new jury charge with an internal dialogue:

> *Does the senate think it a crime to meet someone? No, only to do so for a price; try to convict him of this. How about having many followers? Not*

unless they are hired; show this. What about giving places at the shows or
at dinners? Only if they are given indiscriminately (volgo).[32] *What does*
"indiscriminately" mean? "To all."

(*Mur.* 73)

An address to a third party (the opposing speaker Servius) is combined with a logical or at least logical-appearing argument intended to convince the jury that Cicero's charge is clearly the correct one. What disinterested party could object to so reasonable a lecture? At the same time Cicero minimizes conflict with the jurors' preconceptions on the subject. Given that the global strategy of this speech de-emphasizes formal application of the law (as we will see later), it is also useful for Cicero to employ highly formal, logical-sounding language in those sections which do deal with the law. Thus he avoids the appearance of evasiveness.

This part of *pro Murena* also seems to attempt to set the accusations in some kind of historical context.[33] There are frequent phrases such as "if I may add what is accustomed" (§69), "Do you ask me why we need to do what we have always done" (§70), "by custom and habit and ancestral practice" (§72). However, the relationship between the context and the specific details of the crime is made more problematic in this speech than in *pro Plancio*. The new paradigm of section 73—a narrow focus on deeds and a heavy burden on the prosecutor—is introduced without reference to the general context of Roman custom Cicero has just discussed. Rather, to introduce it Cicero returns to the same argument he made first (§5): that his ethical status as proposer of the law on *ambitus* is relevant only if it is assumed that the defendant is guilty (§67). This is so obviously valid as a local response to the immediate objection (i.e., to Cicero's presence as advocate) that it is easily accepted. But when the hearer accepts this argument, he also absorbs the new, narrowly focused paradigm with it. The winning local argument conceals the globally significant paradigm embedded within and thus serves as a Trojan Horse. When Cicero finally does engage in historical analysis of electoral practice, only one aspect (the gathering of large crowds of followers) is directly justified (§§68–71). Then when the giving of games and feasts is finally discussed (§72), it is largely to explain a loss of electoral support for Sulpicius. Nonetheless the interweaving of more and less sound arguments lends some force to the suggestion (never fully argued) that Murena's actions could be justified if only properly contextualized.

The attempt to add historical perspective is as close to a confession (see note 35 on *ambitio*) as is ever found in Cicero's speeches:

*When was there ever a time, in our memory or our fathers', when it was
not the practice (whether you call it ambition [ambitio][34] or liberality
[liberalitas]) to give seats in the circus and in the forum to friends and
fellow-tribesmen?*

(*Mur.* 72)

But the disjunction between the historical and the legal justifications is best
shown by a change in the basis of the defense.[35] Cicero responds to the charge
that these gifts were improper: "What about giving places at the shows or at
dinners? Only if given indiscriminately *(volgo)*. What is 'indiscriminately'? To
all." Craig (1979:150) argues that this is "not properly a shift to the definitional
stasis [i.e., admitting the facts, but questioning the opposition's definition or
characterization]. . . . That Murena has participated in such activities himself
has been denied, whatever the activities be called." At the beginning of the previous section (on the other side of an intervening lacuna of indeterminate
length) we do find the clause "although Murena did not do it at all." However,
this is a response specifically to the immediately preceding accusation "But
[according to the prosecution] games were given for all the tribes and all were
called to dinners." It seems that at least one new accusation has intervened
where our texts pick up after the lacuna: "the prefect of engineers once gave a
place to his tribesmen" (§73). Hence it is not clear that the strict denial applies
to the latter, definitional argument over *vulgo*. Even if it does in a formal sense,
they stand far enough apart that the rhetorical effect is the creation of distinct
argument, and hence the argument from definition can reasonably be invoked.
The defense of Murena's (and/or his friends') actions on the basis of tradition is never made in detail. The overall strategy of this passage (*Mur.* 67–73)
is similar to that of *Planc.* 45–48, and its effect is not substantially different.
Murena's and Plancius' campaigns were not only acceptable, but, in a strategi-
cally ill-defined sense, conventional.

3. IMPLICIT PARADIGMS FOR JUDGING *AMBITUS*

The previous section considered instances in which Cicero offered the jurors
models for their decision based on more or less explicit rules. Paradigms (as
the name suggests) can, however, take on a less formally structured character.
This section will consider some of these more indirect methods. In a sense,
any argument can be taken to carry within itself a claim for the paradigm within
which it is framed. Making a formal syllogistic argument, for instance, implic-

itly asserts the value of syllogistic reasoning. However, I will deal here only with passages which, primarily or secondarily, establish a paradigm in light of which other materials are to be interpreted.

Early in *pro Plancio* Cicero advances the proposition that "even if a man is passed over by the voters who should not have been, the one who was not passed over should not therefore be condemned by a jury" (§8). The following is his justification:

> *For if it were the case that there could be appeal from the assembly (a power the patricians could not hang on to in the time of our ancestors), jurors would have a power much less to be endured. For at that time, if not ratified by the patricians, the person who won office would not hold it.*
>
> (*Planc.* 8)

He implicitly approves other paradigms by explicitly rejecting this one, wherein the jurors "correct" the errors of the assembly by reevaluating the worthiness of the candidates. Obvious here is his appeal to historical context, a tactic that occurs again in section 11 (discussed above). There is little actual history here, but Cicero makes free use of evocative words like *patres*, "patricians" (literally "fathers"), and "our ancestors." Cicero goes on to employ an interesting *reductio ad absurdum* to dispose finally of this particular aspect of the case. If the court is bound to decide in favor of the more noble candidate, then there is no point in holding elections (similarly again at §14). But the elections are sanctioned by their establishment by the ancestors. Hence one must either accept Cicero's restriction of the charge or reject the *mos maiorum*.

The next example, from *pro Murena*, illustrates a more elaborate invocation of historical models for judging:

> *Since he [Cato] is the accuser, I must beg first, jurors, that you not allow his prestige to harm Murena. . . . Publius Africanus had twice been consul and had destroyed Carthage and Numantia, the two great threats to our empire, when he accused Lucius Cotta. He [Africanus] had the greatest eloquence, faith, and integrity and as much authority as the very empire which had been defended by his efforts.*
>
> (*Mur.* 58)

Yet Africanus' prosecution failed, allegedly because the people did not wish to allow the appearance that Cotta had been destroyed by the whim of one man.

There follows a similar anecdote about the failed prosecution of Ser. Galba at the hands of Cato the Censor, the great-grandfather of the current prosecutor (§59). Here we have two consecutive examples of the most common form of Roman argument from historical context—an anecdote about a specific historical event or personage. On the surface Cicero makes here an argument about how to react to the personal influence of the prosecutor, essentially an ethical claim.[36] However, as Craig (1979:131 and note 16) notes, there is a subtext here which urges a fundamentally different judging paradigm for the entire case.[37] Both defendants seem to have been guilty (or at least thought guilty).[38] Both anecdotes suggest that the greater good lies in protecting weaker citizens from victimization by powerful prosecutors. The implicit paradigm being offered is that of acquitting "guilty" individuals, if the greater good of the state in some sense requires it. As will be discussed in more detail later, this seems to be exactly the decision Cicero wants from the present jury, and the similarity is too close to be explained by coincidence.

The penultimate example of implicit paradigm setting in this chapter is a part of the so-called Juristenkomik of sections 19–30 of *pro Murena*.[39] The passage as a whole effectively lessens the stature of the prosecutor and legal scholar Ser. Sulpicius Rufus relative to that of the defendant and purported military hero Murena.[40] A parody of the complex and formal language of civil law (§§25–26) serves this function admirably, but this is not its only effect. It begins:

> *Although one could well enough say "The Sabine farm is mine.," "No,*
> *it's mine.," then have a trial, they [the jurisconsults] do not allow it. Instead*
> *a flood of words: "the farm which is in the area which is called 'Sabine.'"*

> (*Mur.* 26)

As this fictional narrative continues, the parties go back and forth to their respective jurisconsults obtaining the appropriate legal formulae required to conduct the case. The praetor even takes care "lest anyone think himself charming or pleasant and say anything on his own initiative" (§26). Craig (1979:120) suggests that these points are the weakest in the Juristenkomik. For instance, Cicero's argument that the civil law's opacity was due to intentional obscurantism is largely specious.[41] Furthermore, one can note that the premise of this argument (incomprehensibility of legal language) admits the necessity and expertise of the jurisconsults. This is in direct contradiction to the later argument that law is held in contempt since anyone can learn what he needs of it (§28); the praetor enforces the jurists' standards (§26). These logical weaknesses can be admitted (though the humor of the passage is, of course, not thereby seriously reduced), but we must not ignore the value of the passage for predisposing the jurors to a particular way of judging. They are dissuaded from strict application of the letter of the law (and legal solutions in general) in favor of a more pragmatic approach.[42] This implication then resonates with those of the *exempla* (historical examples) of section 58.[43] Adamietz (1989:231) rightly suggests a similar function for Cicero's ridicule of his opponent Cato's literalist interpretation of Stoic dogma later in the speech.

This section will close with an extraordinary passage in which Cicero makes a very dangerous argument—he tells the truth (in a general way) about politics:

> *You [Sulpicius] demanded an* ambitus *law, though there was one already, the quite severe* lex Calpurnia, *in fact. We humored your will and position. . . . The senate gave in to your pleas, but because of you (and not of its own will) it established a condition harsher for the common welfare.*
>
> (*Mur.* 46, 47)

In a passage more reminiscent of a modern historian than of Cicero's normal approach to law, we are told of the personal motivations behind the passage of the *lex Tullia*. He can make these claims authoritatively because of his personal position as a senator and consul.[44] The law-making process is exposed as highly political and therefore contingent. In effect Cicero has separated law and right. This is all the more noteworthy since bringing the fact up does little to support the local claim that Sulpicius' earlier actions against *ambitus* made him unpopular with the electorate.[45] Instead, it continues to undermine the notion of judicial decision-making in strict accordance with law and instead encourages judicial policy-making. Later, when Cicero is making his final charge in sections 67–73, he reminds the jurors of the contingency of law when he says, "I recall how many votes these senatorial debates cost us, Servius" (§72). Mentioning the division of votes of the senate itself makes this point, as well as reminding the jurors about the more extensive and more pointed account earlier.

Examination of the paradigms Cicero offers to the jurors (both explicitly and implicitly) shows an apparently divided strategy. On the one hand, Cicero seems to demand that the prosecution prove conclusively the fairly narrow hypothesis that the defendant paid for votes. This is not strictly incompatible with the suggestions in my first section above about the social basis of *ambitus*. On this understanding, however, we would have to assume that Cicero has adopted a deliberately narrow view of the crime, not surprising in a defense advocate. On the other hand, both speeches (though especially *pro Murena*) direct the jurors' attention to broader issues of policy—why elections are, have been, and should be held. This potentially gets us closer to the suggestions of the introduction about a tension between gift and market-exchange in relation to campaigning. After exploring one more line of argument within the speeches (section 4), I will try (section 5) to integrate these two paradigms and then reconsider whether they can be made to square with the hypotheses of section 1 or not.

4. THE USE OF ETHICAL ARGUMENT

Instead of looking at what Cicero says he will (or needs to) prove, this section will examine a particular aspect of the actual argumentation—the intersection or overlap between ethical and logical argument. Cicero's argumentative practice can easily be interpreted in light both of our theoretical expectations and of his instructions to the jury, explicit and implicit.[46] These ethical arguments tend to take the following form: a narrative describes an action or actions of a person; from this narrative a general character *(ingenium)* is inferred; then from this character the probability of his taking particular actions (past or future) is inferred in turn.[47] Often, however, this argument appears in truncated form. The chain of inference from behavior may be prematurely stopped after one step (or none) or, on the other hand, the beginning of the chain may be skipped by stipulation.[48] The first parameter we will examine is the formal structure of these arguments as just described. The next is the question of whose ethos is at issue. In principle the following are possible: Cicero himself, the defendant, the prosecutor, or a scapegoat character who purportedly stands in the same relationship to the prosecutor as the defendant does to Cicero. Here we will restrict ourselves to the defendant and his double on the other side.[49]

In *pro Plancio* Cicero's narrative about Plancius is largely designed to show explicitly (§§27-29) or implicitly (§§67, 98-101) his *pietas* toward family, friends, and especially Cicero. In other passages Plancius is defended against Laterensis' character attacks (§§30-31, 33). Very little of this, except the story of Plancius' aid to Cicero in exile, involves extended narrative; it is simply asserted that so-and-so approved of service rendered by Plancius. At the end the audience is left to infer his *pietas*. The situation in *pro Murena* is roughly similar. In sections 11–14 accusations of bad character are denied largely by recounting favorable evaluations by authority figures, such as Lucullus, of Murena's military service or by simply denying Cato's narrative (*nullum turpe convivium, non amor, non comissatio,* "no wild parties, no affairs, no debauchery," §13). Eventually this leads to the conclusion: "We offer as defense the near confession of the prosecution that he is a good and pure man" (§14). In the *contentio dignitatis* the same themes (valorous service in Asia, public approval) continue to resonate (§§15–53). Explicit conclusions are drawn about skills and popularity but not character (Craig 1979 : 110–29). We see in these two speeches various combinations of narrative, inference, and stipulation. There is one notable absence. Neither speech infers from the defendant's general character that he was not the sort of person to commit particular acts of bribery. To anticipate the conclusion of the next section, we can explain this absence as reflecting the relative unimportance of individual acts (as opposed to general electoral behavior) in the judgment of *ambitus*.

Obviously, then, the defendant's ethos is a subject of some interest. Is there any sort of scapegoat figure? No. There is a slight suggestion that some of Murena's friends have gone overboard in campaigning for him ("it was done by his friends," §72), but there is no real attempt to set up an alternate defendant. Perhaps this is because the defense of total denial is available (absent the corpse normally implied in a murder trial). By contrast, at *Clu.* 64ff. (argued under the murder statute) Cicero maintains that the opposition, not his client, bribed the jurors in the trial of the elder Oppianicus. More generally, we will see in chapter five (on *repetundae*) that, even when the very commission of a crime could be denied, Cicero still prefers to point to the opposition as criminals. An alternative defendant in murder cases is (as we will see in the next chapter) a virtual requirement. This expectation in any case is surely a cultural necessity, but not a logical one. Meanwhile, though it might be construed as strictly outside the case, one might expect development of the ethos of defeated candidates, especially those responsible for prosecution. If the actual winner were in fact the "better man," his potential motive for bribery is reduced. This issue is in fact treated briefly, but not in the way one might expect. In both speeches the *good* character of the opposing figure is granted in a list of virtues which Cicero is willing to stipulate (*Planc.* 9, 63; *Mur.* 15, 21).[50] The only narrative about either Sulpicius or Laterensis is that of their respective electoral campaigns. We will have to account for this peculiarity, too, in the general interpretation offered in the following section.

5. THE JUDGMENT OF *AMBITUS*

For the most part we have been able to treat *pro Plancio* and *pro Murena* in parallel. However, before we can treat the judgment of *ambitus* in general terms, we need to take into account some of the individual peculiarities of the speeches. There seems to exist a consensus on the overall persuasive strategy of *pro Murena*.[51] On this account, the bulk of the speech (up to §78) mainly sketches out a *pro forma* argumentative defense against a conventional attack—one against the acts, life, and character of the defendant. It also attempts to increase Cicero's authority while deflating Cato's. Then only at the end do we get Cicero's "real" argument (the only truly persuasive one): if Murena is convicted, there will not be time to elect a replacement before the new term begins, and the government will be weakened accordingly. Thus the danger to the state posed by Catiline is so great as to require acquittal of his client no matter what the details of the case.[52]

Cicero is seen to give the jurors just enough conventional forensic defense to form a pretext for what he will eventually frame as a deliberative decision. This position is often supported by citing Cicero's reference to this case in his later speech *pro Flacco*:

> I, as consul, also defended L. Murena, the consul-designate. As the jurors listened to his noble accusers, none of them thought they should actually judge about ambitus, *since they knew well what I had told them: in the war with Catiline there had to be two consuls on January first.*
>
> (*Flacc.* 98)

While this theory makes some important points, a wider examination of the evidence encourages a less radical hypothesis. In particular we should consider why a supposedly *pro forma* defense would take up most of the speech and why, in any case, that particular form was the one to be observed.

Let us start by considering the context of the passage from *pro Flacco* just cited. Before mentioning Murena's case Cicero had cited those of M.' Aquilius and C. Piso, other men who had (ostensibly) been acquitted of criminal charges for political reasons (the former even admittedly guilty of extortion). The fact that Cicero can now make explicit the policy-oriented paradigm he sought in *pro Murena* (as well as attributing it to these other cases) suggests that it is not so deviant as has sometimes been suggested. This view is confirmed by the charge to the jury which follows in *pro Flacco*:

Prudent and wise jurors always consider the utility of the state, the common safety, and the condition of the republic in their judgments. When your ballot is given to you, jurors, it will not only be about Flaccus, but about preserving the leaders and preservers of our society.

(*Flacc.* 98–99)

Here an appeal to the general good is explicit. The same argument is made in the speech for Rabirius: "Obey this voice, citizens, and you will not remove the hope of liberty, salvation, . . . and dignity from your court nor from the republic" (*Rab. Perd.* 34).[53] If it is this common, the appeal to policy judgment by the jurors would appear, at least in some contexts, to be a legitimate part of the advocate's arsenal.[54] But if the policy argument can be made this openly, why should Cicero have buried it so deeply in *pro Murena*?

It is known that one of Cicero's favorite devices is the *argumentum in utramque partem*: either side of a dilemma is made to lead to the same conclusion.[55] Not only does he deploy such arguments tactically, but, nearly uniquely in extant classical oratory, he uses the form to structure entire speeches.[56] This structural tendency warrants the suggestion that we ought to modify the standard interpretation of *pro Murena*. We have shown above a number of similarities between *pro Plancio* and the supposedly *pro forma* sections of *pro Murena*; others were noted by Preiswerk (1905:43). We should take the first part of *pro Murena* seriously as a normal speech for a case of *ambitus*. To this Cicero adds a second line of defense:[57] Murena is innocent, and even if he were not, it is necessary to state security that he be acquitted. The positioning of this second line and Cicero's own later comments (in *pro Flacco*) indicate that he felt it to be his best, but not his only, argument. The claim of national security should be seen as a gift that fell into Cicero's lap, not as a last line to which he was forced to fall back. One might expect this type of defense to occur naturally in a speech against a charge of, say, *perduellio* (treason), and we will see its like in chapter 4. A crime against the state is by nature a political crime and thus subject to political defense. In *pro Murena* there is, of course, extensive preparation for the shift of paradigm. That, however, is motivated not because overtly policy-oriented argument is strictly illegitimate in *ambitus* cases, but by the fact that it was not normally available in ordinary circumstances. The point here is that, despite *pro Murena*'s being unusual in certain respects, we are entitled to treat it as useful evidence for the actual conception of *ambitus* at the time of its delivery.

So what can we now say about the limits within which *ambitus* is discussed? As for the crime proper, which is at least nominally the justification for the prosecution, there are few surprises. Cicero in both speeches retreats to a paradigm in which the burden of each issue is cast on the prosecutor, and the specific issues are determined by the precise content of the law. This is obviously an advantageous position for the defense. It minimizes the claims they have to defend against. We note also that he assumes this position with what might be considered a relative minimum of rhetorical trickery. The only subtlety involved is the retreat from the (apparently conventional) adoption of a much less favorable paradigm at the beginning of each speech. This may indicate that the eventual paradigm is near to the jurors' preexisting expectations. We should also note that, to the extent that factual issues are discussed in both speeches, Cicero tends to discuss campaign strategy as a whole, rather than specific incidents.

But it is also clear that other issues are at stake in an *ambitus* case and that these cannot be entirely suppressed. Somewhat surprisingly, the "proper" outcome of the election does not seem to be one of these issues, at least not one of the primary ones.[58] Scholars have commented on the rhetorical difficulties (mostly to do with his own ethos) Cicero faced in *pro Murena*, engendered by the fact that he had supported Sulpicius, the prosecutor, in the election (*Mur.* 7).[59] Since a *contentio dignitatis* seems to have been expected of the advocate, he appears to have had a problem. How not to offend his friend and undercut his own credibility by an unfavorable comparison? But if we compare *pro Plancio*, Cicero repeatedly and *voluntarily* puts himself in a similar position. In *Planc.* 13, 16, 18, and 50 he admits that in some sense Laterensis was the better candidate and would have won the election had he comported himself differently—precisely the argument made to Sulpicius in *pro Murena* (§§43–53).[60] To quote two examples, the Roman people are made to beseech Laterensis:

> *Seek the magistracy in which you can be most useful! No matter who the aediles are, the same games are given; what really matters is who the tribunes of the people are.*

> (*Planc.* 13)

Then Cicero explains the options to the prosecutor: "'Why is he elected rather than I?' Either I don't know, or I do not say, or even (the worst case) if I said it, I still could not properly say 'he was not rightly elected.'" (§16). It might be suggested that both of these speeches are affected by unusual personal ties of Cicero's.[61] However, as a matter of general principle we should not declare all extant speeches on this charge abnormal without more specific proof. Furthermore, we can ask just how unusual such ties would have been.[62] If personal ties are not the issue, then we might expect both sides to claim to have the better candidate. Cicero, then, does not find it necessary to show that his client was the better candidate.

The rhetorical imperatives in the matter of the *contentio* are mixed. On the one hand, regardless of the specific courtroom traditions, one might expect one side or the other to bring up the issue of relative merit. It would have been useful to the prosecution to be able to prove underqualification as a motive for bribery (or the defense to prove good qualifications to eliminate motive). Whether or not *ambitus* comes down to specific acts or to broader patterns of behavior, motive could easily be made relevant. On the other hand, the conventionally modest posture of the defendant (and, to a lesser degree, of his advocate on his behalf) might weigh against making strong claims to deserve a particular office. In fact, when Cicero does engage in a *contentio* in *pro Murena*, it has more to do with popularity than with merit in a more abstract sense.[63] There is also some external evidence that Cicero is appealing here to Roman common sense. Rosenstein (1990:114–52) has shown that, as a historical matter, in both electoral and judicial contexts a reputation for personal *virtus* appears to have been required of generals, whereas practical skill and success were merely useful ornaments. This appears to be a particular case of the skills/character distinction that we will see Cicero propose below. That Rosenstein's case is established on broader historical grounds might lead us to believe that Cicero is not simply producing the general principle on an *ad hoc* basis. And perhaps Cicero is drawing from long-standing tradition to find the topos of the fickleness of the voting assemblies used in both *pro Plancio* (§15) and *pro Murena* (§§35–36). In both cases this is figured by storm-tossed seas (examples are collected by Preiswerk [1905:44]). One cannot count on the "right" decision from the assemblies, only an "unbiased" one. Hence there may in fact have been little motive to assert one's "right" to the office.[64] Cicero's lack of zeal in defending Plancius' candidacy (and his relative lack of embarrassment in contending with Sulpicius) should perhaps not then be too surprising.

While the *relative* nobility or talent of the candidate was not so much at issue, we have observed that a general evaluation of his character seems to have been stressed. Here the introduction of the past life as a formal topic (cf. *Mur.* 11) corresponds to the actual practice of both speeches. Cicero devotes considerable space to defending and ornamenting the character of his clients. In neither case does he attack the characters of the opponents or even suggest that they are inferior to those of his clients. In *pro Plancio* he does the reverse:

"I not only confess that Laterensis has the greatest virtues, but I blame you for not listing them while you complain about trivial things" (*Planc.* 63). In fact his discussion of the opposing characters is usually limited to a perfunctory admission of various virtues. The discussion of specific skills as opposed to character (*artes* as opposed to *ingenium*) differs dramatically in the two speeches: Murena is praised for military talent (§§20–22), the *sine qua non* of the well-functioning state, while Plancius is admitted to have had not only no command experience (admittedly early in his political career), but no specific skills at all:

> You ask what [military] camps he saw; he was a soldier in Crete under this man here [Q. Metellus] as his commander and then a military tribune in Macedonia, and as quaestor he took only enough time off from military duties to protect me. You ask whether he is learned. No, but at least he does not think himself so. Does he know the law? As if anyone had claimed that he said false things about the law.

> (*Planc.* 61–62)

Here the admission is so plain (Cicero does not merely duck the issue) as to suggest that technical skills really were, as he goes on to say explicitly, desirable but optional.[65] What is wanted is someone who knows his own talents (and limitations) and can fulfill his assigned role honorably.

We should also recall the historical context in which Cicero attempts to embed both cases. Cicero's claims of adherence to the law and good character discussed above are not made in the abstract but with reference to the behavior of other candidates in the past. Plancius and Murena did what the ancestors did; the ancestors acted correctly; therefore Plancius and Murena were also correct. Furthermore their modes of campaigning were not just acceptable in themselves, but also the key to the operation of the entire received political tradition, as it is described at *Mur.* 70–72 and *Planc.* 44–45, 47 (as well as in the *Commentariolum Petitionis*). This is, allegedly, the crucial area of politics which binds both mass and elite. Hence the entire *mos maiorum* is put at risk by these prosecutions.

Though the evidence is, of course, limited, we may now make a provisional assessment of what was at stake in a case of *ambitus*. On the one hand it is impossible to escape a judgment about certain acts which provide the basis for the law and the charge. Cicero seems to have felt free to minimize and circumscribe these considerations, but they could not be avoided completely—the simple buying of votes for cash. We also need to explain the following characteristics shared by the two speeches: (1) their focus on character in its own right, rather than as a predictor of behavior, (2) their frequent reference to the social context in which actions occur, and (3) their de-emphasis of the comparison of candidates. The defendant is being assessed alone and in terms that are at once personal and social. The more general issue in the jurors' purview seems to have been something like the following: has the candidate's behavior (electoral and general) shown him to conform minimally to the standards of the society he claims to represent (or rather the fraction of society from which candidates and jurors are drawn)? More generally, is the defendant "one of us"? [66] Such a criterion clarifies the motive for the advocate to explain not why his candidate should have won, but how he could have done so. It also takes into account the role of sociohistorical factors in framing the charge. We can now ask whether other aspects of the strategies of the speeches address themselves to the crime as we have defined it here.

If we take this view of *ambitus*, then we can see that the "digressive" material (especially that about Cicero himself) in *pro Plancio* is actually closely tied to the central issue of the rest of the speech. Fairly early in the speech, Cicero praises Plancius' character, particularly his devotion toward his relatives (§29) and notes "to my mind, *pietas* is the foundation of all the virtues." In later sections he returns to the topic of the virtues and rearranges the hierarchy: [67]

> *This [gratitude,* gratia] *alone is not only the greatest of the virtues, but the mother of all the rest. What is* pietas *but goodwill toward one's parents? What citizens are good and beneficial to the state in war and in peace except those who remember the state's benefactions?*
>
> (*Planc.* 80)

Gratia is now made the focus of all virtues, or, more precisely, of all the civic virtues which structure one's relationship to family, state, and gods.

So far this could all be read as self-praise on Cicero's part (after all he is the one who is grateful to Plancius) and a defense against the accusation that he ought not be defending this person at all (*Planc.* 5–6). Now, however, we may note a "digression" on the nature of obligation earlier in the speech:

> *And yet, debts of money and gratitude are not alike. Whoever repays money no longer has what he paid; whoever owes, retains what is another's. But*

whoever repays favor has it and who has it repays it in the very fact of having it.

(*Planc.* 68)

Quamquam dissimilis est pecuniae debitio et gratiae. Nam qui pecuniam dissolvit, statim non habet id quod reddit; qui autem debet, is retinet alienum; gratiam autem et qui refert habet, et qui habet in eo ipso quod habet refert.

Cicero had made the same distinction three years before in nearly the same words (*Red. Pop.* 23) and would repeat it, with an attribution to an anonymous interlocutor, in *de Officiis* (2.69). The rhetorician Antonius Julianus later pointed out that this argument depends on a lexical substitution (Gellius *NA* 1.4). He notes that in *pro Plancio* the phrases *qui autem debet [pecuniam]* and *qui habet [gratiam]* are not parallel and that, while "having" and "owing" are interchangeable in some circumstances, they are not here: if *habet* were replaced by *debet*, the argument would be "absurd and forced" (*NA* 1.4.7). The conflation in this context is possible, of course, because *habere gratiam* is the idiomatic expression for being in a state of gratitude.

This passage brings up an important point about the exchange of favors. A loan of money creates an obligation for that amount of money; when the appropriate amount of money is repaid, the debt is canceled. When, however, one is the recipient of a favor *(beneficium)*, the return obligation is for a state of *gratia*.[68] Doing a favor in return does not end this relationship, for ending the relationship would mean leaving the state of *gratia* and thus reneging on the original obligation. Rather the second *beneficium* creates a reciprocal obligation. Thus gifts of favors and *gratia* show the incommensurability which we have noted as characteristic of gift-exchange systems (section 1). This feature is combined with their temporal separability in a slightly earlier remark in the speech of thanksgiving to the people (*Red. Pop.* 23): "Nor is it just to limit the memory of a favor to a particular time or day." Those who observe their obligations fall ever deeper into each other's debt. It is worth noting that in both passages Cicero speaks of debts and favors in a political context: his recall from exile and his subsequent defense of his allies in the criminal courts. This confirms our earlier suggestion that the Roman elite liked to think of politics in terms of a gift-exchange system.

To return to the specifics of *pro Plancio*: Cicero goes on to say that he would do as much for Plancius as for his own brother or other family member since it is through Plancius that he now has enjoyment of the others (*Planc.* 69).[69] This line of argument about *gratia* converges with the other at the following point: Cicero's debt to Plancius implicates the latter in the economy of *gratia* and *beneficium*, not that of money. Cicero has constructed this economy more generally as the very framework of aristocratic society. References to Cicero's relationship with his own family (§69), and to Plancius' with his family (§29), with his neighbors (§§19–22), and with his superiors (§§27–28),[70] fill out a picture of Plancius woven into all the canonical structures of society. So, if the question in *ambitus* cases is "Is he one of us?," the answer must be a resounding "yes."

In fact, weaving Plancius into the social fabric in this way seems to be the primary goal of much of the speech. We have just noted several passages whose local force is to establish Plancius' social position; now we may also note one substantial argument which, while acting locally as a technical attack on the prosecutor, serves globally to reinforce the significance of Plancius' personal ties to his community. This argument is Cicero's extended complaint about the (alleged) inapplicability of the *lex Licinia* under which the case was tried (*Planc.* 36–47).[71] In particular Cicero objects to Laterensis' refusal to pick for the jury certain tribes that had supported Plancius in the election.[72] The basis of this attack is a little ambiguous. In some places Cicero claims (perhaps disingenuously) that the prosecutor was expected to use his prerogative to pick the tribes that had been corrupted by the defendant and so would have direct knowledge of the case: "The senate thought that, when those tribes were picked which had been bought, they could serve as both witnesses and jurors" (§37).[73] At other points the argument focuses on picking jurors who are familiar *(notus)* with Plancius in a more general sense: "For since you have picked these tribes, you have shown that you prefer strangers, not acquaintances, as jurors" (§42).[74] At least twice the two notions seem to run together. It is general familiarity with Plancius that will allow the jurors to distinguish specific unacceptable electoral behavior from legitimate campaigning:[75]

> *For who would then hear their accusations? What would you say? That Plancius held the money? The jurors' ears would refuse it, no one would take notice. That he is obliging? I am happy to confess that they would listen to that. Don't think, Laterensis, that campaigning and obligation and favors were to be eliminated by the laws the senate wanted passed on ambitus.*

> (*Planc.* 44)

To the extent that the long discussion of jury selection turns on the relationships that exist between Plancius and his social background (his tribesmen and neighbors), it parallels and reinforces the more explicit arguments elsewhere about Plancius and his friends, family, and superiors. Cicero's "willingness" to rely on those who know Plancius best shows that Plancius must be properly connected to them. Laterensis' purported fear of Plancius' connections is taken to confirm Cicero's overall picture of his client.

So far we have drawn a connection between a fairly abstract reading of this claim about jury selection (*Planc.* 36–47) and an equally abstract concept of *ambitus*, defined in terms of economics and of inclusion and exclusion with respect to a social in-group. Is there anything else in the text that would make this complex of issues more concrete? Several times Cicero calls the jurors' attention to precisely the issues he discusses here. This is seen most clearly in the following:

> *Everything I say about Plancius, I say from personal knowledge. I live near Atinia, a neighborhood which retains the old ways of duty and must be praised or even loved; it is not tainted with malevolence, nor used to lies, nor poisoned, nor deceptive, nor learned in the urban and suburban arts of deception.*

> (*Planc.* 22; cf. 29)

In both sections value is assigned by the community, and this is done on the basis of proximity and of standing social relations. Thus Cicero makes explicit the claim that Plancius' position within this network of relationships is what guarantees his worthiness. A little more indirect, but still to the point, is the request at sections 56–57 that the jurors not take into account rumors whose source and thus authority they do not know.[76] We saw in the *Commentariolum Petitionis* and the Pompeiian electoral posters a similar concern for the informational value of social ties. A text (whether an advertisement or an accusation) without a source is also without authority. Plancius' social ties, not least those to Cicero, outweigh anything the prosecution could possibly produce.

All this evidence could perhaps be held to point in another direction. Though Joachim Adamietz has rightly refused to accept preconceived definitions of *ambitus*, and has taken seriously the argumentation of the two speeches, he arrives at a radically different conclusion:

> *The task of the juror in ambitus cases lay not so much in reaching a "guilty" or "not guilty" verdict, but in clearing up which of the disputants*

was more suited to hold the office. That, of course, depends on the question
of whether the accused candidate has conducted himself in the campaign
outside the usual norms, but this was only one part of the larger question.

([1986:117]; cf. [1989:29, 110–11])

But as we have seen above, the judgment is absolute (not relative), and it has
more to do with the connection of campaigning to general social questions than
with fitness for office. This explanation of the offense also makes more sense in
terms of the structure of the Roman "constitution." To accept Adamietz'
model, in other words, is to make the assemblies redundant, as Cicero himself points out (*Planc.* 8).[77] Given the differing composition of the assemblies
and courts, one might imagine that the courts could serve to ensure that the
assemblies did not return candidates whose agenda was antithetical to the interests of the aristocracy as a whole (probably a rare occurrence). But at this
level of abstraction, such a view could be taken as a restatement of the conclusions reached above. In other words, the courts serve only to ensure that
the winning candidate respects the canons of aristocratic behavior in general
terms. Furthermore, Adamietz' definition means that he cannot give any extra-
ethical interpretation to Cicero's discussion of himself in *pro Plancio*, a discussion which then seems excessively long and digressive even by Ciceronian
standards.

One problem remains: we have given the jurors two paradigms which, on
the surface, need not be compatible. One is the question of social worthiness
and contextualization; the other is a narrowly defined issue of fact (paying and
dividing voters, and so forth). Yet they must render a single verdict. We may
account for both aspects of *ambitus* if we define the word by recourse to the
notion of "prototype." Linguists have found (perhaps unsurprisingly) that
certain linguistic categories are not definable by their borders.[78] This is not
merely to say that two or more persons may define the category differently, or
that there are categories like "tall" (often defined relatively) or "justice" (often
defined tentatively). Rather, we are speaking of categories into which some entities clearly fit, some (perhaps) clearly do not, while others are of intermediate status. Often these categories are best described by taking a clear case as
the "prototype" and evaluating other entities as more or less good examples of
the category to the extent that they more or less resemble the prototype. The
prototype of *ambitus*, then, is the candidate's exchange of cash for vote(s) in a
quid pro quo. To put this in the terms used in the first section, the prototype of
ambitus is also a prototypical case of the market-exchange of votes.

The core or prototype case described above would, by definition, have been clearly recognizable as *ambitus* and therefore would require the defense of denial. However, as we move away from this core case in various ways, for instance by removing one or the other of its defining characteristics, we (with the ancient audience) have to deal with more difficult cases. Some of these cases were eventually addressed by explicit legislation: the paying of an entourage (in which there is not a direct exchange for votes), distribution of bribes through *sectores* (in which the candidate is not involved), or *sodalicium* (in which cash is not involved). Even more distantly related offenses were forbidden by statute, such as Cicero's *lex Tullia*, which forbade giving games shortly before a campaign. However, even this mass of legislation did not (and could not) rule on all possibly related actions. Depending on one's perspective, these other actions may or may not be close enough to the core for them to count as *ambitus*.[79] It is the advocate's job (and opportunity) to introduce the appropriate perspective to draw the line to his client's advantage. Cicero denies the prototype case (and tries to minimize the opposition's opportunity to "prove" him wrong); otherwise, he must convince the jurors that the candidate's exchanges were more of the gift variety than of the market variety.

CHAPTER 3

Murder (and How to Spot It)

1. THE *LEX CORNELIA DE SICARIIS ET VENEFICIIS*[1]

The law under which Cicero argued homicide[2] cases was enacted during Sulla's brief domination of the state in 82–79. It was also the statute that remained in effect (albeit in amended form) down to Byzantine times. Hence we have an unusually large amount of information about its contents, even if they are sometimes hard to interpret. As its name suggests, the *lex Cornelia de sicariis et veneficiis* (on "'dagger-men' and poisonings") established a compound court. There is direct attestation of a separate court *de sicariis* (also *inter sicarios*) as early as 142 to prosecute armed murders (*Fin.* 2.54; cf. *Att.* 12.5b). Prosecutions *de veneficiis* are recorded several times in the first half of the second century (Livy 39.41.5, 40.37.4, 40.43.2; *Per.* 48), and a standing court for that charge seems to have been established by the early nineties.[3] The charge of *veneficium* covered not only the use, but also the manufacture, sale, and purchase of poisons (see below).

The title of Sulla's law is the first evidence that both crimes were brought together under a single statute, but an earlier joining is certainly possible.[4] Additionally, a passage of Cicero's *de Inventione* (2.58) shows that parricide (the killing of a close relative) was brought into the purview of the court *de sicariis* by the time that text was written, perhaps in 86. Later, parricide continued to be tried under the composite *lex Cornelia* (see below). Both the parricide and the simple murder sections seem to include clauses against arranging a killing, as well as the act itself: "or by whose malicious intent this is done" (Marcianus *D.* 48.9.1[5]; Ulp. *Coll.* 1.3.1[6]). The *lex Cornelia* also incorporated a law of the 120's against abuse of capital process, conventionally referred to today as "judicial murder" (*Clu.* 154; more below). Finally in imperial times the statute was expanded to cover abortion, arson, castration, and the concealment of shipwrecks; none of these provisions is attested for the Republican period.

Before considering the purpose of the law as a whole, we must consider the purposes of three of the four main components: *sicarii*, parricide, and abuse of practice (poisoning, for the moment, will not be problematic). The normal sense of the word *sicarius* in the early first century is not "murderer," but "gangster" or "racketeer" (Cloud 1969:270–80). A *sicarius* is a member of an organized group using violence and the threat of violence to further its ends; *sicarii* are perhaps roughly the urban counterparts of rural *latrones* ("bandits, highwaymen") or a more general version of the same type.[7] The section of the *lex Cornelia* that appears to have covered simple murder seems to have read:

Hold a capital[8] trial of any man who was or will have "been with weapon" for the sake of killing a person or of committing theft, or who has killed or shall have killed a man, or by whose malicious intent this has been or shall have been done.

de eius capite quaerito qui cum telo fuit fuerit hominis occidendi furtive faciendi causa, hominemve occidit occiderit, cuiusve id dolo malo factum est erit.[9]

An ancestor of this prohibition may be paralleled as early as Plautus, probably before 186 (*Aul.* 415–20). Kunkel (1962:65–66) notes that the clause which forbids actual killing is added almost as an afterthought. He and Cloud point out that the emphasis of the law makes best sense if its object is not the repression of murder as such. If we see the law as primarily directed against conspiracy and large-scale threats of violence, of *sicarii* as Cloud has defined the term, then the phrasing is easily understood. The clause about actual killing is a legalistic addition ensuring that *sicarii* may not escape prosecution by carrying out their threats and intentions of force instead of merely "going about." Apparently it also, incidentally, removes the necessity that the killing have been done by one of the enumerated means (weapon, poisoning, and so forth). This is the origin of legislation against *sicarii*; later we will consider its further evolution.

Parricide *(parricidium)* has a murky early history; there is no need here to go into the much-disputed etymology of the word or its possible connection to the term *paricidas* in a purported law of the regal period (Festus 247L).[10] In the Late Republic parricide included the murder of relatives (parents, grandparents, siblings, cousins, assorted in-laws, step-parents, and children) and of patrons (Marcianus *D.* 48.9.1).[11] We have already noted that these cases would have been coming before the court *de sicariis* by 86 at the latest. The last known legislation *de parricidiis*, a *lex Pompeia*, apparently served to bring parricide cases under the *lex Cornelia de sicariis* (*ibid.*).[12] The most distinctive feature of earlier parricide law was the "penalty of the sack," *poena cullei*—the offender was sewn into a sack with a dog, a rooster, a snake, and an ape and thrown into the sea (*Rosc.* 70, Just. *Inst.* 4.18.6; Radin 1920). The main substantive effect of the *lex Pompeia* seems to have been the elimination of this spectacular punishment in favor of the normal (capital) punishment of the *lex Cornelia* (Cloud 1971:47–60).

Cicero's speech for Cluentius provides the only direct contemporary evidence for the text of the rest of the law (§§148, 157). Our later sources are all imperial juristic texts: *Digest* 48.8 (especially paragraph 1 from Marcianus), Ulp. *Coll.* 1.3.1, and *PS* 5.23.[13] There is a reference to the law in the younger Seneca, but it is too general to be of use.[14] Cicero breaks up the law for rhetorical effect, and clearly leaves out a few words (note, for example, that he quotes the same phrase in slightly different form in the same section: *quicumque fecerit* . . . [148.3C] and *qui venenum* . . . [148.15C]). Nonetheless, from what he says we can reconstruct roughly the following:[15]

> *Hold a capital trial of him who has made or will make, sold or will sell, possessed or will possess, or given or will give poison. And also try on the same terms him who, as tribune of soldiers for the first four legions or quaestor or tribune of the plebs . . . [other offices] . . . or as one who has spoken or will speak an opinion in the senate, conspires or will conspire, plots or will plot, connives or will connive, or gave or will give false testimony so that someone may be condemned by a iudicium publicum.*

[Cap. 5] De eius capite quaerito qui hominis occidendi causa venenum malum fecit fecerit vendidit vendiderit emit emerit habuit habuerit dedit dederit. [Cap. 6] Deque eius capite quaerito qui tribunus militum legionibus quattuor primis, quive quaestor, tribunus plebis *[other offices]*, quive in senatu sententiam dixit, dixerit, qui eorum coit, coierit, convenit, convenerit, consensit, consenserit . . . falsumve testimonium dixit dixerit . . . quo quis iudicio publico rei capitalis condemnaretur.

The exhaustive lists of verbs with variation in tense, the disjunctive asyndeton, and the list of minor offices are all characteristic of Roman legal style. Thus there is hope that Cicero reports nearly the precise words of the legislation (though he could doubtless have imitated that style in free composition if he had wished). In any case, all of this squares with the later sources.

The most contested issue regarding this law is the distinction allegedly made in chapter six between senators and others. This is the "judicial murder" clause which is sometimes assumed to outlaw bribing jurors. Senators are always liable under this provision, while others (i.e., *equites*) are so only if they have held particular offices. This rather arbitrary distinction is to the advantage of Cicero's nonsenatorial client, and so some have been hesitant to accept his word on this point. Of the late legal texts, Ulpian and the *PS* do not appear to address the issue, while Marcianus (*D.* 48.8.1) seems to support the distinction.[16] Thus there is no textual reason to suspect that Cicero has made any substantive changes.

It is also historically plausible that the law would have made such a distinction between the two orders. Cicero says at section 153 that M. Drusus the Younger once attempted to extend the same legal liability to equestrian jurors but was successfully resisted. This information on Drusus' "reform" attempt, repeated at *Rab. Post.* 16, is also independently reported by Appian (*BC* 1.35). Drusus' failed attempt was revived in 61 (*Att.* 1.17.8; cf. *Att.* 1.18.3, 2.1.8). The distinction seems to have been a well-established principle of law. Furthermore, the *lex Cornelia* dates from 81 (a time when *equites* did not serve on the juries at all), so what we have could easily represent the original state of the law. We may then reasonably ask why, when forces existed in 70 which would put the *equites* back on the juries via the *lex Aurelia*, those same forces would also bring about change in a different law (the *lex Cornelia de sicariis et veneficiis*) to increase their liability.

A third legal point has to do with the real object of the "judicial murder" clause. Paulus treats the giving of *falsum testimonium* along with poisoning at *Coll.* 1.2.1 (there is a similar report at *PS* 5.23.1, while the taking of bribes by jurors does not appear until a later passage [5.23.11]). The involvement of money thus seems to trigger a different part of the law than the clauses we have been considering so far. At *Brutus* 48 Cicero quotes a supposed Athenian law containing a slightly abbreviated formula, derived from the *lex Cornelia*, as an explanation of why the Greek speechwriter Isocrates (allegedly) gave up writing court speeches for others. The law also contained the words "so that someone be wrongly convicted by a court" *(quo quis iudicio circumveniretur)*, and allegedly Isocrates feared liability under it for writing forensic speeches for others. The story is likely apocryphal, but it seems to show that the issue at stake is receiving bribes, not giving them. *Clu.* 151 and Marcianus *D.* 48.8.1 show that this abbreviated version was the original (Gracchan) formulation of the "judicial murder" section eventually incorporated in the *lex Cornelia*. Ewins (1960) has pointed out that the historical circumstances of Gracchus' original legislation do not lend themselves to a concern for bribery. The sixth chapter of the *lex Cornelia* is not, in fact, concerned with bribery *(per se)* at all; rather it is directed at any abuse of official power (particularly in the courts, standing or special) resulting in the death of a citizen. Thus jurors are only a small part of those covered, so amending the law to cover a new group of them would not be a pressing matter. In any case, the law is certainly directed at the officials in power, not at outside givers of bribes.[17] Hence, not only is Cicero's text of the *lex Cornelia* probably sound, but his interpretation of it would have been quite plausible.

There has been a great deal of discussion in the secondary literature of the precise section (or sections) of this complex law under which Aulus Cluentius was tried in 66.[18] In particular, was he charged with "judicial murder," poisoning, or both? Cicero's surviving defense is, perhaps surprisingly, unhelpful. Alexander's (1982) work fortunately allows us to cut the Gordian knot.[19] He makes his argument in the context of a discussion of the Roman concept of double jeopardy. To wit, a prosecution on a given charge included all instances of that crime up to the date of the trial, thus any acquittal insulated the defendant from any later trial on the same charge not based on events postdating the original trial.[20] Though not incontestable his case seems reasonable. If so, then a highly specific indictment would be unnecessary; a Roman prosecutor probably never had to make a complete accounting of his intended accusations, and almost any of the several poisonings alleged would have sufficed to get the case heard. Nor was he bound by procedural rules of relevance while arguing in court. Once there Attius, the prosecutor in this case, could argue whatever charges he thought most damaging, whether or not the relevant section of the law happened to apply to the particular defendant. It would be up to the defense advocate to point out any abuses.[21] The only defense against such a prosecution strategy would be precisely what we see in Cicero—a blanket, multilevel denial of any and all charges. The charge of *pro Roscio*, Cicero's other homicide defense, is much simpler. Roscius had allegedly had his own father killed (no one seems to have suggested that he had committed the crime himself).[22]

If we now have some idea of the several fact-situations prosecutable under the *lex Cornelia*, it is possible to speculate on the function of the law as a whole. As we saw above, simple murder seems to have been forbidden by the *de sicariis* part of the *lex Cornelia*. Yet at the time of the *lex Cornelia* the term *sicarius* still largely retained the sense "gangster." From this fact and the lack of emphasis on actual killing in the law, Cloud (1969:282–86) argues that the section *de sicariis* of the composite law was still directed at its original target (racketeering), not at murder in general.[23] On the other hand, Kunkel (1962:70) suggests that the law *de sicariis* had, at least in practice, already been reconceptualized as a simple murder law. He supports this claim by noting, for instance, the existence of provisions in the Sullan law directed at slaves who kill their own masters (hardly prototypical *sicarii*; Gaius *D.* 29.5.25.pr). This seems to be the sounder position. The whole idea of a composite law, and particularly the appearance of the word *sicariis* in its title, supports the notion that it is meant to be read generally. Poisoning, parricide, and "judicial murder" are connected precisely by being varieties of homicide. Only if we accept that the clause *de sicariis* had come to be thought of as attacking simple murder will it fit into the set.[24] So we should think of the joint title as reflecting the two central means of murder (blade and poison), and the law as bringing all homicides under a single criminal jurisdiction.[25] Thus, I think we should see an evolution of the notion of *sicarius* from Cloud's original sense to something much more like our "murderer" already by 81.

For the sake of completeness, mention should be made here of the existence of three "exceptions" to the homicide laws throughout our period. A person could kill his or her own slaves (but not those of another; see note 24), and a father theoretically had the authority to execute his children regardless of their age or place of residence.[26] The significance of these exceptions will be discussed in chapter four. Finally, the text of the *lex Cornelia* refers only to intentional homicide; note the repetition of phrases like *hominis occidendi causa*. At some point after Hadrian's time unintentional homicide was included but given a lesser penalty (Marc. *D.* 48.8.1.3). This seems to represent an extension of the law rather than a reduction in severity.[27] While issues of intent arise only peripherally in the speeches, I do wish to make one point here in anticipation of the investigation of those speeches. While the defendant's intent is a matter of fact of a different order than, say, whether he held a knife, it is (as the notion is used) nonetheless a matter of fact. The defendant intended "to kill a person or commit a theft" or he did not; more complicated questions of intent do not arise.[28] The notion certainly does not involve the sorts of contextual and political judgments familiar from our treatment of *ambitus*.

2. JUDGING PARADIGMS IN *PRO ROSCIO*

Cicero's two homicide speeches—*pro Sexto Roscio Amerino* and *pro Cluentio*—differ more between themselves than the *ambitus* speeches discussed in the previous chapter. As a result we will begin this discussion with an analysis of *pro Roscio* entire and follow this with a comparison with *pro Cluentio*. In this way it will become evident that *pro Cluentio* is built on a similar plan, even though a large superstructure of other issues has been added.

It is worth noting that (once again) Cicero opens his speech with a charge to the jurors that on the face of it lays a tremendous burden on himself:

> But if some reason for accusation or ground of suspicion of the deed or finally anything at all, however minute, is found which suggests that the opposition has been pursuing anything at all real in bringing their indictment, and if (finally) you find some other motive beyond the value of these farms of which I have spoken, I have no problem with handing Roscius' life over to satisfy their desires.

(*Rosc.* 8)

The slightest *(vel minima)* cause for suspicion is grounds for a conviction. Here, as in *pro Plancio*, the burden is initially laid totally on the defendant's side. While the topic is not defined at all clearly, words like *quaelibet* ("whatever you will") and *quicquam* ("anything") suggest that issues of character are at least potentially included. Once again the defense advocate apparently offers to prove that his client is completely upright.[29] This is made clear a little later (§18): "But as for that which has up to now been a matter of suspicion, if the very facts shall not have made [the guilt of the prosecutors] evident, judge this man [Roscius] guilty"; and finally again later: "If suspicion is found in these things, I will concede guilt" (§76). This first of these two sentences is an incidental remark in the midst of the narration. It also introduces a subsidiary element that will recur later. Only by proving who the actual criminal was will Cicero show that his client did not commit the crime. The second introduces the second major argument of Cicero's proof, namely, that Roscius had no opportunity to kill his father.

Between these two sentences, however, there are several other charges of a significantly different character. Cicero employs an apparently standard topos about the horror of parricide; from this general discussion he slips into its supposed implications for the case. Parricide is a crime of such prodigious evil that prosecutors are compelled to prove (by past deeds) that accused parricides are themselves prodigiously evil (*Rosc.* 38). The argument is one we have not seen before, since it is (at least as stated) specific to parricide. Parricide is the worst of crimes; thus the individual parricide must have the worst of *ingenia* ("characters"), and this would naturally be visible in his *vita ante acta*, "past life." Cicero makes character—a standard weapon of the prosecution—

into a burden by application of a broadly accepted psychological principle. Essentially the same argument is repeated later, but with an extra step added. The putative motive for murder was to prevent the father from disinheriting the son. The prosecution then needed to show the same kind of character in the son for a different reason. In this case such a motive is necessary to justify the claim of such drastic action on the father's part:

> *Although you should have enumerated all the causes — and this was the duty of a prosecutor who charges so great a crime: to unfold all the flaws and wrongdoings of a son which could fire a parent to overcome his natural affection and eject that deep-seated love from his spirit, and even forget that he is a father — these things could not, I think, have come about without great wrongs on the part of my client.*

> (*Rosc.* 53)

This revised paradigm is soft-pedaled by being embedded in both an address to the prosecutor and an elaborate *praeteritio*.

As the speech progresses Cicero continues to reiterate this theme. He appeals to shared views on inherent character and the natural strength of blood ties, comparison with lesser cases, and an explicit attack on the failure of his opponent to carry these points. His presentation of this paradigm grows bolder and bolder. Much of the highly evocative vocabulary of the individual instances is repeated from one section to the next (especially §§61–63, 68): "unique," "boldness," "terrible," "nature herself," "portent," immensity": *singularis, audacia, atrox, ipsa natura, portentum, immanitate.*[30] One interesting twist in the midst of this repetition is this: "I would almost say that the jurors must see hands splattered with a father's blood before they believe so great, so monstrous, and so terrible a crime" (*Rosc.* 68). It is interesting to note that being caught red-handed is only "almost" necessary here *(paene dicam)*. Elsewhere we saw Cicero attempt, in the main body of his speeches, to reverse completely the burden established in the various introductions. We will consider later whether this passage deviates significantly from his previous tactics.

In any case, the theme of the depravity needed to commit this crime is eventually sounded one last time and in its briefest form:

> *The present case is about parricide, which cannot arise without many reasons; however, it is being argued before men of judgment who understand that no one commits even the least evil without some reason.*

> (*Rosc.* 73)

The final charge serves as a conclusion in several ways (though the speech is only half over). First, it returns to address the prosecutor. Second, the longest version of the charge (§§61–63) is echoed both verbally (cf. §61: "A case of parricide is at issue," and §62: "many causes") and in the usual argument comparing lesser crimes to greater. More unusual is the *captatio benevolentiae* (by pure flattery) that accompanies the instructions. This marks the end of a series of charges from section 8 to section 73, which are spaced throughout the first major argument of the speech (that about motive and character) in roughly increasing order of assertiveness. The return to the paradigm still strongly biased against the defendant in section 76 ("if suspicion . . ."; cited above) is part of the introduction to the second argument (that about opportunity).

As we noted above, Cicero offers not just to prove his client's innocence but to identify the guilty party. In the course of his counteraccusation he several times remarks on the superior quality of his own evidence and accusatory procedure. This explication of the duties of an accuser constitutes indirect advocacy of a particular paradigm using Cicero himself as the *exemplum*: while only summarizing his own points, he will still produce the weighty proofs that accusation requires (*Rosc.* 83). He continues with rhetorical questions:[31]

> *Should argument be sought in manifest facts* (perspicuis rebus) *or taken from conjecture? Should you not come to see with your eyes the things you have heard, jurors?*
>
> (*Rosc.* 98)

Here in the counteraccusation Cicero precisely reverses the themes he rehearsed in his original statements of the case (§§8, 18; quoted above). Mere *suspicio* is contrasted to that which is obvious *(perspicuus)*. Cicero also claims that he can bring to bear the multiple proofs of bad character and criminality that he himself demanded repeatedly in earlier sections. Thus these passages are largely a repetition of earlier themes cast in a slightly different form.

At this point we can ask what it is that Cicero puts at issue in the case of Sextus Roscius. For the most part the question is simple: did he or did he not engineer his father's death? Are the jurors convinced that certain actions took place? There is no attempt to claim that there were circumstances which justified the crime or that any definition of the crime was not met. Finding the best answer to the factual questions subsumes three equally factual (though not readily decidable) issues treated in the second half of the speech (as prescribed by the rhetorical handbooks; *Inv.* 2.14–51). Did the defendant have a motive

(§§37–73), did he have the opportunity (§§74–81, 92–94), and was he the sort of person who could commit such a crime (see following section)?[32] Formally we also see Cicero again shifting the eventual burden of proof to the prosecution: they must show that this (assumedly unlikely) event did in fact occur. At the end of the next section it will be possible to define this shift in burden more precisely. For the time being I note that Cicero's emphasis on observable fact as opposed to value judgment allows considerations not purely internal to Roman elite culture to be brought to bear on how the case is to be judged. The constant use of *perspicuus* (in contrast to *suspicio* and *coniectura*) implies that anyone should be able to identify a parricide.

3. ETHOS AND *EXEMPLA* IN *PRO ROSCIO*

The modes of ethical and exemplary argument used in homicide cases suggest that homicide is best seen in terms of specific events, not general situations. Ethical argument is narrowly directed toward assessing the likelihood of specific events—an "instrumental" use of ethos. I mean "instrumental" to have a technical sense here. Obviously any ethical argument is used instrumentally in that it is a device meant to persuade the audience. In the narrower sense I propose here, however, an ethical claim is "instrumental" only if it is used to provide the premise for a further argument. Rhetorical *exempla* are drawn from a variety of different contexts; since the notion of homicide is not defined by reference to its context, *exempla* do not depend on reference to particular social, political, or economic situations for their value.

Vasaly (1985) discusses certain pervasive stereotypes *(personae)* used to guide audience interpretation of the characters involved in the trial.[33] It appears that Erucius, the prosecutor, portrayed Roscius (the defendant) as an uncouth thug, only at home in the country ("he never stayed in town," §74), a man who shunned society ("Erucius cleared [him] of luxury when he said he had almost never even been around a party," §39), even a wild man ("a fierce and untamed man," §74). Cicero does not dispute the "fact" of Roscius' rusticity. Instead he offers a different, but still standard, stereotype of the rustic.[34] Erucius had attempted to evoke a grim, older farmer (§39); Vasaly (1985:10–11) compares such blocking figures as Knemon in Menander's *Dyskolos* and Demea in Terence's *Adelphoi*. The figure on which Cicero bases his characterization is a much more likable, younger rustic such as Gorgias in the *Dyskolos*. This is all the more easily accomplished since Roscius' role in this "drama" is explicitly that of son. Cicero can then argue for the superior reliability of his stereotype on grounds not of further specific evidence but of ideology

(§§50–51). Since the founding fathers of Roman history are often depicted as farmers first and soldiers or lawgivers second, the jury was to accept the positive view of the rustic.[35] Note here that the local reason for this ethical argument is to set up a factual inference that is drawn immediately: dispatching the younger Roscius to the country could not have been a sign of paternal displeasure, and so he had no motive for murder. Globally, however, it argues for Roscius' good character in a more general sense.

Conversely, other members of the prosecution (Magnus, Capito, and Chrysogonus) are depicted as "urban scoundrels" (Vasaly 1985:13–17). As urban characters they are given over to luxury *(luxuria/luxuries)*, which leads to greed *(avaritia)*, and thence to the daring *(audacia)* which produces crime.[36] Chrysogonus' luxurious lifestyle is described at great length (§§133–35): his fine art, precious metals, skilled slaves, and riotous parties. Cicero concludes: "You see that he looks down on all men, that he thinks no one greater than himself, that he thinks that he alone is blessed and powerful" (§135). The depiction of Erucius' prosecution (and his response to the beginning of Cicero's speech; §§59–61) confirms his characterization as the tool of the powerful freedman (May 1988:25). Admittedly, both these passages about Chrysogonus are pure ethical narrative; that is to say, no explicit conclusions are drawn. Contrast the stories of Magnus and Capito, which are at least tangentially part of a claim as to how the elder Roscius was killed. The defendant's character is inferred from a few negative statements taken from the prosecution (he did not go to Rome, he did not go to parties, and so forth) so no further narration is necessary. In either case (and this is more typical of this speech than the treatment of Chrysogonus) the characterization is advanced to support some specific inference.

The connection of these characterizations (good rustic vs. urban scoundrels) to a particular judging paradigm is first made explicit early in the second half of the speech:

> *I pass over the fact that . . . evil-doing does not ordinarily arise amidst rustic habits, meager sustenance, and a rude and uncultivated way of life like his. Luxury must come from the city, avarice from luxury, audacity from avarice, and it is from audacity that all crimes and evils are born.*
>
> *(Rosc. 75)*

On this first attempt the argument is framed in a *praeteritio*. The theme returns in direct form at sections 117–18, where the directness of the charge is reinforced by a precise, formal future imperative *(putatote)*.[37] A third statement of this charge is nearly Cicero's last word on the case:

> *Is there any doubt where the evil lies when you see on the one side a thug, enemy, assassin, and accuser all in one, and on the other a son impoverished, but dear to his own, on whom not only guilt, but even suspicion cannot rest?*

> *(Rosc.* 152)

Roscius could not have done the deed because he is not that kind of person.

Thus the use of ethical argumentation in this speech is largely instrumental and thereby differs from that in the two *ambitus* speeches. There the defendant's character was an issue in its own right, particularly in the discussion of Plancius' community support. There is also a parallel difference in the types of *exempla* adduced. In principle, *exempla* may be drawn from (at least) literature, history, and mythology, the boundaries between these categories not being clearly drawn. Within these categories is a subset of historical examples which are marked for their value as part of specifically Roman tradition, that is, those which illustrate the *mos maiorum*. In both the *ambitus* speeches there was a strong tendency to use only such *exempla*; in *pro Roscio* (and to some extent *pro Cluentio*) Cicero allows himself a much broader range. I will argue (and Cicero himself nearly makes this explicit) that this is a reflex of the putative universal meaning of homicide. Any part of human experience should be relevant.

The first type of culturally unmarked example is that of historical but obscure figures. Such is the story of the unfortunate T. Cloelius of Terracina (§§64–65).[38] He was killed while sleeping in a room with his sons. They, however, were acquitted of his murder against all other probability when it was seen that their consciences allowed them to sleep undisturbed afterward. Cicero's insistence on every possible proof of criminal character is given a precedent, but of a very general kind. This is immediately supported (§§66–67) by an even more general example—that of the Furies and their pursuit of Orestes.[39] Proof of parricide is said to require a showing of "fury and madness" in the alleged killer (§66). Another, later mythological example is that of Jupiter himself (§131). Even he cannot keep track of everything that goes on in the world, and so he is used to set a limit to what can be expected from Sulla.[40] The main literary example is used in a somewhat different way. In making the argument that relegation to the countryside does not show paternal disapproval, Cicero refers to a play of Caecilius Statius (§46), where apparently the rustic son, Eutychus, was well loved by his father.[41]

For all three categories (historical, mythological, and literary) Cicero makes explicit arguments that his *exempla* are relevant, and in all three cases this claim is based on a notion of a transcultural (probably universal) human nature; parricide can be understood (so it is claimed) outside the categories of Roman thought. Historically, Roman law is superior to that of the Athenians because it recognizes the possibility of parricide (as distinct from ordinary murder) and so better protects ties of blood. This law is better not just for the Romans, but absolutely, because it takes better account of the possibilities of human nature (§70). The Furies are psychologized as a figure for the workings of conscience: "His own offense and fears most try each person, his own crime drives each person and makes him mad" (§67). Finally he can say of Caecilius' characters that it doesn't matter whether they are real. "For I think that poets compose their works so that we see our own habits played out and the very image of our daily life in other persons" (*Rosc.* 47). This passage is to be read a little more narrowly than the others, with *nostros mores* referring specifically to Roman character (at least in the local context), but even here authority does not rest with special culture heroes. It is accessible to anyone without being licensed by rank, social standing, antiquity, or other social factor. Naturally Cicero also uses some historically prestigious *exempla* as well (Fimbria/Scaevola §§33–34; Atilius §50; Scipio Africanus §103), but they are only part of a much wider spectrum.

All this goes to illustrate that murder is not defined by reference to social circumstances. As a result no special cultural knowledge is required to evaluate murder charges. Hence considerations other than the fact of killing (or not) are rarely introduced by Cicero. Other issues might not be universal. Similarly, the evidence of character is not introduced as a topic of judgment in its own right. Rather it is used to support arguments about who did or did not actually kill the elder Roscius. For the Romans (much as for ourselves) homicide was an act in the physical world, not a social situation. While the blood-ties involved in this case alter the probabilities and the punishment, they appear not to change the basic issue at stake (who killed Roscius?) nor the standard ways of finding an answer to that question.

In concluding this section I want to return in detail to the final charge. Given that the speech only continues for another two sections afterward, this passage takes on particular significance. It sums up a number of themes including one major point not yet discussed, so I will quote it in its entirety again:

Is there any doubt where the evil lies when you see on the one side a thug,
enemy, assassin, and accuser all in one, and on the other a son impover-
ished, but dear to his own, on whom not only guilt, but even suspicion
cannot rest?

(*Rosc.* 152)

The first aspect to be noted is the dilemma which is established.[42] The jurors are offered a choice of two hypotheses: either Roscius was responsible for
the death of his father or Magnus, Capito, et al. were. Cicero offered the same
choice earlier in his counteraccusation:[43] would the guilty party (or parties)
have come out richer or poorer? would they have been frugal farmers or bold
criminals? urban folk or rural (*Rosc.* 88)? As in the conclusion, there are only
two possibilities offered to the jurors: Roscius or the prosecution. The jurors
must choose which of the two had a stronger motive, which had the better opportunity, and which was more inclined by character to commit murder. This
kind of dilemma is used to structure not only these charges but also the individual arguments. For instance in investigating opportunity Cicero asks:

How did my client kill him? Either he struck the blow himself or had others
do it. If you say the former, he was not at Rome; if the latter, I ask who did
it? Slaves or free men? If free, then who? Were these assassins from Ameria,
too, or from the city? If the former, who are they? Why are they not named?
If the latter, from where did Roscius know them given that he had not been
at Rome in many years and had never been there more than three days
at a time?

(*Rosc.* 74)

This form is picked up a little later: "I must differ with you, if the following is
relevant to this crime — either he did it with his own hand (which you deny) or
through some slaves or free men" (§79).

Furthermore, there are several individual uses of dilemma sprinkled
throughout the speech, not directly connected to the central choice of which
side is more likely to have done it (*Rosc.* 39, 72, 119, 128). Why the frequent use
of dilemma? Discussing *pro Caelio*, Craig (1989:314) argues that "a great part
of Cicero's persuasive power inheres in his ability to argue extra-rationally in
a way that seems superficially to be rationally compelling."[44] As the quintes-
sentially rational(-seeming) figure, dilemma is particularly appropriate to the

topic of murder; it appears to deal systematically with facts, facts which should be at the core of the case.

To return to the final charge (152: "Is there any doubt . . ."), we note the probabilistic arguments used. We have already seen the predominantly instrumental use of ethos in this speech, the drawing of factual inferences from personal character. We have also seen the lengths to which Cicero went to establish characters to support these inferences. In the final charge this process of inference is extended to motive and opportunity (as anticipated in §§78 and 88). The convergence of explicitly probabilistic argumentation and dilemma produces a very different judging paradigm from what we saw in the two *ambitus* cases. There the prosecution was eventually asked to refute conclusively and concretely a rather vague claim about the social worthiness of the defendant. The relationship of this claim to any particular acts of the defendant was problematic. Here the commission of a crime is certain—the Elder Roscius *was* murdered[45]—hence punishment is clearly in order for someone. Cicero must show that it should not fall on his client, that someone else is more deserving. He does this by arguing that another hypothesis is more likely.[46] Ironically here, where the issue is clearly one of fact, the decision turns on relative probability. In cases of *ambitus*, the decision is phrased in absolute terms. When Cicero says that the *almost* bloodied hands of the defendant are needed for a conviction (§68), he may merely refer to the fact that a defendant need not have done the killing himself to be criminally liable. More likely, however, is a different reading: the prosecution need not prove that the defendant is guilty, only that this is the better possibility.[47]

4. POLITICS IN *PRO ROSCIO*

Despite the strong tendency to focus narrowly on the offense itself, certain political considerations clearly do slip into *pro Roscio*. They deal in various ways with the relationship between the trial and the recent Sullan coup. The most straightforward example of this reference is the depiction of the trial as a simple test of allegiance to Sulla. Cicero goes to some lengths to establish his own conservative credentials. Sulla was in complete control of the situation at Rome, yet he had also assumed the consulship in 80 to make a political point of his traditionalizing values (App. *BC* 1.103). Cicero's discussion of the virtues of agriculture may not have been of direct political importance but would at least constitute sounding the "party line" of cultural and political conservatism. Similarly, his use of the term *audacia* to characterize the opposition is part of conservative political vocabulary.[48] Perhaps even more pleasing to the ears of conservatives would have been the defense of existing property relations at section 111. Finally, Cicero makes his political position explicit:[49]

> *I rejoice, jurors, because these things are finished and each has his proper rank and honor again, and I delight when I see that all these things were done by the will of the gods, the earnestness of the Roman people, and by the council, command, and good fortune of Lucius Sulla.*

> (*Rosc.* 136)

Conversely, Cicero attempts to use ideological means to detach his opposition from their (purported) close connections to Sulla. He insists repeatedly that Sulla was never aware of what Chrysogonus and his henchmen were doing and that his approval of such criminal activity would be unthinkable (§§21–22, 25, 91, 110, 127, 130–31). Eventually there is an extended argument that a verdict against Chrysogonus (as an acquittal is described[50]) is precisely in line with the goals of the Sullan program (§§137–42). If one accepts Cicero's premise that the jurors' vote is about Chrysogonus and the recent upheaval,[51] his conclusion makes sense. As a Greek freedman, Chrysogonus is almost as far as possible from the old nobility whom Sulla and his associates set out to empower.

Somewhat more complicated is the alleged relationship of this trial to the suspension of the courts and to the proscriptions earlier in Sulla's reign. For instance, Cicero asserts that the prosecution was relying on public opinion that the first person tried before the revived courts would be convicted to mark their return to force (*Rosc.* 28; cf. 11). This is hard to believe; Romans may have felt a desire for a return to law and order in 80, but surely one more death, even with a sound legal basis, after the uncontrolled killing of the proscriptions would be at best irrelevant.[52] Rather, an acquittal would be the surer sign of normalcy. In fact, this is very much what Cicero says at one point earlier in the speech (*Rosc.* 13). The issue of proscriptions is explicitly raised at the end of the speech, immediately after the last charge to the jurors:

> *But if you undertake this and offer your labor to this project, and if you sit here so that the children of the proscribed may be brought before you, beware, by the immortal gods, lest you seem to have restored a new and still crueler kind of proscription!*

> (*Rosc.* 153)

We may hypothesize that the supposed public opinion in favor of a conviction was (by and large) a fiction. The general desire was for stability. He uses the fiction to introduce the sensitive topic of the proscriptions in a gentler way.

We can make four observations about the use of this political argumentation in *pro Roscio*. First, Cicero does not deny the propriety of political argumentation from the other side; that is, he never objects to actual political argument in open court, as opposed to the application of extrajudicial *potentia*. He only claims that, properly understood, political considerations argue *for* his client. This is further justification for the contention in the previous chapter that open arguments from political consequences were sometimes acceptable in a criminal court context. We also note that such arguments in this speech are not restricted to the conclusion as in the other two. Only the most pathetic example (§153) is found at the end of *pro Roscio*. This confirms the contention that overt political argument is not restricted to particular, rhetorically marked contexts. Third, we may point out explicitly something that has already been implied—that the overtly political arguments which do exist here are not specific to the defendant or the actions at issue, as they were in *pro Murena* and *pro Plancio*. Instead they deal with more general issues of the relationship of the courts to society at large.[53] Finally, the political argument presupposes Cicero's view of the facts of the case, that is, that his client is innocent and that members of the prosecution were in fact responsible for the murder.

5. JUDGING PARADIGMS IN *PRO CLUENTIO*

Although *pro Cluentio* is longer than *pro Roscio*, it contains fewer explicit charges to the jurors. These, however, fall into the general pattern familiar from all three speeches previously discussed, particularly *pro Roscio*. In the exordium there is the nearly ritual assumption of the burden of proof:

> *You are accustomed to listen to accusations then ask for rebuttal of all of them from the other orator, and you think that no more should be given to the defendant's health than what the defense advocate accomplishes in proving and disproving claims in his speech.*

> (*Clu. 3*)

A little later in the exordium Cicero accepts responsibility for making a counteraccusation as he had done in *pro Roscio*. He will demonstrate, he says, that a jury was bribed "not by Cluentius, but against him" (*Clu. 9*). Then eventually in the heat of argument, and as usual in an address to his opponent, Cicero reverses the burden:

> *Show what money Cluentius gave, whence he gave it and how; at least show some one trace of the money which came from Cluentius. Then show that Oppianicus was a good man, that nothing different was ever thought nor any previous case decided against him.*

> (*Clu.* 124)

The trial in which this bribery is alleged to have taken place is the notorious *iudicium Iunianum* in which the elder Oppianicus (father of the current prosecutor) was convicted of poisoning.[54] Cluentius (the current defendant) was the prosecutor. The immediate context of this charge should also be noted. The initial premise ("Let . . . be removed") is backed up by a substantial *reductio ad absurdum* which argues against always following censorial judgments (§123). We will return to the political implications of this argument shortly.

One point on which *pro Cluentio* differs from the other speeches we have examined is its constant insistence on the narrow scope of the trial. The jurors are to consider only specific criminal acts. For instance, section 3 (partially quoted above) continues as follows:

> *As for* invidia *("hostility"), however, you should treat the matter by considering not what I say, but what ought to be said. For these criminal charges are Aulus Cluentius' own personal danger;* invidia *is a matter of common cause.*

> (*Clu.* 3)

The distinction between criminal charges and *invidia* (to be discussed at length below) is introduced mainly to reduce the value of certain legal precedents but is also given a general enough form to focus the entire trial. Here in the introduction this part of the charge is meant to look like a minor (and therefore reasonable) request for relief by contrast with the burden accepted just before and again in section 9. Later in the speech, however, Cicero actually lectures the jurors on this point:[55]

> *For it is up to the wise juror to take into account the fact that the Roman people have given him as much power as they did, to remember that they gave not only their power but their trust, . . . and to keep in mind under*

> *what law the defendant is charged, about what defendant he judges, and*
> *what is at stake in the trial.*
>
> (*Clu.* 159)

One might think at first glance that the claim of the elder Oppianicus' bribery (§124; quoted above) forms an exception to this pattern. Note, however, that a single sentence here is essentially the only reference in the speech to Cluentius' character, and an oblique one at that.[56] Additionally, in this passage his character and the precedents *(praeiudicia)* are made subordinate to the issue of the crime proper ("show . . . then show"). This suggests that the implicit ethical argument is that of *Inv.* 2.32–33: unless a pattern of criminal activity is established, no evidence can reliably support the accusation of a single crime. Hence the use of ethical argument is instrumental here; it goes to the plausibility of Cluentius' committing the crime, and so the focus remains fairly narrow. In any case there is a remarkable insistence throughout the speech on this very narrow focus of judgment.[57] This pattern (and the slight deviation of §124) would be an appropriate response to extensive attacks on the *vita ante acta* of Cluentius by the opposition.

More interesting than the explicit charges discussed above are the many implicit paradigms suggested throughout Cicero's narration and proof. On Cicero's description, much of the case rested on the results of various prior trials.[58] Cicero uses the opportunity of recounting these trials to offer advice about judging philosophy to the jurors he addresses. The main cases are the trials of Scamander, a freedman and alleged accomplice of the elder Oppianicus (§§50–55; further discussion in section 8 below), and the Fabricii, also Oppianicus' henchmen (§§56–59). His emphasis is on the utter certainty of the evidence by which they were convicted. For instance, Cicero (who happened to have been the defense advocate in Scamander's case) claims that he was given no respite by the prosecution:

> *I acted, fought, and struggled in every way and (as far as I was able)*
> *resorted to all remedies and refuges with the result that I achieved this one*
> *thing, which I will say timidly — no one will think that this cause wanted*
> *for an advocate. But as soon as I laid hands on anything, the accuser imme-*
> *diately twisted it away.*
>
> (*Clu.* 51–52)

Locally these arguments support Cicero's inferences that (1) Oppianicus was guilty in an earlier murder and hence that (2) he—rather than the prosecutor Cluentius—was responsible for the bribery when the case came to trial. These trials were held in the same *quaestio de veneficiis* in which Cicero was arguing. Hence, globally they provide a hint of the high level of proof Cicero claims is appropriate to such a trial: the defendant must be left without argument.

More complicated is Cicero's use of the *iudicium Iunianum* itself, which he treats twice (§§66–76; 106–7). In both passages Cicero gives a breakdown of the jurors' votes and an account of their underlying motivations. He finds a reason to praise almost everyone except his already selected villains (minor characters named Staienus, Bulbus, and Gutta). Eventually, however, he picks out one group of jurors (those who had voted *non liquet*) for special praise of their wisdom. They refused either to absolve a guilty man or to convict in circumstances which might give the appearance of impropriety (§106). This praise is then amplified by a list of most of the individual jurors who voted thus and of their respective virtues (§107). The best jurors were those who were torn between the belief in Oppianicus' guilt and the political principle that no one should be convicted because of the personal malice of the jurors. The latter principle would apply to Cluentius' situation as Cicero has described it.

Yet these jurors did not vote to acquit Oppianicus, as Cicero wants the current jury to acquit Cluentius. So why does Cicero use them as his preferred *exemplum*? First, a vote of *non liquet* has the same practical effect as an acquittal, and so a similar verdict here would be acceptable. Second, the scenario Cicero has produced (and probably had to produce, since the trial was well known) requires that the verdicts in the past and present cases be opposite but equally valid. This leaves a dangerous ambiguity of interpretation in the story.[59] If Cicero picked either of the other groups of jurors to privilege, there would be potential conflict between transfer to the present case of their actual votes and transfer of the supposed principles on which they made their decisions. That is, one group decided on the basis of the facts alone, as Cicero claims to want, but they voted guilty. Cicero cannot praise them and risk privileging their severe verdict. Those who voted to acquit, which Cicero surely wants in this case, must be in the wrong since his main premise is that Oppianicus was forced into bribery by his flagrant guilt. Praising this corrupt group would compromise Cicero's ethos. In the third *(non liquet)* group either the judging paradigm or the actual vote is acceptable in practical terms, and this group carries no moral stain.

6. ETHOS AND *EXEMPLA* IN *PRO CLUENTIO*

Just as the basic argumentative structure of *pro Cluentio* corresponds to that of *pro Roscio*, so the uses of ethical and exemplary arguments are roughly similar in the two. Explicitly ethical arguments (i.e., those that make specific claims about the character of some individual) are several times used instrumentally in *pro Cluentio*. About halfway through that speech Cicero sets up his great false dilemma: that either Cluentius or Oppianicus (but not both) attempted to bribe the jurors. Then he reasons that Oppianicus bribed the jurors because he had no other hope of salvation and because he had always been characterized by "singular audacity" (*Clu.* 64). Here we see, in condensed form, the argument from character (as well as from motive) that figured so heavily in *pro Roscio*.[60] Later, after reviewing a list of Oppianicus' alleged crimes (§125), he asks:

> As long as these things about Oppianicus all fit together, I say, and the accusations about Cluentius' money are not supported by proof, how can that whim (or, if you will, "opinion") of the censors be used to aid you or crush this innocent man?

> (*Clu.* 125)

In the first example the same facts support both an argument about character (and thus tendency to commit a crime) and one about motive. In the second only the character argument is present, though by this point the jurors may not need much further reminder of the other half. Both, however, illustrate the instrumental use of ethical argument.

We also see a good deal of description of various activities of the opposing characters (the elder Oppianicus, Staienus, Sassia). This serves two functions. First Cicero has explicitly committed himself here, as in *pro Roscio*, to producing a counteraccusation. If he is to produce the kind of character evidence that is vital to a convincing case, he must provide this kind of narrative himself. The amount of space devoted to ethical narrative shows that he takes counteraccusation seriously.[61] The other function is simple character assassination. The fact that the defendant's own mother was (apparently) appearing for or at least with the prosecution must have created extraordinary credibility problems for Cicero. His response was the equally extraordinary attack on her character; the extensive descriptions of her behavior are never used to support specific conclusions, and her actions have no direct connection to the trial.

Cicero simply attacks her character as a countermeasure. Much of the similar freestanding ethical narrative of other characters can be read in the same way. Since further detail at the moment would take us out of the realm of judging paradigms, we may now move on to the use of *exempla* in this speech.

Again we see a mixture of high and low prestige *exempla*. One of the low-prestige type is the story of a client of Cicero's, one D. Matrinius, described as a "little man" and an "aedile's scribe" (§126). His story illustrates the uncertainties of censorial judgment. Cicero even goes so far as to say, "I will not use the great store of *exempla*, I will not bring forth an ancient fact or some powerful or popular man." As in *pro Roscio* he explicitly notes the relevance of such a story. Another example is even more peculiar:

> I remember a certain Milesian woman from the time when I was in Asia who was condemned because she had induced an abortion by drugs after accepting money from the second-rank heirs.

> (*Clu.* 32)

A sordid story, perhaps Cicero's Milesian tale reminded his audience of Aristides' fictional *Milesiaka*, recently and famously translated into Latin by Sisenna.[62] Fundamental issues of murder and kinship are not supposed to be matters of legitimate cultural difference; contrast, for example, forms of government. Though Rome was not to be ruled by kings, monarchy might be perfectly proper for other states. A Greek example is therefore relevant. Here there may even be a special point to the external example. Sassia, alive at Rome, had exceeded in wickedness even a character nearly drawn from Greek fiction.

There are also a few very high prestige *exempla* in the speech. At one point Cicero makes passing mention of the resistance of P. Popilius and Q. Metellus ("very great and notable men") to unchecked tribunician power (§95). Then we get the example of the great P. Cornelius Scipio Aemilianus, who refused (as Cicero tells the story) to take away the public horse of one C. Licinius Sacerdos on his own authority as censor. Cicero says:

> For I must not pass over the example of a noble and famous man, Publius [Scipio] Africanus. . . . Though both the Roman people and foreign nations were content with his judgment, he was not himself content to condemn another to ignominy on his own authority.

> (*Clu.* 134)

It should be noted that both of these prestige examples generally occur in a political context: discussion of the censorship and its evidentiary value. In particular, are the censorial marks against some of the jurors in the earlier *iudicium Iunianum* to be given probative value (§119)? Based on the four speeches
we have considered so far, there is a clear pattern to the use of the *exempla*.
When Cicero discusses an issue that is perceived as part of Roman social practice, he uses examples of the *mos maiorum* that authorize that practice. If the
issue is more "universal," the situation can best be described as unmarked. Examples are chosen merely to give a convenient fit with the immediate point
Cicero is trying to make. The only potential exception is the Matrinius story
(§126). Even here though, the force of the story rests not on the admittedly
minimal authority of Matrinius but on that of the magistrates involved, hence
more prestige is in play than might appear at first sight.

7. *PRAEIUDICIA* AND *INVIDIA* IN *PRO CLUENTIO* [63]

In the foregoing we have seen that the basic argumentative strategy of *pro
Roscio* can also be picked out in *pro Cluentio*. The jurors are to consider only
a limited, factual question. Character and opportunity argue that Cluentius
would not and could not have committed the charged crimes. Despite these
parallels, it cannot be ignored that there are also many things going on in *pro
Cluentio* which do not occur in *pro Roscio*. We have, moreover, not confronted
the fact that the bulk of *pro Cluentio* deals with the various rumors, decisions,
and decrees before the case came to trial. This section will attempt a brief survey of these issues and examine how overt and covert political issues interact
in the "apolitical" environment of a homicide case.

Cicero opens *pro Cluentio* by bemoaning the fact that his client is faced
not only with a criminal charge but by long-standing *invidia* (*Clu.* 1). *Invidia*
should, according to Cicero, be irrelevant. He goes on to stress that the jurors should not bring any preconceptions *(quid . . . praeiudicati)* to the trial
(*Clu.* 6). At this point he maintains the position that it is the absolute duty of
the jurors to disregard any pretrial prejudices. But it soon becomes clear that
jurors are not, after all, meant to come to court with a completely open mind.
In discussing the trials of Oppianicus and his alleged henchmen, he brings up
a dilemma that faced the earlier jurors:

> For what were those jurors able to do? If they had condemned the "innocent"
> [to be taken ironically] Fabricii, nevertheless they ought to have stayed
> with their judgment in Oppianicus' case and agreed with the previous judg-

ments. Were those men to rescind their own judgments on their own by them-
selves, when other jurors normally look out lest they disagree even with
others' judgments?

(Clu. 60)

Here Cicero clearly wants to assume that there is an obligation of consistency
with one's own legal precedents.[64] The last clause also suggests the existence
of an obligation, perhaps a weaker one, to accept other past legal judgments.
Certainly this kind of appeal to consensus is coherent with the valorizations of
legal precedent. The importance of precedent is later implied (§114), and in at
least one passage, following precedents *(praeiudicia)* is depicted as an absolute obligation:

Jurors were led to believe not only that a defendant could be rightly con-
demned by one who had not sat in judgment the whole time, but, if a juror
had known nothing other than the precedents which are known in this case,
that he ought to listen to nothing else.

(Clu. 104)

Thus sometimes it is said that jurors must not use certain preconceptions,
sometimes that they may, and sometimes that they must. Is there a pattern
here, or has Cicero allowed himself multiple self-contradictions because of the
varying tactical demands of the different parts of his speech?

Obviously the distinction in practice is that those decisions which favor
Cicero's client are (allegedly) important while those that do not are to be disregarded. This is not, however, all that can be said on the topic. Cicero opens
his discussion of the decisions subsequent to the *iudicium Iunianum* thus:

But many other cases indicated that the jury was corrupted by Cluen-
tius. . . . I have prepared and strengthened myself to show you that what
judgments were said to have been made later about that trial were, in part,
more kangaroo-court than a real trial, in part did not tell against Cluen-
tius, in part were even for him, and in part are of a sort that have never
been called or even thought of as iudicia.

(Clu. 88)

"In part did not tell . . ." makes it clear that only some of the cases involved
are simply irrelevant even on Cicero's interpretation. The others either must

be read in Cluentius' favor or are defective. At one point in the introduction Cicero had conflated *invidia* and *praeiudicia* (§6). Here he makes the crucial distinction between "true judgments" *(iudicia)*, which are to be followed, and "false" ones. And while this section draws a novel distinction within the speech, it does seem very similar to one drawn between *iudicia* and open public meetings *(contiones)* elsewhere in the introduction:

> *For just as in other places truth has too little basis and strength, so here false* invidia *ought to be weak. Let it reign in mass meetings, let it give way in the courts; let it be strong in the opinions and speech of the great unwashed, let it be repudiated by the wise.*

> (*Clu.* 5)

In a somewhat different vein is the long discussion of the unreliability of censorial judgment (§§117–34). The rejection of both these categories (popular and censorial judgment) is defended on similar and very general grounds. Cicero's repudiation of censorial judgments contains a number of different arguments, of which I will discuss only one representative type. It concerns the collegiality of the censorship, the fact that two men held the office simultaneously and with equal authority: "If Lentulus did not stand by the judgment of Gellius and Gellius was not content with Lentulus' evaluation, . . . why is it that any of us thinks that all censorial marks ought to be fixed and perpetually valid?" (*Clu.* 132). Here are two examples of censorial verdicts refuted by an equal authority—the other censor. Therefore one cannot rely on the judgment of either.[65] A similar conclusion is derived from the story of Aemilianus and Sacerdos (§134; quoted above). Although Aemilianus knew that Sacerdos had perjured himself, he would not require the surrender of Sacerdos' public horse on his own authority as censor. Cicero's spin on the story is instructive here. Scipio's censorship was noted for its severity, but we know that in practice his attempts to penalize various citizens were frequently blocked by his colleague Mummius (Astin 1967: 119–21, 254–56). In this case, too, the actual issue was presumably less Scipio's willingness to proceed alone than his legal authority. Nonetheless, Cicero here makes the question one of a single censor questioning his own judgments. The censor's sole knowledge *(dixit se scire)* is not treated as a secure basis for others to make their judgments.

Support for this view of individual knowledge can be found in another passage of Cicero's. This point is made by Minyard (1985:32): "Real knowledge cannot be the product of the private insight of one man alone, since the test must always be historical and social, and in looking for truth we must not make up things in our heads, . . . but share in public thought." This view is illustrated by the following passage from the *de Re Publica*:

> *For [Cato the elder] used to say that no talent was so great that there would ever have been anyone whom nothing would escape, nor would all the talents brought together into only one man be able to foresee at one time so that everything would be included without experience and antiquity.*[66]

(*Rep.* 2.2)

From this perspective judicial use of censorial judgments is illegitimate because it relies too heavily on individual talents.

Despite the raw number of people involved, Cicero also reduces the case of mob judgments to that of one-man rule. The *contio* is exposed to (and therefore produces) only one opinion, that of the person who calls and addresses it:[67]

> *Why is it that now our defense is heard in such silence, while back then Iunius' power of defending himself was taken from him? . . . He lacked the opportunity not only to speak, but even to rise.*

(*Clu.* 93)

Without being exposed to different points of view, one tends to adopt the bias of one's source. How can this be asserted of such great assemblages? Here lies the important political/ideological point at which Cicero hammers away throughout the speech. Most of the population does not possess sufficient *gravitas* (weightiness) or sufficient *constantia* (constancy) to produce a consistent decision; therefore they are not a reliable source of knowledge. This is shown in part by the frequent descriptions of the *contio* as a storm, a random force of nature:[68]

> *From this it could be understood (as has often been said) that as the sea, which is tranquil by nature, is agitated and disturbed by the force of the winds, so the Roman people are calm by nature, but can be stirred by the voices of seditious men as by violent storms.*

(*Clu.* 138)

Essentially the same simile was used in both *ambitus* speeches as part of a topos on the unpredictability of the formal voting assemblies. However, there is a crucial difference in *pro Cluentio*. In the *ambitus* speeches there is only one-place correspondence in the simile; the meeting equals the sea, but no one holds the place of the winds. The point is the (limited) randomness which allows a lesser candidate to win legitimately. In *pro Cluentio* disturbance is not purely random, but directed (or at least generated) by a demagogue associated with the wind that drives the sea. Twice elsewhere in this speech the people are carried away by these metaphorical winds (§§77, 130). This graphically illustrates their alleged lack of moral *gravitas*.[69] Thus susceptibility of the mob to manipulation by a single figure (such as Quinctius) makes them an unreliable source of information.

One might then question the choice of the word *invidia* in the context of quasi-random hostility. The normal sense of the word seems fairly clear—it is hostility directed at the (usually rightful) position, success, property, or other advantage of another person. A common context for use of the term is resentment of the weak toward their rulers or superiors (Hellegouarc'h 1972:196). *Invidia* is used pejoratively of those who feel it (like "resentment"), and it can even imply the moral correctness of its target.[70] Cicero explicitly invokes the uni-directionality of *invidia* by making references to the hostility of the mob toward the senatorial class:[71]

> *Lucius Quinctius, a noted populist, . . . thought that* invidia *toward the senate had given him the opportunity to grow stronger, because (he thought) the judgments of this order were little approved by the people.*
>
> (*Clu.* 77)

The fact that *invidia* is normally unjustified fits with Cicero's epistemological evaluation of popular opinion.[72] These points of contact make it possible for Cicero to assign most popular judgments to the category of *invidia* (to which they would not naturally belong) and hence to discredit them. At the same time, the repeated use of the loaded word *invidia* constitutes an extra-rational strategy for persuading the jurors that popular opinion actually had these dangerous characteristics and therefore should be disregarded on grounds both of intellectual value and of class interest.[73]

We may now consider the relationship between these broadly political claims and the arguments we identified in *pro Roscio* (and to a lesser extent in *pro Cluentio* itself) as appropriate to homicide cases. The difference between *ambitus* and homicide is as follows. The former focused on the relationship between the (political) character of the defendant and Roman traditions of political practice.[74] The latter was a question of the occurrence or nonoccurrence of particular events without the same close regard to the social context. *Pro Cluentio*, however, shows how overt political considerations could intrude even in a murder case. The existence of previous decisions does not directly affect the question of guilt or innocence, yet it does bear on the appropriateness of this particular body rendering official judgment on the question of guilt or innocence. It may sometimes be more important to guarantee stable verdicts than the truth. Questions of the distribution of authority are by definition political. In this sense this speech is highly political. On the other hand, the political solution offered is (nominally) dictated by the "apolitical" character of the crime. The political issue of court authority is framed as a more abstract epistemological issue. What procedures are best suited to discovering absolute truth?

8. THE TRIAL OF SCAMANDER

We may conclude with a brief account of one of the few ancient murder trials for which we know essentially all the salient facts (at least for present purposes)—the trial on a charge of poisoning of the freedman Scamander in 74 (*Clu.* 50–55; see above). This was an obscure prosecution, which we know of only because it forms part of Cicero's narrative of the events surrounding the trial of Oppianicus (also in 74); this narrative forms the centerpiece of Cicero's defense of Cluentius Habitus in 66. On Cicero's account Scamander was acting as the elder Oppianicus' agent in an attempt on Cluentius' life. Cicero aims to show Oppianicus' manifest guilt (and thus explain Cluentius' success in prosecuting him) by making Scamander's guilt as clear as possible. The particular strategy he uses is to show how the prosecution was able to parry all the arguments of the defense advocate—Cicero himself. The more lines of defense Cicero can bring into play, the more effective this strategy will be. Furthermore, offering a story of a poor defense would unnecessarily make Cicero look bad and so reduce his *auctoritas* within this trial.[75]

The case was old and apparently not well known, which is what makes it so methodologically appealing for present purposes: Cicero can engage in more-or-less free composition in constructing an ideal prosecution and defense. Any other facts about the actual *pro Scamandro* (which we admittedly do not have) are therefore irrelevant to an analysis of Cicero's rhetoric in *pro Cluentio*. All these considerations suggest that we should expect a summary of all the ways one should defend against a homicide charge and the ways to defeat them. He starts by running through the standard categories of opportunity, motive, and character (§52). Then there is a more unusual argument. He claimed Scamander was tricked and thought the poison was medicine (§53). The implication is that Scamander had no idea what he was actually doing and so lacked the necessary intent to commit a crime. All of these arguments cohere with the "factual" view of homicide we have proposed.[76] Cicero could have credited himself with some kind of political or contextual defense, especially since it would have been easy to produce the necessary matching refutation on behalf of the prosecution, but he did not.[77] This is best explained if such lines of defense did not appear to be relevant to the charge. Hence this quasi-fictional trial provides clear confirmation that homicide was, by this time, essentially a question of "whodunit."

CHAPTER 4

Vis: *A Plague on the State*

1. VIOLENCE AND LAWS *DE VI* [1]

While the *lex Cornelia de sicariis et veneficiis* remained the framework for homicide law for centuries, the Republican laws concerning *vis* (literally "force, violence") were soon superseded by *leges Iuliae* under Augustus (and probably under Caesar before that).[2] As a result, reconstruction of the text of the *vis* laws is uncertain, even more so than for the laws on *ambitus*. A major problem is that later sources such as the *Digest* do not generally attribute material to original Republican laws which have been superseded; Romans, not surprisingly, thought of their laws as law, not as history. Our information about the Republican laws comes, therefore, largely from a collation of very scattered later sources with passing allusions in Cicero and other early authors. Hence we must cast our nets more widely than before and allow for a greater degree of speculation. The rest of this section will examine some of this legal detail. Then Cicero's four speeches *de vi* will be considered in chronological order. The final section will attempt to correlate changes over time in the argumentation of these speeches both with changes in the laws concerning *vis* and with underlying changes in ideology.

Criminal legislation against *vis* is a relatively late development in the Roman republic. There is no trace of a Sullan law or court *de vi* (nor of either before Sulla).[3] The first such law seems to have been a *lex Lutatia* of 78:[4]

> *Before you is a charge of* vis. *This law protects empire, majesty* (maiestatem), *the state of our fatherland, and the safety of all; Q. [Lutatius] Catulus carried this law at what was nearly the end of the Republic amidst armed disputes among citizens; after that fire had died down this law also extinguished the embers of the smoking conspiracy [of Catiline] during my consulship.*

(*Cael.* 70)

The puzzling thing about this passage (the only known reference to such a *lex Lutatia*) is that all other mentions of the law under which the Catilinarian conspirators were tried agree that it was a *lex Plautia*.[5] The best solution to the contradiction seems to be that the *lex Lutatia* was passed originally and specifically to deal with Lepidus' insurrection (in 78), and that a later *lex Plautia* succeeded it and, in normal "tralatician" Roman fashion, absorbed it (presumably adding new provisions also).[6] Thus Cicero's reference in *pro Caelio* to the earlier law is figurative, but not without point. Lintott (1968: chapter 8) argues plausibly that the distinction lay in extending the scope of the law from only full-scale insurrections (in the original Lutatian measure) to any act of violence which could be construed as *contra rem publicam* (in the *lex Plautia*).[7] (This phrase, quite common in surviving Latin texts [see note 16], can be translated as "against the state/republic/commonwealth"; to avoid prejudicing certain later arguments, I will retain the Latin.) The remainder of this section will provide additional support for Lintott's view.[8] We will defer consideration of the *lex Pompeia de vi* of 52 until the final two sections. Its innovations seem to have been largely procedural, and its scope was in any case limited to three specified past events.

We should also take a look at actual trials and accusations. Lintott (cited above, especially his appendix B) considers a number of trials *de vi* in the period 63–50 and concludes that they all have political overtones that could make the violence involved *contra rem publicam*. Here I will quickly note one other trial listed in *TLRR* (Alexander 1990) as conducted certainly or possibly under the *lex Plautia de vi*. If Lintott is right, then any criminal prosecution for *vis* should at least assert that public interests are at stake.[9] The trial of Asicius for complicity in the murder of the Alexandrian emissary Dio (*TLRR* 267; mentioned in *pro Caelio*) is normally taken to have been on a charge of *vis*. The same accusation figured in Caelius' trial *de vi*, and Ulp. *D.* 48.6.7 appears to bring attacks on foreign dignitaries *(oratores)* under the heading of *vis*.[10] The implications of such an act for the reputation of the Roman state are clear, so Lintott's thesis is at least weakly confirmed by this trial. *TLRR* lists a few other possible *vis* trials between 70 and 50, but the details are sufficiently uncertain that they cannot be used to argue for or against the thesis (my Appendix C).

Cicero's remarks on the *lex Lutatia* suggest an affinity between *vis* and *maiestas*. The latter is often translated "treason," but the full name of the offense—"diminishing the majesty of the Roman people"—illustrates that it has a much broader scope than the American "aid and comfort to the enemy." A look at *maiestas* trials of this period can shed some light on the nature of *vis*. If the *lex Plautia* extended the jurisdiction of the *vis* courts to all acts of violence *contra rem publicam*, then it would not be surprising that the remaining *maiestas* trials after the date of that law (there are very few) would concern non-violent acts. This is not a legal necessity. *Maiestas* law from at least the early first century encompassed seditious violence, as did imperial law on the subject.[11] These facts (as well as the generally conservative nature of Roman law-making) make it very unlikely that such activity was removed from the scope of *maiestas* law in the Late Republic. Yet *maiestas* is a vague, default category for offenses that are otherwise difficult to prosecute.[12] A violent offense might therefore be a more obvious example of *vis* than of *maiestas*. It would therefore have been prosecuted in the *vis* courts in the first instance.

The first and most famous example is the trial(s) of the tribune Cornelius (*TLRR* 203, 209). He was tried twice for reading the text of a bill (his own) despite a veto by another tribune.[13] In this incident there is no violence in the conventional sense. We must also consider one of the trials of Gabinius (*TLRR* 296) in 54. A letter of Cicero (*Q. fr.* 3.1.15) notes explicitly that he was accused *de maiestate* (before a spate of attempts to prosecute him *de repetundis*). Later historical sources say that he was tried for restoring Ptolemy Auletes to the Egyptian throne contrary to the wishes of the senate (Dio 39.55.4; Appian *BC* 2.24). Under the *lex Iulia* this could constitute *repetundae*, but that does not mean the offense could only be tried under that heading. This was a military operation so it could easily have been construed as an act of violence, yet that is not how our sources frame it. As provincial governor Gabinius was legitimately in command of troops, and his victims were Egyptians; this operation bears little resemblance to what was ordinarily recognized as sedition, such as Lepidus' insurrection in 78. Gabinius was prosecuted because (1) he left his province of Syria and entered Egypt, and (2) he did so against the instructions of the senate.[14] While it is easy to imagine how a prosecutor could have argued this as *vis*, the violence (despite its scale) in fact seems incidental to the offense. Rather, his crime was overstepping general and specific restrictions on his authority as governor. Hence all these possible *maiestas* and *vis* trials are compatible with the hypothesis that the *lex Plautia de vi* covered all and only acts of violence against the interests of the Roman state. (For a few other possible *maiestas* trials which do not ultimately affect this argument, see Appendix C.)

It seems that the *lex Plautia* prohibited the usucapion of property which had been taken by *vis* (Iulianus *D.* 41.3.33.2; Gaius 2.45), though it should be noted that the legal sources speak of a *lex Plautia et Iulia* (or *Iulia et Plautia*) rather than a distinct *lex Plautia*. (Usucapion is essentially the acquisition of legal title by continuous good faith possession for a sufficient period of time.[15])

Even if we grant the usual (and reasonable) assumption that this is in fact the same *lex Plautia*, that does not show that it extended criminal liability to private violence (*pace* Gruen [1974:227, note 30]). First, while the Iulianus passage might be taken to invoke the rule against usucapion in a context of private violence, that tells us nothing about how "by violence" *(vi)* would have been construed originally. Criminal *vis* had much expanded scope after the *lex Iulia*, to which Iulianus also refers. Second, even if we do take "by violence" broadly in this passage, it establishes nothing about the criminal law. The civil law had long tried to restrict the role of force in the acquisition of property (see notes 3, 9), and the *lex Plautia* could simply have expanded that attempt without expanding (in what must in any case have been a separate provision setting up the *quaestio*) the criminal offense.

As a final angle of approach to the character of *vis* law, I want to turn to two more purely discursive issues: the more general use of the phrase *contra rem publicam* and a particular use of the term *vis*.[16] Nowhere is *contra rem publicam* directly attested as part of any law *de vi*; do we really want to read it into the *lex Plautia*? We have references to eleven actions which were decreed (or proposed) to be *contra rem publicam* by the senate, including six prospective declarations, that is, ones referring to potential events which had not yet occurred.[17] One of these instances contains a direct quotation of a *senatus consultum* which suggests that the phrase was in fact part of the decree in all these cases (*Fam.* 8.8.6). Hence the phrase was probably a conventional one, even if not a part of statute law. It would add particular point to the several prospective declarations if they automatically carried a more concrete sanction. We can also note that *adversus/contra rem publicam* is attributed to the *lex Iulia maiestatis* four times in the *Digest*:

> He is subject [to this law] by whose effort or malicious intent plans will
> be made for men armed with weapons or rocks to be present in the city or
> to gather together contra rem publicam, *or to seize [elevated?] places or
> temples, or for anyone to bear arms* contra rem publicam, *or for the ene-
> mies of the Roman people to be assisted deliberately and* contra rem publi-
> cam, *or for soldiers to be recruited or incited to bring about or an uprising*
> adversus rem publicam.

> (Ulp. *D.* 48.4.1.1)

Tenetur is cuius opera dolo malo consilium initum erit, . . . quo armati homines cum telis lapidibusve in urbe sint conveniantve adversus rem

publicam, locave occupentur vel templa . . . quove quis contra rem publicam arma ferat, . . . quo hostes populi Romani consilio iuuentur adversus
rem publicam, quive milites sollicitaverit concitaveritve, quo seditio tu-
multusve adversus rem publicam fiat.

At least two of these clauses (seizing public places, *seditio*) were covered by
Republican *vis* laws, so their wording may have been brought over, including the *contra rem publicam* qualification, from the *lex Plautia*.[18] Finally, we
should emphasize a passage already noted by Lintott (1968:117). In his speech
de Haruspicum Responsis, Cicero reports:[19]

> *[The senate decreed that] whereas [Clodius] devastated my house with fire
> and stones and iron, the senate decreed that those who participated should
> be subject to the law on* vis, *which is directed against those who assaulted
> (*oppugnassent*) the republic as a whole. . . . [T]he same crowded meeting
> of the senate decreed that he who had violated my house had acted* contra
> rem publicam.

(*Har. Resp.* 15)

Here the difference between "those who assaulted *(oppugnassent)* the republic as a whole" and "who had acted *contra rem publicam*" could be explained
as variation for stylistic reasons. If so, then we have a direct connection between violence *contra rem publicam* and prosecution for *vis*. At the very least
we have both of them in the same context. As Lintott points out, this passage
gives a context for most of the senatorial decrees discussed above. The decrees
provide a powerful tool for accusers in *vis* trials by giving them an external basis for their claim that some act of violence was *contra rem publicam*.[20]

Another point worth making explicit is that *vis* requires actual violence in a
fairly narrow sense. This has already been indicated by the contrast with the
charge of *maiestas* (discussed above), but it is also true that in ordinary usage
vis can take on a variety of metaphorical senses (*OLD*, s.v.). However, Robert
Cape's (1991:74, 89–94) recent reading of Cicero's second speech against
Catiline confirms the narrow, literal reading in this context. In this speech
Cicero maintains that he did not exceed his legal authority in bringing about
Catiline's flight from the city after the first speech. In particular, he rejects the
claim that Catiline was "ejected by force and threats" (*eiectus . . . vi et minis*;
2.14). Cape (1991:90) plausibly suggests that Cicero may even have been an-

ticipating a prosecution *de vi*. A few sections earlier Cicero had expressed his preferred view of what had happened:

> *There are those who will say, citizens, that I ejected Catiline. Could I ac complish such things with a word, I would eject those, too, who say this. For it was a timid and respectful man indeed who could not bear the voice* (vocem) *of a consul.*

> (*Cat.* 2.12)

This argument is compelling only if the audience feels there is a strong opposition between *vis* on the one hand and *vox/verbum* on the other.[21] There is certainly some room for slippage here, as "force and threats" shows, but *vis* seems prototypically to involve the actual use of physical force.

Thus there were apparently two distinct elements of criminal *vis*. The first was an act of actual, not just symbolic, violence (contrast the trials of Gabinius and especially Cornelius for *maiestas*). The second was that the act be *contra rem publicam*. In the analysis of speeches that follows we will see a considerable variety of ways to deny one or both of these contentions.

2. THE *ORATIO PRO SULLA*

In 62 Cicero defended P. Sulla on a charge of *vis* based on the latter's alleged complicity in the Catilinarian conspiracies.[22] The irony of Catiline's great enemy defending an alleged conspirator was not lost on Cicero (or, apparently, on the opposition); in fact, it becomes the central fact of the defense. The essence of the defense is much like that used in the murder trials: someone was killed, but not by Cicero's client. If Sulla had been involved, Cicero (so he claims) would have known about it or at least have heard rumors. Furthermore, the burden of proof is made to lie heavily on the accusers:

> *But in trials I think it is necessary to ask not whether someone has been cleared of charges, but whether they have been proven. . . . I do not ask whether Cassius cleared Sulla; it is enough for me that he gave no evidence against Sulla.*

> (*Sull.* 39)

Ethical argument is also employed much as in *pro Roscio* and *pro Cluentio*. That is, Cicero uses the whole chain of inference from known behavior through underlying character to the possibility of other behavior:

In all grave and significant matters, jurors, it is necessary to weigh what
someone wished, planned, and actually did, not on the basis of the accusa-
tion, but of the character of the defendant.

(*Sull.* 69)

Here we even have an explicit theoretical justification of the inference of character from past action which will be drawn over the next eight sections. Nor
does the similarity to the homicide trials end here. Cicero even uses the argument (also expanded at length in *pro Roscio*) that the defendant had no opportunity to commit the crime because he was a long distance away: he was not
centrally located at Rome, nor in the most unsettled regions (Camertum, Pi-
cenum, Gaul), but in the allegedly stable area of Naples (*Sull.* 53).

There are, however, few other explicit assertions of any specific judging
paradigm in this speech. Most of our evidence for the model that Cicero wishes
the jurors to employ is based on his division of the defense strategy. The partition of the defense between Cicero's co-counsel Hortensius (who had discussed the so-called first conspiracy of Catiline[23]) and Cicero (dealing with
the second[24]) is explained as follows: each will argue about the phases of the
conspiracy of which he has personal knowledge based on his government service (*Sull.* 13-14). The theme is repeated when Cicero responds to charges
brought by the younger Cornelius:

If those were the older matters, unknown to me but not to Hortensius, he
has already responded; but if, as you say, it is that attempt of Autronius and
Catiline, when they wished a slaughter in the Campus Martius at the con-
sular elections which I conducted, then we saw Autronius in the Campus —
but why do I say "we"? I saw him myself.

(*Sull.* 51)

Particularly interesting here is Cicero's blanket and hypothetical denial of the
possibility of the earlier crime: if anything had happened, Hortensius would
have known about it. Sulla has irrefutable fact on his side.[25] The defense is
summed up early on:

Later, when Catiline had been ejected (or allowed) out of the city, that man
[Autronius] sent arms, horns, insignia, standards, and legions, and that
man who had been left within the city, but was awaited outside, once he was
cowed by the punishment of Lentulus turned to fear, not good sense; this

> man *[Sulla], on the other hand, was so quiet that he spent the whole time
> at Naples, where no one has even imagined that there were men joined to the
> conspiracy and where the setting itself is more conducive to consoling the
> spirits of the crushed than inflaming them.*

> (*Sull.* 17)

Sulla cannot be tied to the crime itself (that is to say the conspirators or their
arms); in fact physical distance at the time and the lack of expected witnesses
positively demand that there was no connection. If the prosecution cannot
show such a connection then their case has failed.

This, at any rate, is the core of Cicero's argument. There are, however, some
interesting twists which do not appear in the earlier homicide cases. Let us
start by examining one of the minor characters—P. Sittius, a client of Sulla and
allegedly a sub-conspirator sent by him to foment insurrection in Hispania Ul-
terior (§56). Sittius is defended on this point by an ethical argument like that
used for the benefit of many actual defendants: he was not the sort of person
to do such things. But Sittius' good character is defined in unusually specific
terms. He allowed a substantial part of his estates to be sold off so as to pay
some debts (*Sull.* 58–59).[26] Sittius is a good man because he values his financial obligations over his own wealth. This kind of respect for property rights
is certainly in line with Cicero's views, but ethical defense normally makes use
of well-known character types (as in *pro Roscio*) or of cardinal virtues like *pietas* (as in *pro Plancio*). Nor does the passage on the avoidance of debt form part
of a larger denunciation of luxury, as will occur in *pro Caelio*.[27] What we see
here is a highly political notion of virtue and in particular a kind of virtue
peculiarly lacking in the Catilinarian conspirators as Cicero had always described them. For instance, in the second speech *in Catilinam* Cicero gives a
catalog of five types of conspirator, one of which is described as:[28]

> *One group is that of those who, although deeply in debt, hold extensive prop-
> erty, their love for which will not permit them to sell off any of it. This is
> the most honorable group among them at least in appearance (for they are
> wealthy), but their allegiance and cause is most rash.*

> (*Cat.* 2.18)

Such passages attack in similar terms those who would preserve their own
property at the expense of social destabilization. It is (allegedly) the program
of revolutionaries like Catiline to exploit this class. Sittius, however, has resisted temptation. Thus ethical and political argument merge.[29]

Cicero implicitly politicizes the standard ethical argument, which is based on the *vita ante acta*. Then in a second theoretical discussion, which caps the detailed comparison of Sulla and the "real" conspirators, he makes that political aspect explicit: [30]

> *It is very much in your [the jurors'] interest, since you have lived with great fastidiousness and integrity, that the cases of honorable men be weighed not on the basis of caprice or slander nor on the whim of witnesses, but rather that in great inquiries and dangers which happen to arise each man's life serve as his witness. Do not allow, jurors, that the honest life be stripped of its arms, cast denuded to envy, and handed over to suspicion; fortify the common citadel of the good, block the escape of the evil.*

> (*Sull.* 79)

Note first the contrast between the jurors (members of the elite) and their potential accusers. The latter are characterized by the *levitas* and *invidia* which we have already seen to be characteristic of the mob. References to the *boni* and *improbi* are even more specifically politically loaded.[31] Cicero reserves ethical defense for the social elite and in particular the political conservatives—the self-styled *boni* ("good men") and *optimates* ("best men").[32]

The status aspect of the argument is emphasized by the passage immediately preceding. There Cicero had just produced a standard argument against testimony extracted from slaves under torture. In itself the topos is unremarkable ("the questioner is in control, desire misleads, hope corrupts, fear weakens" and the like). But its position within the broader discussion of character is significant. For Cicero, truth is the exclusive property of the free or even the elite. A similar epistemological issue arose in *pro Cluentio*, but there it was in a context formally secondary to the issues of the case. In *pro Cluentio* the question was how to evaluate the worth of previous judgments; here the central question of guilt or innocence is at stake. This shift suggests that, despite earlier appearances, the issue in this case may not turn on a simple matter of fact after all.

If we now turn our attention to a single one of these politically loaded terms, *bonus*, we see repeated reference to political judgments the jurors are expected to make. For instance, in discussing his own testimony to Sulla's innocence, Cicero gives the jurors the following instructions:

> *Under the circumstances, jurors, if I am found inconsistent or unreliable* (levis), *no weight should be attributed to my testimony, nor authority to my*

defense; but if I show consideration for the republic, reverence for my per-
sonal duty, eagerness to retain the good will of the boni, *then the accuser can*
say only that Sulla is defended by me while Autronius was injured by my
testimony.

(*Sull.* 10)

To evaluate Cicero's testimony the jurors must evaluate (among other things) his political correctness, that is, his eagerness to retain the goodwill of the *boni*. Cicero again justifies himself by his adherence to the *boni* (§21). Conversely, he claims Sulla's would-be colleague in the consulship, Autronius, was guilty because he seemed to be "opposed to the higher orders, hostile to all good men, an enemy of our fatherland" (§15). Autronius' national treason takes pride of place but is only one of three charges along with class and political disloyalty. Finally, Cicero expresses surprise at the basically virtuous Torquatus (the prosecutor), on the grounds that any accuser (and hence enemy) of Sulla should, by definition, have been "an enemy of the *boni*" (§41).[33]

In the instances discussed in the previous paragraph, the question of political affiliation is said to be important not to the central issue of Sulla's guilt or innocence but to secondary issues like Cicero's credibility or Autronius' guilt. This is much like the treatment of social validation of knowledge in *pro Cluentio*. However, a turn toward the specifics of the case is marked by the following passage explaining why none of Sulla's character witnesses had appeared previously for Autronius:

Why so? Because in the case of other offenses, good men think they need not
desert even a guilty man, so long as they are friends; in this case you would
be subject not only to charges of "liteness," but even to a certain guilt by as-
sociation, if you were to defend a man you take to be the parricide of his
country.[34]

(*Sull.* 6)

So horrible is this crime that none of the *boni* can be associated with someone who has committed it, even as an advocate or witness. If this is the case, how much more implausible would it be for one of the *boni* to have committed it himself? This is very much like the discussion of the *vita ante acta* in the *ambitus* cases and reminiscent of the argument of *pro Plancio* in particular. The basic form is a simple factual inference. One who has not committed any crimes in the more distant past is not likely to have committed a particular recent one. In this case, however (as later in the speech), Sulla's *vita ante acta* is defined largely in political terms, thus blurring the character of the defense. As in *pro Plancio* the defendant's status is assured by his adherence to the appropriate community (here the *viri boni*, there his *vicini*) and theirs to him, especially as mediated by Cicero himself.

In short, the basic line of defense in *pro Sulla* is simple denial. It is in line with the paradigm which Cicero sketches briefly and looks much like that used in murder trials. Obviously some violence took place (at least in the case of the second Catilinarian conspiracy), but Sulla had nothing to do with it. On the other hand, many of the subsidiary arguments and even the central denial take on political overtones. Sulla is defended on grounds of his political allegiance. In the terms developed in the first section of this chapter he never resorted to violence (*vis* nontechnically), nor did he act in other respects against the interests of the state *(contra rem publicam)*.[35] In fact Cicero perhaps suggests in this speech (as he will do more clearly in *pro Sestio*) that a *vir bonus*—a highly politicized notion—cannot, by definition, act *contra rem publicam* and so cannot commit *vis*. This will take us even further from the homicidelike defense that is prominent in *pro Sulla*.

3. THE *ORATIO PRO SESTIO*

One difference between *pro Sulla* and the speeches examined in the first two chapters is that in Sulla's defense Cicero rarely offers the jurors an explicit paradigm. The same difference exists, and is even more marked, in *pro Sestio*. In fact, nowhere in this speech is the jury offered a specific rule to guide their deliberations. Cicero does, however, frequently direct the jurors' attention to the main points he intends (or claims to intend) to prove. Only by implicit arguments does he attempt to show that these points justify an acquittal.

Cicero's defense is structured around a narrative of Sestius' entire career generously supplemented by the story of Cicero's own political fortunes. After discussing Sestius' earlier offices, his role in suppressing the Catilinarian conspiracy, and his role in the immediate aftermath of Cicero's exile, the orator finally offers his audience an apologetic explanation of this plan of attack:

> *I fear that one of you might happen to wonder what this speech of mine . . . aims at, or how the crimes of those who have troubled the republic before his tribunate are relevant to Sestius' case. However, I intend to show that Ses-*

tius' whole mind and every council were directed as far as he was able to
curing a weak and failing state.

(*Sest.* 31)[36]

At this point he is proposing not to give a particularly controversial account of
what Sestius has done, but an interpretation of why he has done it. Later the
focus shifts slightly from Sestius' internal motivation to the external forces that
motivated him: "But to return to what I intend to do in this speech, showing
that the state was beset by all evils in that year [58] by the crime of the consuls"
(§53). After a brief digression on the sufferings of himself and his family during his exile, Cicero turns to yet another version of his main topic:

But to depart from my own case, recall the remains of the plague of that
year [58]—for in that way will you see most easily how great a force of all
possible remedies the state demanded from the next set of magistrates — the
mass of laws, both those which were carried and those which were merely
suggested.

(*Sest.* 55)

Of particular interest here is the parenthesis explaining what conclusion the
jurors are to draw from the historical narrative. Given the connivance of the
consuls with the state's enemy, the next year's magistrates (including tribunes
such as Sestius) had to come to the aid of the *res publica* by armed struggle in
the streets. It cannot be coincidence that in this speech the state is said to require "the *vis* ("force, quality")" of all remedies." The word *vis* is quite frequently used of the effectiveness of drugs and so fits naturally into the metaphor here (*OLD*, s.v. [15]). However, given the context of a trial on a charge of
vis the audience will also understand that Cicero hints at a justification of *vis*
in its more concrete sense. The republic is in an unprecedented state of crisis
because its leaders and would-be defenders, the consuls, have been co-opted.[37]
Under these extraordinary circumstances Cicero will show that any use of
force by Sestius was undertaken for the good of the state. He never expressly
admits to *vis* (even in the nontechnical sense of any violence) but effectively
concedes that it was used.

Once Cicero has finally come to the tribunate of 57, the form of Sestius'
"cure" for the state becomes clearer, as does Cicero's rationalization for it. He
responds to the opposition's claim "You [Sestius] have bought, collected, prepared men" not with a denial but with an analysis of Sestius' possible motiva-

tions. (The parenthetical *credo*, below rendered "I have no doubt," is a reliable marker of heavy irony in Cicero's orations):

> *To do what? Besiege the senate? Exile citizens without trial? Steal their goods, burn and shatter buildings? Burn the temples of the immortal gods . . . [more crimes follow] . . . ? I have no doubt that it was to do these things, which could not be done without crushing the state by arms, that Sestius assembled his band of troops.*

> (*Sest.* 84)

While the focus has narrowed to the keeping of troops, Cicero's strategy remains the same: he does not deny the version of the accusation but addresses Sestius' motivation and context. On Cicero's account, Sestius did not intend various clear acts of sedition, some of which were likely outlawed expressly by the *lex Plautia* (e.g., arson, besieging the senate). By contrast, the opposition's claim, or rather Cicero's paraphrase of it, is free from legally loaded words. Hence Cicero's near admission costs him relatively little.

The argument about motive is made in more positive form when Cicero moves on to praise one of the other tribunes of the same year, T. Annius Milo (§§86–95). Milo, who had apparently been used already as a positive example by the opposition (§86), is offered as a model for Sestius' resort to the use of force in an intolerable political situation:[38]

> *We prefer to avoid both of these [sc. law (ius) and force], but one or the other must be used. We want force to be extinguished, but law must prevail, that is, the courts in which right is manifested; when the courts fail us or cease to exist, force must rule. . . . [Milo] wanted to use the one, so that virtue would conquer audacity; he had to use the other, lest virtue be conquered by audacity. Sestius' reasoning . . . was the same: the necessity of defending his own safety and preparing a defense against violence.*

> (*Sest.* 92)

Earlier extreme measures were justified on the grounds that the consuls, the natural and legal defenders of the state, had been co-opted. Here another natural line of defense for the republic had (he claims) fallen: the courts.[39] This failure causes a breakdown in the normal societal guarantees of personal safety. Since a political situation has arisen in which *vis* (in the general sense) is unavoidable, good men must see to it that what force is used is directed to good ends. If this principle holds for Milo, then it should also hold for Sestius. In essence, Cicero has argued that both their actions have been *pro re publica* ("to the benefit of the *res publica*"). If, as we have argued, criminal *vis* is defined as force *contra rem publicam*, then Sestius should be acquitted. One should note the frequency in these two passages of the word *necesse* and its derivatives. Although Cicero does not make the argument that what is necessary is *ipso facto* acceptable, it was a well enough known topic that he would have no need to do so explicitly (*Inv.* 2.98–100, 170–75).

Another kind of political theorizing is given potential juridical content by two *exempla* of courtroom situations. The first is Cicero's interpretation of what will happen if Sestius is convicted. The precedent would pose a danger to the "best citizens" by exposing them not only to banditry, crime, and violence (the characteristic instruments of evil men) but also to legal sanctions at the hands of the "best men," that is, the jurors (*Sest.* 2). This argument, and especially the juxtaposition of "to the best citizens" *(optimis civibus)* to "by way of the best men" *(per optimos viros)*, asserts the unbearable irony of political conservatives convicting one of their own number and thus doing the work of their enemies. We will have a great deal more to say about these *optimi viri* later; for now, let us consider the more specific judicial *exemplum* proposed by Cicero. For him the beginning of the year 57 marks the resurgence of the traditionalist forces in the state. One of the particular manifestations of this is as follows: "Whoever there was who had any part in my grief at the Clodian crime, wherever he went, whatever court he entered, he was condemned" (*Sest.* 68). In *pro Murena* Cicero had invoked the trials of Cotta and Galba, who were acquitted despite their technical guilt (perhaps like his client).[40] Here the relevance of the example is somewhat more indirect. In the context of the passage (broad popular support for Cicero's recall and the few hold-outs against it), the phrase "Clodian crime" seems to refer to support for Cicero's exile, not any kind of "recognizable criminal offense." The courts had, according to Cicero, convicted persons on the basis of their Clodian affiliations. If this practice is acceptable (and Cicero seems wholeheartedly to approve), then might it not be appropriate to *acquit* someone simply because he was a supporter of Cicero and therefore an opponent of Clodius? Thus Cicero twice uses the outcome of trials to make the oblique suggestion that the jurors should decide Sestius' fate on the basis of his political affiliations.

We encountered the rhetoric of political alignment in *pro Sulla*. Interwoven with the central assertion that Sulla had had no part in the Catilinarian conspiracies was the suggestion that to accuse one of the *boni* of *vis* was *ipso facto* nonsensical. Various individuals of proper political leanings might be subject to occasional lapses of moral or practical judgment which would lead to other crimes, but they could not, by definition, be involved in *vis*. In *pro Sestio* the rhetoric of political alignment comes to the forefront. While the descriptions of the trials just discussed merely suggest the judicial significance of political affiliation, the famous discussion of the "tribe of optimates" (*natio optimatium*, §§96–132) explicitly gives the reasoning which might support such a position. Acting *pro re publica* could have two senses. One is to act for the common good, the other is to act in accordance with the common will. On Cicero's account, Sestius has, of course, been doing both.[41] We have already seen Cicero's claims that Sestius was acting in the interests of the state (§31, and *passim*). Now we can examine his arguments that adherence to an optimate position constitutes truly popular politics.

Cicero initially offers the following definition of the *optimates*, "optimates, best men":[42] "Whoever want what they do and say to be pleasing to the multitude are styled *populares*; whoever work to make their counsels acceptable to the best men are called *optimates*" (*Sest.* 96). So Cicero's *optimates* and *populares* differ from each other not in policy or rank, but in the extent to which they believe ranking among aristocrats should depend on broad popular support. Whether or not this reflects any real political division, it would be easy enough to represent political differences in these terms and make aristocratic jurors sympathetic to Cicero's partition. This definition, however, does not help Cicero make his immediate point, so he offers a "clarification":

> *Then who is that "best man"? . . . The number of this group is, as I have said, spread far and wide; but the whole group can be circumscribed and defined briefly so that error may be avoided. All are* optimates *who are not criminals nor evil by nature nor mad nor troubled at home.*

> (*Sest.* 97)

Here the *optimates* are defined more as a community of character and interest, and less as one of political belief (much less economic class).[43] And he goes on to argue that this community is nearly universal: "This thing which all reasonable and good and peaceful men desire most of all—an honorable state of tranquility *(cum dignitate otium)*.[44] All who desire this are optimates" (§98). Here optimate support of the common good is made equivalent to support of the common will. Cicero can use this kind of definitional bait-and-switch since it is the opposition which has attached the optimate label to Sestius.[45] He can then take the characterization (and its opt- 'best' root) for granted and run with it.

Cicero goes on to argue more specifically that Sestius and his cronies have the support of the people, whereas Clodius is popularly hated. He suggests three fora in which popularity can be measured, so long as distorting forces such as bribery or armed force are absent (*Sest.* 106): public meetings *(contiones)*, formal voting assemblies *(comitia)*, and the gladiatorial and theatrical games. He expresses the same hope (and hints at the same fear of distortion of the people's true feelings) again at section 119: "I will easily achieve this if I shall have expressed the true and uncorrupted judgment of the whole people and the deepest feelings of the citizenry." A *contio* held by the consul Lentulus, in which Pompey spoke for Cicero's return, is given as an example of the first category (§§107–8).[46] Cicero claims that Lentulus' words were so effective because they told the people what they wanted to hear, that "nothing so 'popular' *(populare)* seemed ever to have fallen on the ears of the Roman people" (§107). The *comitia* are considered in sections 109–14. Here he concentrates on magisterial elections and the bill for his own recall. What he explicitly passes over are the legislative votes of the tribal assembly, held separately from the elections.[47] These legislative votes are precisely those in which the upper classes were the weakest (Taylor 1949:59). In the tribunician elections Cicero again takes a very broad view of what counts as optimate and a narrow view of what is *popularis*, thus ensuring that the candidates elected can be counted in the former category (§§113–14). Finally there is a series of anecdotes about theater crowds cheering for lines that appeared to support Cicero's cause and for Sestius himself and hissing at Clodius (§§115–27). The applause at all these events showed "that there was never a greater or more obvious consensus of the entire Roman people in any cause" (*Sest.* 124).

At this point it will be appropriate to consider a few details of the way Cicero makes these arguments about the popularity of the optimate cause (usually equated with his own cause). Cicero uses many literary citations in this speech in what has manifestly become a highly political case (§§120–23, 126). We suggested earlier that such a context would favor higher-prestige *exempla*. In particular one might here expect traditional Roman historical examples. The examples he actually does use suffice here for two reasons. First, their primary force lies not in the very words of the poetry themselves but in the crowd's political interpretation and approbation of them. After all, the original, second-century author of the lines (Accius) cannot have had any sentiment about Cicero in mind. Cicero also attributes some force to the delivery of these lines by the actor Aesopus. To the extent that his or Accius' authority is invoked, it is to shame Cicero's higher-status contemporaries who did not adopt the "correct" position as early as they should have: "Was it right, then, that

Aesopus or Accius say these things on my behalf (were the Roman people free), rather than the leading men of the state?" (§123). The other main point of the argumentation is Cicero's selective use of the *contiones* and *comitia*. After having announced that *contiones* are a sure sign of the opinion of the Roman people (§106, cited above), Cicero makes a significant distinction:

> *Is there some other populace of evil citizens, who feel hate and envy for us? . . . Do you see then how great is the difference between the real Roman people and a* contio*? And that the lords of the* contiones *are marked out for every hatred of the people, while those who were not permitted to stand up in the meetings of thugs are decorated by every sign of the favor of the Roman people?*

> (*Sest.* 125, 127)

The case against the Clodian *contiones* is essentially the same as that against the "invidious" judgments that played out against Cluentius. The only new twist here is the addition of money as the specific force which binds the group to the will of a single man ("hired" men and assemblies, §106; "mercenary voices," §126). The antisocial force of money has already been discussed in the context of *ambitus*.

Milo is used (as detailed above) as an *exemplum* of the appropriate use of political violence. But Milo is also a contemporary figure, and therefore the possibility of his political alignment with Sestius is raised. Presumably his popularity with some group led the prosecution to introduce him in the example in the first place. Similarity to Milo is used like the generalized argument about the common will discussed above; it shows that Sestius acted not only for the common good but according to the common will (one-half of Cicero's definition of "popular"). Praise and defense of Milo parallel the argument that those aligned with him (like Sestius) support the common good (§§12, 60–62). Sestius' connections with Milo confirm that he meets the other half of the modified definition of "popular"—that he acted for the general good. This is the half that only the "optimates" can truly claim. Thus Sestius is aligned both with paradigmatic individuals and with the more abstract *natio* of the optimates, and the whole group is shown to conform to Cicero's explicit definition.

In *pro Sulla* Cicero argued that there was no evidence to support the specific charges against his client. He also argued that a person of Sulla's political affiliations could not in any case have been involved in *vis*. The argument of *pro Sestio* is different. Whatever Sestius had done (this remains rather vague), it was justified because it protected the state and particularly the conservative interests therein. One might ask whether this difference in arguments is an artifact of the accident that we do not have the defense speeches which preceded Cicero's. He himself remarks:

> *But because the others have responded to the individual accusations, I will speak of the overall situation of Sestius, his way of life, his nature, his habits, his incredible love for the good, and his zeal to preserve the common safety and peace.*

> (*Sest.* 5)[48]

If the speeches preceding Cicero's *pro Sestio* were of a radically different character than his own, it might suggest that the apparent differences in defense strategy are merely matters of organization, not content. Perhaps the other speeches were more like *pro Sulla*. However, there are several reasons to suspect that the apparent differences are real. First is the fact that Sulla's defense was also partitioned. But there both Cicero and Hortensius dealt with specific accusations (*Sull.* 12–14). The division of charges in *pro Caelio* is less even, but Cicero is still left with some real specifics to refute.[49] Thus the de-emphasis of specific actions in *pro Sestio* is deliberate; Cicero could have been given "real" charges to defend against even though speaking last. Also if defense of specific events were crucial to a successful defense, Cicero might have been hesitant to publish a speech that was, in isolation, fatally flawed. The third reason to suspect that the speech we have is characteristic of the style of the defense as a whole is the fact that Cicero not only does not deny Sestius' use of force, or even simply ignore it, but almost admits it. We have already seen the example of the "'force' of all remedies" (in §55); another instance is a little earlier: "And since he consumed all the effort *(vim)* of his tribunate in saving me, it is necessary that my past circumstances be conjoined to the present defense of this man" (*Sest.* 31). In both cases the use of *vis* is metaphorical, but it is a metaphor that he could have avoided if he had wished.

These structural differences between *pro Sestio* and *pro Sulla* reflect the different inferences drawn from political alignment in the two speeches. In *pro Sulla* it is primarily instrumental—used to dissociate Sulla from certain actions. In *pro Sestio* it is used to decriminalize actions that probably were taken. The jurors are being asked to acquit on the basis of political alignment alone.

Sestius' aims are *pro re publica*, so his actions are *pro re publica* (that is, not *contra rem publicam*), and so he cannot have committed *vis*.[50]

4. THE *ORATIO PRO CAELIO*

The strategy of the speech for M. Caelius Rufus is substantially different from the approaches of the previous two speeches. Once again there is a combination of factual and political defenses, but both the character of the combination and the nature of the political defense are novel compared to what we have seen so far. The following analysis of the speech will be selective and will generally follow previous readings.[51] For the most part it will involve selecting particular points of interest and translating them into the framework adopted here.

In murder trials Cicero argued as if the issues at stake revolved around the performance of specific acts. He tried to define those actions (and thus the competence of the court) as narrowly as possible and to place as high as possible a burden of proof on the prosecution. Examples of this kind of argumentation are not hard to find in *pro Caelio*. For instance, Cicero mentions specific charges which had been refuted by the other counsel, Crassus ("the sedition at Naples, the attack on the Alexandrians at Puteoli, the goods of Pallas," §23), or which he would refute himself ("the [death of] Dio," §23; "two crimes: one of gold and one of poison," §30).[52] In between, he attempts to limit the case to such specific issues by complaining that the prosecution has been attacking his client on overly general grounds: "But you seemed to me to wish to stir up some hostility towards Caelius on the basis of the common ill-repute of youth" (§29). Cicero, of course, is happy to make these stereotyping arguments when they suit his purposes, but here he asks the judges in their "wisdom" to take a stand against them. Cicero repeatedly claims that with the responsibility to accuse a specific person comes the need for specific evidence. Early in the speech he makes the following distinction between accusation and invective:

> But it is one thing merely to speak ill and another to accuse. Accusation requires a specific accusation so as to define the facts, to mark the man, to prove by argument, and to confirm by witnesses; speaking ill has no object beyond invective; if this is done more petulantly it is called insult, if more cleverly, wit.

> (*Cael.* 6; cf. 30)

So there are some traces of the narrow argumentation of homicide cases in this speech. A subject *(rem)* must be specified, then proven, or else the accusation fails.

In this speech Cicero also tries to narrow the scope of the jury's competence, but never quite to the extent found in the speeches analyzed in the previous two chapters. For instance, the distinction between inherent and instrumental arguments from character is never made; he never absolutely rules out the former. He does, however, deny that the jurors should take notice of some (hypothetically) admitted wrongs, whether criminal or not in themselves:

> *But it is for your wisdom, jurors, even if there is a just cause for real men to attack Caelius, not to think that you must therefore concern yourselves with another's pain rather than your own honor.*

> (*Cael.* 21)

The jurors are not to redress injustice in general, but only to uphold their oath to this particular court *(fides)*.

In *pro Roscio* Cicero used his own scrupulous attention to detail and argument to emphasize the prosecutor's sloppiness. In *pro Caelio*, too, Cicero contrasts his handling of the case to the opposition's in order to illustrate a particular judging paradigm. Immediately after the section just cited his criticism of the opposing witnesses moves into a discussion of how he will conduct his own case. Witnesses (who can be "distorted" and "fabricated") will be pushed into the background. Rather, Cicero will privilege the use of "arguments," "evidence," and "facts" (*Cael.* 22). These ideas are reiterated when he produces his own (allegedly more credible) witness (*Cael.* 55). Differences in the quality of the two sides' witnesses are allegedly paralleled by differences in the quality of their evidence and argumentation:

> *There is no suspicion of the crime, no argument about the fact, no trace of words or time or place in respect to what is said to have been done; no witness and no accomplice are named, the whole accusation comes from a hostile house, an infamous one, a cruel one, a criminal one, and one full of lusts.*

> (*Cael.* 55)

He refers to arguments about the absence of confederates and lack of opportunity (by way of place) just as in *pro Roscio*. He also points out the failure of the prosecution to carry its burden of proof (or rather any level of proof).[53] The opposition has no grounds for suspicion and no arguments. All they can produce are witnesses, and probability weighs heavily in favor of Cicero's witness. A few sections later (§66), the opposition is once again described as having neither evidence *(signa)* nor arguments, only inherently incredible and already overmatched witnesses. They have failed even in their basic obligation to prove that Caelius did anything at all, much less anything illegal.

This set of passages in which Cicero lists the rhetorical failures of the opposition resonates with another series of arguments in the speech. Craig (1989) has examined the dilemmas in *pro Caelio*. Most of these are variations on the following argument. Clodius' sister Clodia (who is allegedly responsible for the prosecution) either does not have a relationship with Caelius which would make her alleged knowledge of his crimes plausible, or, if she does have such a relationship, she is thereby implicated in such immorality that no weight can be given to her testimony. (There is, of course, a sexual double standard at work here.) The individual passages are structured so that the latter possibility is implicitly preferred, though Cicero does not come down clearly on this side until the conclusion.

Parts of many of the passages just cited (e.g., *Cael.* 55: "a rash, insolent, enraged woman [seems] to have fabricated the crime") support this preferred reading of the various dilemmas. In return the dilemmas, more common in this speech than in any other of Cicero's but one,[54] add the appearance of rational argument to the passages I have discussed, with which they resonate. This appearance is due to the form of dilemma—the systematic evaluation of a purportedly exhaustive set of possibilities. Such apparent rationality is important in an argument which, as with the homicide speeches, is allegedly designed to discover the facts about particular real-world actions.

There is, however, another strand to Cicero's argument:

> So why has Caelius been called into this court? He has neither been charged
> with the particular crime of this court (proprium quaestionis crimen), nor
> anything not strictly covered by the law, but perhaps still relevant to your
> severity.

> (Cael. 72)

Not only does he admit the particulars of the case, narrowly defined ("the particular crime of this court"), but also more general questions, so long as they are of some gravity. By itself this could have been a bluff, a broadening of the burden to win audience sympathy, as in the homicide and *ambitus* speeches. In this speech, however, it is part of a larger pattern.

In *pro Caelio* practically the first words out of Cicero's mouth assure the jurors that the case before them is not worthy of their attention. Should an imaginary visitor come to Rome and visit this trial, he would assume that a matter of great importance was being tried since the jurors were forced to serve on a holiday. This traveler would be surprised to discover that "no crime, no audacity, and no violence" were at issue (*Cael.* 1). In mentioning the holiday Cicero refers to the fact that this trial was being held during the celebration of the *Ludi Megalenses* (games in honor of Magna Mater), something that was apparently possible only for a trial on this charge (*Fam.* 8.8.1). He suggests in general terms the triviality of the issue, especially by contrast with the urgency implicit in the extraordinary procedure. Later he ties this triviality to the central legal issue in the passage we saw at the opening of this chapter:

> *Before you is a charge of* vis. *This law protects empire, majesty* (maiestatem), *the state of our fatherland, and the safety of all; Q. Catulus carried this law at what was nearly the end of the republic amidst armed disputes among citizens, and after that fire had died down this law also extinguished the embers of the smoking conspiracy [of Catiline] during my consulship.*

> (*Cael.* 70)

In the terms developed earlier, a hypothesis is advanced in this passage that Caelius has not acted *contra rem publicam.*[55] He may not have done anything noble or productive like Sestius, but his dalliance with the meretricious Clodia simply does not reach the threshold necessary to bring about a successful accusation of *vis* (i.e., effect on the state). His actions were too trivial to constitute the crime. The opposition seems to have anticipated this kind of objection by referring to the (presumably successful) prosecutions of two men named Camurtius and Caesernius on charges of *vis* (§71). It is implied their offense was purely moral. We know nothing else of their cases, but it does show orators other than Cicero using the same techniques (here *exemplum*) to establish a judging paradigm.[56]

The claim of triviality is only explicitly advanced in the frame of the speech (§§1, 70–72), but it is supported throughout. The most important method for this support is discussed in Katherine Geffcken's *Comedy in the pro Caelio* (1973), which argues that Cicero uses comic tactics throughout his defense. The "use of comedy" in the speech takes two forms. The first is the use of devices which are comic or humorous in a general sense: bathos, conspiracy with the audience, ridicule, and so forth. The immediate effect (as Geffcken points out) is usually the demolition of the credibility of Clodia or some other figure in the prosecution. But here we might add the observation that these same tactics also resonate with the framing argument that the issue at hand is itself insignificant. Particularly notable for this effect are the confrontation between Clodia and the "ghost" of her forefather Appius Claudius Caecus (§§33–34), the mock-heroic description of the "battle of the baths" (§§61–67), and the wonder of the hypothetical spectator of the introduction (§1). The other use of comedy consists of frequent references to characteristic practices of the Roman comic stage. Examples include the paratragic characterization of Clodia as a "Palatine Medea" (§18), the overt invocation of the stock fathers of comedy (§§37–38), and the explicit description of the opposition's narrative as (bad) drama:

> *Like this whole little tale—the work of an aged and experienced poetess—which is without plot (*argumento[57]*) and can find no conclusion!... The ending is fit for a mime, not a real play; since no denouement is to be found: someone flees from their hands, then the castanets rattle, and the curtain is dropped.*[58]

(*Cael.* 64–65)

This set of "comic" tactics also has an (at least) dual effect. Locally they offer the comic theater as a full and complex paradigm for the "drama" of the crime and the trial.[59] This paradigm evokes audience expectations of characters, roles, and plot outcomes (Geffcken 1973:46, 53–54). Thus the audience/jurors know that the young comic hero/Caelius is "supposed" to win in the end. Globally they reduce the whole affair to the level of lightweight fiction—not merely theater, not merely comedy, but mime. This was a low-brow, often quite risque, genre in antiquity, various parts sit-com, porn film, and dime novel.[60] This generic identification reinforces the argument that Caelius has done nothing worthy of judicial notice.

Similar to the use of comedy is Cicero's treatment of the prosecutor, Atratinus. Quintilian (11.1.68) noted Cicero's patronizing tone: "Cicero employs this moderation against Atratinus in *pro Caelio* so as to seem not to attack him in the manner of an enemy, but to warn him as a father." Geffcken (1973:9) points out the need for Cicero to adopt an ethos which will minimize sympathy for the seventeen-year-old prosecutor created by the contrast with the ex-consul. The rhetorical issue was familiar to Cicero because he had carefully exploited this kind of sympathy early in his own career. Cicero frequently "pardons" Atratinus for pious errors of judgment (§§2, 7–8) and sympathizes with the young man when he is given a racy part of the prosecution to which his tender years are not suited (§7).[61] Atratinus, unlike Caelius, has led a sheltered existence. The prosecution, as Cicero depicts it, is distinctly minor-league in its form as well as its content.[62]

The elimination of the chief prosecutor as a serious rival allows Cicero to be more aggressive than usual in his early addresses to the jurors on the matter of their responsibilities (§§21, 29). He speaks adult-to-adult with unaccustomed equality, though still with more respect than he accords Atratinus. Of course both these features parallel the contrast made from the very beginning of the speech between what Cicero regards as the apparent seriousness of the situation and its actual triviality. It has been briefly noted that the *ludi Megalenses* gave Cicero a convenient hook on which to hang this defense by dismissal, but the point deserves more attention (Geffcken 1973:10). The courtroom is a serious setting and lends gravity to the content of the proceedings. Cicero relies on a slightly broader context as a source both for comic elements and for the license to use them. From what we have seen above the charge itself encourages such a line of argument. Whatever the details of Caelius' actions (except the alleged murder of Dio, which is largely suppressed), their societal insignificance is probably a legitimate, and certainly not an irrational, defense.

A few words are in order here on Cicero's defense against the charge that Caelius had been involved in the murder of the Alexandrian ambassador Dio (§§23–25). He is brief but to the point. He argues that the person responsible was known (Ptolemy, the king of Egypt) and admitted his responsibility, that the person through whom Caelius was connected to the death of Dio had been acquitted on the charge, and that some of Dio's hosts in Rome (the brothers Coponii) were prepared to testify in Caelius' defense. Austin (1960:153) thinks that there must be a deeper truth which Cicero is attempting to conceal. This is possible, but it seems equally possible that the charge is simple character assassination, hardly unusual in a Roman court. In any case Cicero presents a straightforward, rationalizing argument that Caelius had nothing to do with the crime. Any further argument might lend credibility to an accusation Cicero would like to treat as ridiculous.

In this speech Cicero characteristically offers two different lines of defense for Caelius. First, Caelius "didn't do it." Second, whatever he did do, it was not of social consequence, and hence he cannot be convicted of action *contra rem publicam.* The relationship between the two arguments is novel compared to that of multiple arguments in *pro Sulla* or *pro Murena.* The latter is expressed only in framing passages of the speech, while the former appears in the body. However, we have noted that other compositional features, particularly the use of dilemma and of comedy, support both of these explicit arguments. The interweaving of these features makes it hard (and unrewarding) to demarcate the areas in which the two arguments appear. In particular the audience is reminded of the assertion of inconsequentiality throughout the speech. Cicero's two implicit paradigms are logically incompatible: one is that the jurors should evaluate the claim that "he did it," the second is that they should ask whether "he did anything that meets the threshold of the law." The burden is not clearly set in the first case, since the opposition's evidence is dismissed as trivial by any standard. In the second case the references to Catulus' and Cicero's suppression of rebellions implicitly set a high standard of proof. Cicero could have dealt with the tension between these two paradigms by somewhere arranging them in hierarchical form ("he did not, and even if he did, it does not matter"). We have seen such a hierarchical arrangement in *pro Murena,* but Cicero chooses not to use it here. The two arguments are never articulated either structurally or conceptually. The audience is simply left with its choice of two different options, but in either case Cicero and Caelius win. This may be why there is no explicit judging paradigm. Why expend argumentative effort to force the jurors to make a choice that is not necessary?

Finally, we should make explicit reference to a radical technique for establishing judging paradigms which is illustrated in *pro Caelio.* We have already recalled one of Geffcken's most interesting observations on this speech. Cicero pointed out that the performance in the court had taken the place (for the jurors) of a theatrical performance. He went on to draw parallels between figures and actions in the case and certain characters and plots of drama (especially comedy). By establishing these homologies Cicero invites the jurors to view themselves as a comic, not a judicial, audience. As such they would naturally support the young hero (Caelius) in preference to agelasts such as the prosecutors. Axer (1979) and Vasaly (1985) have made similar arguments for the role of comedy in other speeches. Axer (1989) points out that the use of comedy is not the essence of this tactic. In principle the orator might re-create for the audience any conventional "communicative situation"—the theater, the classroom, and so forth. What paradigm(s) is at work in *pro Caelio?* I would argue that what Axer described as remodeling the communicative situation is in turn a specific application of what has recently been described as "the game-playing paradigm" (Zarefsky 1987). In game-playing the advocate redefines the rules of the forum from the ground up—in this case by substituting the rules of another forum wholesale. Of course Cicero does not openly ask the jurors to make this substitution; this would imply a disrespect for the institution which would damage Cicero's ethos. Instead he hints at it and emphasizes the insignificance of this particular case. This licenses the jurors to make the substitution themselves. If Cicero is successful, the jurors will apply the conventional standards of the substituted situation rather than those of the courtroom.

Pro Caelio is usually the prime example of Cicero's rhetoric of irrelevance, for those who have argued that trials in the *iudicia publica* had little to do with the cases nominally at hand (see above). In that light it may be worth reemphasizing here how difficult a rhetorical trick Cicero pulled off here. He in essence asked the jurors to use a general (theatrical) metaphor to govern their behavior in the court.[63] Once he has done this Cicero's view of specific issues (e.g., the proper outcome of the case) seems to flow naturally. A modern parallel might be use of the "war on . . ." metaphor by politicians speaking to a citizenry generally suspicious of increases in state power or expenditure. If, however, the public can be made to feel that "war" (on drugs, on poverty, on cancer) is being waged, then unspoken consequences follow naturally. Of course, then, costs should not be counted carefully; of course, the situation demands unusual obedience to central authority. The trick here lies in trying to replace an entire metaphorical system. As an example of such a system, one can say that arguments are structured by *(inter alia)* the war metaphor: they can be won, lost, fortified, demolished, and treated in many other ways as military exercises. To impose such a structure, then, is to convince your audience of many things at once. The one advantage that a speaker attempting such a task has is that the different parts of the structure come packaged together. Once you have sold your audience on several connections between, say, argument and war, the rest fall out "naturally."

Cicero had to convince the jurors of similarities between their present situation and the desired (theatrical) metaphor on the basis of similarities that were not obviously tendentious (the then ongoing games, the rash youth, the older woman of questionable reputation). Cicero's ability to radically restructure the jurors' understanding of the trial was thus dependent both on internal peculiarities of the case and on external factors (the *ludi Megalenses*). He was helped in addition by the charge that was made. *Vis* (as opposed to homicide, which could perhaps also have been charged) required a certain level of significance;

hence a reply that ridicules the accusation is a legitimate response. Thus Cicero's persuasion in this speech, while perhaps "extrarational," is not in the larger sense irrelevant. And he goes even that far only because unusual circumstances allowed him to do so.

5. THE *ORATIO PRO MILONE*

In April of 52 Cicero defended T. Annius Milo on a charge of *vis* under the new *lex Pompeia*.[64] Milo was on trial for the death of his rival P. Clodius at the hands of Milo's slaves. This fact, at least, was agreed on by all parties (and appears to have been "common knowledge" in any case). Cicero thus cannot use the defense of simple denial. But he can and does offer a variety of other lines of argument. Some are advanced only to be dropped, but two are retained throughout the speech. Adverse circumstances may have prevented Cicero from delivering the speech as well (or perhaps as completely) as he had intended; the published version almost certainly contains later additions, the nature of which will be discussed later.[65] For the moment, however, we may consider the text as it has come down to us.

Let us begin with the defenses which Cicero says he will not use. The first is that the crime was committed by Milo's slaves without his knowledge, which he claims "not to displace the crime, but just as it happened" (*Mil.* 29). Even if this description of events were true, it may not have established a valid defense. Since slaves were not legal persons, the Romans took measures to make their masters responsible for their actions.[66] A possible parallel to the present case is found in the civil law interdicts *unde vi* and *de vi armata*. These required restitution of property to the aggrieved party if force was applied by a principal, his agent, or his slaves (*Tul.* 44, *Caec.* 55; cf. *FIRA* 1.8.18).[67] But if, as has been suggested, the *lex Pompeia* specified only the actual criminals or those by whose criminal intent *(dolus malus)* the crime was committed, then this argument of Cicero's might have been to the point.[68] In either case Cicero does not return to this issue; it seems to be a weak point, and is accordingly subordinated by *praeteritio*.

More important are the two distinct but related arguments about the public good which are rejected in section 6. First, Cicero renounces the argument that Milo should be acquitted on the strength of the general benefits to the community of his career ("Milo's tribunate and all his acts for the salvation of the state") as he had pleaded for Murena and Plancius and, to some extent, Sestius. Second, he claims he will not defend Milo on the grounds that his specific action ("Clodius' death") was itself the salvation of the state. Later he reassures the jurors on this second point (*Mil.* 30); he will not defend Milo on the basis of the social utility of the death of Clodius. But it is this very argument, twice denied, which in fact resurfaces later; the argument about more general benefits to the people does not reappear.[69] (I will refer to the specific line of argument by the unlovely term "popular benefit argument/defense.")

Instead of these arguments Cicero's main defense is a claim of self-defense ("Milo was ambushed by Clodius"). The question of self-defense is to be the judging criterion:

> *But if the plottings of that man will be clearer in this light, then I will beg and beseech you, jurors, even if I lose on the other points, that this at least be left to us, that it be permitted to defend one's life from the daring and weapons of enemies without fear of punishment.*

> (*Mil.* 6)

In the course of the speech Cicero puts forward the self-defense issue in two slightly different ways. The first, using a "definitional" orientation, appears in section 15: the identity of the killers is clear, but Milo "sees that even with a confession of the deed, a defense of law can still be undertaken." That is, did Milo's admitted action fall within the scope of the law? He reiterates this point a little later and goes on to provide a criterion for answering the question:

> *Although there was no controversy of fact, the very mover of the law wished there to be a consideration of the legal issue, and the sort of jurors were picked, and a man put in charge, who would sort these things out justly and wisely; it remains, jurors, that you should ask nothing except which man laid a trap for which.*

> (*Mil.* 23)

The legal question is reduced to the factual question *(constitutio coniecturalis)* of who ambushed whom. Section 31 goes so far as to repeat the two versions of the question back to back. It is possible to make too much of the different bases of argument—legal versus factual.[70] Either way the case amounts to making a factual judgment of whether Clodius was more likely to have intended murder than his alleged victim (as in *pro Roscio* and *pro Cluentio*). Cicero takes advantage of the discrepancy between the two formulations only once, when he denies the usefulness of torturing Milo's slaves on the grounds that the question before the court is one of law not of fact ("for a question of fact belongs in the torture chamber, one on law in the court" [§57]). Otherwise the "who against whom" and "murder or self-defense" formulations are largely equivalent.

The defense, until about two-thirds of the way through the speech, is actually conducted very much along the announced lines.[71] First Cicero disposes quickly of the easy juridical point that self-defense does not count as criminal violence (§§7–11). Then he spends most of his time establishing the more controversial conjectural point that there was an ambush, which would mean that the self-defense argument was actually applicable in this case. To this end the argumentation follows the same standards for factual cases that we first saw in *pro Roscio*.[72] The motives of the two principals are compared (§§32–34). Opportunity is also compared in terms of the standard categories of time (§51), place (§§53–54), and equipment (§§55–56). Cicero analyzes in order actions before (§45), during (§51), and after (§§61–63) the fact to decide who is more likely to have laid the ambush. All this follows closely the requirements of the rhetorical textbooks. Not required by the handbooks, but still characteristic of the homicide speeches, is the apparent need to convict *someone* of the crime. Obviously, Cicero cannot usefully argue that both men premeditated the conflict; his client would still be guilty, if not alone. But it is less obvious that accident could not have been a legitimate defense: Asconius for one seemed to think that at least initially the struggle began by chance (41.18–21C). In the absence of the text of the *lex Pompeia*, it has been speculated that features of the law required the defense which was actually offered.[73] Nonetheless, it is more economical to see Cicero's primary motive in attacking Clodius as the general tendency in disputes of fact to produce an alternative defendant, a scapegoat.

Cicero's argument, however, takes a sharp and sudden turn a little more than two-thirds of the way through. He claims that Milo could, if he wished, shout "openly and proudly" that he had killed Clodius (*Mil.* 72). The alleged social benefit of the killing, which Cicero had originally refused to exploit, comes back quite suddenly, if only in hypothetical form. This form serves essentially as *praeteritio*; it soft-pedals the introduction of a new argument (or more accurately an old one which Cicero had sworn to eschew). Cicero proceeds to back up the new line of defense with prestigious *exempla* of men killed for the good of the republic (Maelius, Gracchus; §72), a list of the crimes of Clodius (§§73–75), and a more precise catalog of the dangers he would have posed to the state in the future (§76). Then Cicero reiterates the thesis of this line of defense, shifting into a more definite mode:

> Remember this, jurors. I hope that you and your children will come to see many good things under the republic; in each case you will realize that you would have seen none of these were P. Clodius still alive.

(Mil. 78)

After this Cicero offers the jurors another paradigm. This one is also hypothetical, as well as being highly creative:

> Consider (for our thoughts are free and gaze on what they wish, so that we spy what we do not see[74]), consider, then, the offer I make, if we could bring it about that you should absolve Milo but only if Clodius were to live again—why do your faces show fear?

(Mil. 79)

Thus his basic question to the jurors is "Are you better off for what Milo did?" This curious argument is recalled to the jurors' minds twice in other contexts. The first instance is primarily part of the argument that the *Clodiani* have no respect for symbols of the state (the *curia*) and hence the state itself (§91); the second is part of Cicero's invocation of his own ethos (§103).[75] Both, however, resonate with the hypothetical choice of resurrecting Clodius. On the one hand Cicero appears to be very generous here. He offers to pay for an acquittal with the return to life of his own and Milo's worst enemy. This generosity makes the paradigm attractive. On the other hand, the jurors do not really have the option of bringing Clodius back, so Cicero has nothing to lose.

In the later part of the speech, therefore, Cicero adopts the narrow argument from political good that he had most strongly disclaimed. This paradigm allows (even forces) him to make certain arguments which contradict what he had said earlier. One is the argument from divine providence. If Cicero can describe Milo as the agent of divine providence and enforcer of natural law (§§83–91), then he is no longer the passive, unknowing victim depicted in the self-defense argument. Another contradiction lies in the contrast expressed in section 89 to show who was on the side of virtue: "So that an effeminate individual [Clodius] tried to kill a powerful man." Earlier in the speech this description would have been dissonant with the arguments that Clodius was unencumbered, accompanied by soldiers, near home, and otherwise more likely to have been an aggressor. Hence in this part of the speech, Cicero follows the new paradigm not only against his earlier declarations but also at the expense of his earlier argumentation.

The formal situation in this speech is much like that presented by *pro Murena*. The speech begins with an extensive plea that the defendant did not commit the crime (though the basis for this claim differs radically in the two speeches). This is followed by the subordinate claim that, even if he had committed the crime, it is in everyone's best interests that the defendant be acquitted. There the benefit was prospective, here it has already been tendered. It was argued in chapter two that Cicero expected both arguments of *pro Murena* to be taken seriously, although any individual juror only needed to believe either one. The contradictions between the two arguments in *pro Murena* were small enough that a reasonable person could hope to win both arguments. Here the central contentions are much harder to reconcile. The remainder of this section will consider the relative valuation of the self-defense and state benefit paradigms.

It is possible that, as some have suggested for *pro Murena*, only one of the arguments is real, that is, expected to be persuasive, the other being added *pro forma*. Suppose that Cicero had serious doubts over the value of the self-defense claim. One possible sign of anxiety as to the value of that argument is the digression on whether it is *ever* right to kill another human being (§§7–11). By contrast, there is no explicit justification for the popular benefit argument. However, there are good reasons for a different reading of this passage. First, this digression would be the only overt sign of concern over the strength of the argument. Another is the literal textbook status of the story of the soldier who killed a superior who had threatened his chastity (*Inv.* 2.124 and *IO* 3.11.14[76]). The series of *exempla* of men (Ahala, Nasica, Opimius, and Marius), even private citizens, who had killed for the good of the state would at least have been familiar to previous auditors of Cicero's, if they were not yet part of general rhetorical currency (§8).[77] Hence little or none of this line of thought should come as a surprise to the audience. The references to justifiable man-slaying (in the laws of the Twelve Tables and, apparently, the *lex Cornelia de sicariis*) seem to be irrefutable legal arguments.[78] I would suggest that the whole digression is of this sort. The strongest part of Cicero's argument, which would probably have been accepted even if left unexpressed, is the principle of self-defense. This he naturally develops at length. The weakness of the self-defense claim is that it does not (apparently) correspond to the facts. Hence Cicero suppresses relevant details of how Clodius was actually killed (*Asc.* 32.7–13C).

There is far more actual anxiety surrounding the use of the popular benefit defense. The most obvious manifestations of this are Cicero's repeated denials that he will use it (§§6, 30, quoted above) and his reference to the whole line of argument as "outside the case" (*extra causam*; §92). When Cicero so distances himself from his own arguments, it can serve other functions, for instance as a bluff, but other indications suggest that here it is simply what it appears to be—a hedge.[79] One such indication is the fact that Milo's confession is consistently expressed in conditional and contrafactual terms. The necessarily hypothetical character of the discussion of Clodius' resurrection resonates with the conditionality of the whole argument: "Even if Milo had committed murder, it would nonetheless have been justified." Going outside the speech, we might also contrast Cicero's soft-pedaling of this issue to *pro Sestio*'s more forthright opposition of force to force. Outside the corpus altogether we find perhaps the most significant piece of evidence for Cicero's evaluation of his own argument. Asconius reports that, despite the recommendations of friends and allies to use the "philosophical" defense (i.e., the popular benefit defense), Cicero actually used only the self-defense argument (41.9–18C). Hence Cicero seems genuinely uncertain of the possibility of justifying Milo's actions with the state-benefit defense.

This last argument brings us face-to-face with the question of the relationship between the delivered and published versions of the speech. We know from the explicit statement of Asconius that the original was transcribed and preserved for decades (42.2–4C).[80] Hence Asconius would have had a firm basis for his assertion about the content of Cicero's actual speech: "Cicero contended and argued that Clodius had laid a trap for Milo and his whole speech dwelled on this point" (41.16–18C). Stone (1980:96–102) considers the wide variation in the respect and attention granted Pompey and his allies in different parts of the speech and partitions the text accordingly; on this basis he speculates that the *extra causam* section (§§72–91) and a few other passages (§§67–69) were inserted into the original and that relatively little further editing was done to unify these sections with the original text. This is compatible with Asconius' comments. Let us accept this hypothesis with the understanding that any reconstruction at this level of detail cannot be certain.

Starting from this basis, Clark and Ruebel (1985) have discussed the motivation for the later additions. They are primarily interested in the similarity of the popular benefit argument to certain doctrines of the Stoic philosophical school. Notable characteristics of the argument are (1) the treatment of the tyrant (as Clodius is figured) as inhuman and, in fact, a threat to human society, and (2) the identification of the will of God and the intent of the "truly wise man" *(sapiens)* that will lend coherence to the two halves of Cicero's defense. Clark and Ruebel then compare other works (particularly *de Republica* and *de Finibus*) to establish that Cicero's adoption of this Stoic view of the duty of tyrannicide dates from after the original delivery of *pro Milone*. We know that Brutus and others specifically urged the philosophical defense for Milo (and we might have assumed that Cicero was in any case aware of such arguments), yet, as Asconius says: "It was not pleasing to Cicero that, even if some one could properly be condemned to the good of the people, he should be killed without trial" (41.12–14C). The central conclusion of the article is:

> *What Cicero must have objected to in Brutus' argument was that Milo, without authority, had killed a citizen (albeit a harmful one) who had not been tried. Cicero presumably felt that the legal situation was untenable in that case, and was unable or unwilling to use the arguments of philosophy.*

> (Clark and Ruebel 1985:70)

They go on to argue that Cicero could not have made this argument (which they assume would have been much more effective than the self-defense claim) until he had worked out to his own satisfaction the philosophical issues surrounding the figure of the tyrant, something he accomplished only in the wake of Milo's conviction. This is an unsatisfactory explanation. Clearly objectionable is the premise that Cicero's use of this argument is dependent on his belief in it. Consider the fact that the Gracchi, normally used as *exempla* of legitimate political killings, are treated as solid statesmen at *Leg. Agr.* 2.10. And consider the exaggerated respect Cicero shows for the will of the people in *pro Plancio*.[81] This suggests external reasons to doubt that Cicero avoided this argument merely because he was unconvinced of it.

There are also more concrete reasons to question a belief-based analysis. One is Cicero's execution of the Catilinarian conspirators. In that case there was at least a claim that the state had authorized the act, but that claim was far from generally accepted. Cicero may have learned the dangers of testing the limits of legality from his exile in 58. Lintott (1968:53–64; 1974) has suggested that Cicero took a permissive, if not yet formalized, attitude toward political violence in a good cause from as early as 59. Note for instance his approving reference to the use of Milo's forces to impede a vote ("with great glory and to the delight of the people; *Att.* 4.3.4). Cicero even foreshadows Clodius' death at Milo's hands in the following section of the letter.[82]

Clark and Ruebel are aware of this work, but they do not really engage with it. Lintott's examples all seem to hold. Only one counterexample is proposed: "I follow Pompey, not his cause (believe me) as in *pro Milone* (*Att.* 9.7.3)." But this refers to Pompey's ends (personal domination), not his means (violence). Hence Clark and Ruebel confuse the development of a particular line of argument about the tyrant with the entire development of Cicero's thinking about political violence. Cicero did not categorically object to such violence. The problem is aggravated by the fact that they exaggerate the novelty even of some aspects of the tyranny argument, especially its dehumanizing tendency.[83] Thus, even if Cicero had qualms about the killing of a citizen without proper authority, such beliefs would not sufficiently explain why he did not originally make use of the same compensatory defense which after all forms the basis of the entire *pro Sestio*. In light of Cicero's fondness for multiple lines of defense, moreover, the omission clearly requires further explanation. I would claim that the choice is purely pragmatic. Cicero felt that self-defense was the only argument that the jury might accept—the only winning argument. In the next section I will explore some of the conditions that may have brought about this situation.

6. VIOLENCE AND THE STATE IN THE LATE REPUBLIC

Let us begin this section by reviewing the conclusions reached so far. The crime of *vis* has two defining characteristics. The first is the actual act of violence. The second is an adverse effect on society as a whole. Perhaps by statute, and certainly in fact, it is *vis contra rem publicam* that is criminal. Lintott's (1968:28–34, 52–66) comparison of the treatment of violence in criminal law with that in civil law and in literary and philosophical texts is revealing. Rome had a long tradition of reliance on popular justice, usually in symbolic forms but even to the point of violence (Usener 1901). This does not so much indicate a "permissive" attitude toward violence as diffuse the authority to use it. Texts from the middle of the first century indicate that these attitudes were still broadly held and that violence in the pursuit of legitimate goals was itself legitimate, if not as a first resort.

This reconstruction of *vis* gives a principled explanation for the variety of defenses Cicero offers in trials *de vi*: the advocate may question whether his client's actions have met either or both parts of the definition. In *pro Sulla* he claims that there was no violence on his client's part. For Sestius he argues that any violence was in the interests of the republic. And Caelius, who supposedly did nothing in the first place, should be of no interest to the state ei-

ther way. These options correspond to the possible defenses against the similar charge of *maiestas*: simple denial, or "I have increased the majesty of the
Roman people," or both (Bauman 1967:51, 150 and *passim*). In light of this
flexibility we have already asked why the *pro re publica* defense is broached so
timidly in the published *pro Milone* and not at all in its original.[84] Our curios-
ity should be increased by the fact that the celebrity of the event and the wording of the law (specifying the murder of Clodius as one of three crimes to be
considered) would have predisposed the jurors against accepting a factual denial.[85] What else, then, influenced Cicero?

Max Weber famously defined the "state" as that political institution which
claims for itself a monopoly on the legitimate use of violence.[86] Later sociolo-
gists have pointed out problems with extending this definition to the premodern period, but we can still use Weber's insight to organize our thinking about
the social context of violence.[87] In particular, it will be argued in this section
that the rise of the Roman principate involves the creation of a Roman state in
roughly the sense of Weber's definition. Or perhaps we should say that the two
phenomena (the rise of a particular government of and the underlying "state")
are different aspects of the same political process of centralization of authority.
We can also see that those changes had already started to take place in our period.[88] Once we have sketched out the trajectory of this process, we may return
to *pro Milone* and reconsider Cicero's rhetorical decision to stick with a strict
self-defense argument in light of the social circumstances which were beginning to radically reshape the government.

Before I examine individual cases, let me address a general issue that relates
to all of them. Powers exercised by or under autocrats are potentially attribut-
able to personal authority instead of abstract state authority. Hence one might
object that the creation of the principate merely mirrors certain effects of the
later rise of nation-states. The two possibilities are not, however, exclusive.
As Ian Morris (1992:48–49) has pointed out, the rise of tyranny was a major
factor in the shape of state-formation in much of ancient Greece. Giddens
(1987:94) finds a similar role for the absolutist state (and particularly its con-
stitutive notion of sovereignty) in the creation of the modern nation-state.
Concentration of power in the hands of a state centered on a single individual
is still, *a fortiori*, concentration of power in a state. So, on to the examples.

One aspect of the changing relationship of state and violence is an expanded
use of force by the state apparatus, particularly in internal matters. An example
brought to the fore by *pro Milone* is the use of troops to enforce order in the
city. Pompey (in 52) was the first to bring troops inside the *pomerium*, the
sacral boundary of the city, as a police force.[89] This was only a temporary mea-

sure, but it was eventually institutionalized by the creation of the *vigiles* (a police/fire force), the urban cohorts, and the praetorian guard under Augustus.[90] Another aspect is restriction of the private use of force. In *Mil.* 10 Cicero tries to treat the right to bear (and so to use) arms as virtually incontestable ("What good are our posses and our swords, which we would not be allowed to have if they could not be used under any circumstances?"). However, some slight restrictions had already begun (see below). A significant expansion occurs during Pompey's third consulship (again, 52). Pliny the Elder (*HN* 34.139) mentions that at this time Pompey outlawed the bearing of weapons within the city of Rome. And a similar measure is attributed to Antony in 48 by Dio Cassius (42.29.2).

These laws seem to have been temporary measures originally, but they, too, were eventually followed by more permanent weapons restrictions. The earliest known case is the *lex Cornelia de sicariis et veneficiis* of 81. It forbids, among other things, possessing a weapon *(esse cum telo)* for the purpose of killing someone or committing a robbery (*Rab. Perd.* 19; Marc. *D.* 48.8.1.pr). In the context of homicide law, this has reasonably been understood as being directed against attempted murder rather than simple possession or self-defense. That interpretation is less compelling for the same provision when it was, apparently, taken over a few years later into the *lex Plautia de vi* (*Att.* 2.24.3; Asc. 55.10–13C; Sall. *BC* 27.2). The *lex Iulia de vi* then seems to have prohibited any possession of weapons in *contiones* or *iudicia publica* (Ulp. *D.* 48.6.10.pr). Finally, the restriction may have come to include any public place (Marc. *D.* 48.6.3.1; *PS* 5.26.3). Contrast the very late Republican and imperial situation to that as late as 70. In that year Cicero could note with surprise that in Sicily slaves (not citizens) were not allowed to *esse cum telo* and that even this was acceptable only because of a long history of slave revolts there (2 *Verr.* 5.7). Thus the history of weapons laws shows a dramatic restriction of the means of violence from the mid- to late first century. We should probably also see the history of homicide law (as discussed in the first section of chapter three) in the same light. Originally only certain kinds of homicide are the object of public courts. By perhaps 86 any killing becomes, in and of itself, subject to public prosecution. Before restricting weapons in general, the state first claimed a monopoly on deadly force.

It is important to note that these regulations do not mark the end of a period of unconstrained weapons use. That never existed. At least in the politically prominent circles, of which we have some knowledge, there was a very low level of armed violence through the third and most of the second centuries.[91] Then, starting in 133, a number of political figures were assassinated, often along with a number of their followers: Ti. Gracchus, C. Gracchus, Saturninus, and M. Livius Drusus. In most of these cases our sources refer to the role of "armed" mobs on either side.[92] A closer reading, however, shows that these "arms" are largely of an improvised sort. Ti. Gracchus and his supporters were attacked with rocks and boards (Plut. *Ti. Gr.* 19), Tiberius himself with fragments of a bench (Liv. *Ep.* 58, *ad Her.* 4.58.68). C. Gracchus and two of Flaccus' sons are singled out as having swords, apparently implying that the rest of their "army" of supporters had at most improvised weapons (*ingens agmen*, Oros. 5.12). Gracchus' ally Antyllius was killed with writing implements (Plut. *C. Gr.* 13). Saturninus and Apuleius also fell to sticks and stones (Flor. 2.4; [Vict.] *Vir. Ill.* 73), though their side had made use of swords (Vel. Pat. 2.12). Finally, Drusus was killed with a mere knife (Vel. Pat. 2.14; App. *BC* 1.36).

Among the elite real weapons would have been kept as protection for travelers (*Mil.* 10; Shaw 1984:9–10); more generally we may suspect that past and potential soldiers would have been in possession of military-style weapons (Aigner 1976:3–7). This would have included much of the elite. Many more citizens may have owned such weapons for other reasons, though there is little evidence either way.[93] In any case armed violence (even in these extreme cases) seems to be held in check more by inclination than by opportunity. Thus the passage of legislation marks not the initial imposition of controls on violence but rather the transition from informal to formal modes of control.

On a different level, one might compare the restriction of the command of legions (at least in terms of the formal command or *imperium*, if not direct control) to the emperor, the fixed center of the state, not the officials of the moment. A logical consequence of this, though one that seems in practice to have occurred independently earlier, is the restriction to members of the imperial family of the full triumph for a major victory over a foreign power.[94] The Augustan developments on this score are again foreshadowed by Pompey's sole consulship in 52.[95] The most obvious similarity is the rule of the single individual. Historians agree that Pompey manipulated the political situation with the intent of producing some such result: he and his troops remained in their legal place, outside the city, while gang warfare prevented the consular elections for 52 until late in the intercalary month of that year (Ruebel 1979:239–40). At this point he entered the city under the authority of the *senatus consultum ultimum*. This is a vaguely worded decree that calls on the chief magistrates to "see to it that the republic suffer no harm."[96] The situation convinced the senate (and apparently the people) that it was in their interest to grant Pompey extraordinary powers and in particular unprecedented power to arrogate all armed force to himself. Augustus' rise to power is for us a matter of main force, but after the fact he reconstructed it in a fairly similar way: "I recruited an army at my own expense and on my own initiative, through which I freed the republic which had been oppressed by the domination of a faction" (*RG* 1). This interpretation was perhaps made more acceptable because the pattern had been set and could then be appealed to as "tradition." In both cases resort to a strengthened central authority is the cure for an intolerable but otherwise irremediable social situation. In Pompey's time the crisis and the extraordinary measures for its solution were short-lived, but they sprang from a social matrix which remained largely in place and allowed the establishment of a more stable dictatorship.

A few words may be in order here on the effectiveness of the Roman state's claim to a monopoly on violence. Premodern states have generally had a difficult time enforcing this monopoly (Giddens 1987:57, 60), and the Romans did not escape the difficulties. Shaw (1984) engages with precisely these issues in a discussion of banditry in the Roman empire.[97] He claims that broad regions outside the cities (and especially outside Italy) were prey to bandits. The problem was particularly acute in areas in which Roman governors had neither their own troops nor local assistance (Shaw 1984:14–19, 36–39). Several of the individual types of evidence for the extent of bandit activity available are ambiguous (9–12). As Shaw notes himself, it is hard to tell whether a mention of two bandit attacks in a letter of Pliny (6.25) is to be understood as typical or extraordinary. Given the usual reticence of sepulchral inscriptions on cause of death, the handful employing the formula "killed by bandits" may well stand in for a much larger number of actual victims. On the other hand, something about this particular death may make it particularly worth recording. In both cases in Pliny's letter the victims simply disappeared; we should wonder whether bodies of those killed by bandits were ordinarily recovered. That, in turn, might explain the tombstones of those who were.

Perhaps more telling is the perception expressed in Cicero's letters that bandits constituted a significant threat to the delivery of mail, especially in time of war (Nicholson 1994:55). In any case, the accumulated evidence seems to justify Shaw's (24) eventual conclusion: "Whatever their absolute numbers (probably small) bandits were a common phenomenon in the Roman empire and presented the state with specific problems of integration."[98] On the other hand, there seems to have been more success on the ideological front. Roman law put bandits "beyond the pale." They were subject to a summary punishment, often in the form of ostentatiously cruel public executions (Shaw 1984: 19–23). The use of *latro*, "bandit," as a term of abuse, much like "gladiator," suggests that the demonization of bandits was not merely a legal construct.[99]

Their violence remained practically unchecked in most places, but it was certainly delegitimized (at least among the elite).

In any case, the ideology was one that hardened over time. A brief look at a text from the Augustan period may be illuminating here. Consider the story of Horatius and his sister (Livy 1.26.2–12). Horatius killed her for weeping for an enemy soldier (her fiancé) he had just slain in battle. This is one of many episodes in Livy's early books in which the needs of family are subordinated to those of state—Romulus kills Remus for leaping the new city wall (1.7.2), Brutus has his sons executed for treason (2.5.8), the elder Torquatus has his son executed for fighting a duel with a Latin enemy without authorization (8.7.20–22).[100] Horatius' words to his sister (1.26.4: "May whatever Roman woman mourns an enemy perish thus," *sic eat quaecumque Romana lugebit hostem*) even recall Romulus' words to his brother (1.7.2: "Thus also to whoever else leaps my walls," *sic deinde quicumque alius transiliet moenia mea*). Normally the actions of Livy's protagonists are accepted, if not actually celebrated, by both the narrated audience and the narrator.

Horatius, too, escapes punishment, but his case is somewhat more complicated than the others'. He is put on trial; the charge is *perduellio*, the archaic form of treason.[101] The conventional and quite plausible explanation of this charge (in contrast to the more obvious one of *parricidium*) is that in taking his sister's punishment into his own hands, he has usurped the state's right to pursue her treason.[102] Horatius is acquitted, as legend required, but according to Livy the judgment was made "more out of admiration for his prowess than from the justice of his cause" (1.26.12). Her death was approved by her father's say-so (*iure caesam*, 1.26.9); at least later, real Roman law would have encouraged such a killing (Marc. *D.* 11.7.35; cf. Ulp. *D.* 3.2.11.3). Nonetheless, Livy still feels a need for an extralegal justification of Horatius' acquittal. This marks growing acceptance of the state's claim to a monopoly on the legitimate use of violence.[103]

The crime cannot, at least in Livy's version of the story, have been usurpation of the father's right to punish his daughter (even if that had qualified as *perduellio* at some period). If it had been, then the father's eventual approval, not Horatius' *virtus*, would have been the deciding issue.[104] However, this aspect of the tale raises a slightly more general issue, which first came up in the discussion of homicide law. Legal sources seem to be in agreement that, at least in theory, a father had the right to execute his own children and that this authority was not restricted until at least the time of Hadrian.[105] On its face this is an exception, if a narrow one, to the argument that homicide was not taken to be dependent on social context (and thus to the present contention that the

Late Republican/early imperial state tried to gain a monopoly on violence). It is then interesting to note that the jurist Gaius described *patria potestas* (usually considered the ultimate source of this legal authority) as an institution known only to the Romans (and, he adds, perhaps the Galatians): "This is a right peculiar *(proprium)* to Roman citizens (for there are practically no others who have such power over their children as we have)" (*Inst.* 1.55). This suggests that the exception, even if real, was perceived as an unnatural one. And, in practice, the exception seems to have been a very narrow one indeed.

Harris (1986) collects alleged examples of the use of this power to kill an adult child. Many involve fathers who simultaneously hold political or military authority which would suffice to authorize the execution. Many are in the legendary past. In several of these cases the son commits suicide in the wake of a lesser penalty, and in one case the father is himself exiled for his actions (Harris 1986:82–86). One of the two clearly historical and clearly private cases is that of A. Fulvius, who was executed by his father for his participation in the Catilinarian conspiracy (Sall. *BC* 39.5; Val. Max. 5.8.5). Strikingly, Dio notes in his telling that some thought that Fulvius was the only person ever so killed by a *privatus* father (37.36.4). In the other case one Trichio required the protection of Augustus from an angry populace after he had his son beaten to death (Sen. *Clem.* 1.15). Killing of daughters seems to have been somewhat more accepted, but even there clearly historical cases are rare (Harris 1986: 87). In practice, then, the theoretical power of life and death seems to have been largely a mirage.[106]

I would like to suggest that on these issues of violence elite opinion was moving ahead of legislation. In particular, the struggles of Milo and Clodius seem to have had a major impact.[107] Historians have ordinarily considered these events in terms of the immediate opportunity created for Pompey. What were the longer-term manifestations and effects of this violence? There had already been murders in the Forum in 57 (*Sest.* 76–77), and both sides packed *contiones* with their forces in 56 (*Q. fr.* 2.3.4). The elections for 53 and 52 were enormously delayed (Asc. 30.20–31.3, 33.25–34.2C). The disruptions of 53 and early 52 were merely the climax of a long series of events. It is easy to imagine that this long-term pressure could produce long-term determination to restrict violence, as later legislative history bears out. At the time of Milo's trial (52), then, the removal of violence from private hands is both a popular desideratum and a natural side effect of the resulting moves toward centralization of power.

This social trend precedes most of the corresponding legal change, but oratory cannot afford to wait for law; it must address the jurors of the moment.

This has consequences for the argument of *pro Milone*. One is the self-imposed restriction to the self-defense argument. After suffering Clodius' and Milo's reign of terror, the Roman people (and especially the jurors from the same aristocracy which had summoned Pompey) were beginning to have grave doubts about the wisdom of traditional Roman permissiveness toward private violence. Self-defense, however, would always constitute a legitimate excuse, as Cicero takes great delight in pointing out (§§7–11). In the published version Cicero can afford to offend some readers whose fundamental presuppositions will be questioned by the argument that Milo's ends justified his means, if he can thereby convince others of the truth of that argument. In the delivered speech more caution was required. Thus this version may lay the groundwork to defend further violence in good (i.e., Cicero's) causes, by arguing for the principle of state-defense. Even in publication he is careful to subordinate this argument as described above; he still wants to persuade.

These political conditions may also explain the distribution of an important metaphor. We noted in *pro Sestio* (note 36 above) the frequent description of extraordinary political action (especially political violence) as medicine for the state. It would seem natural for this figure to recur in *pro Milone*, at least in the later parts. In fact, it occurs only once, in two words, and in a reference to Pompey, not Milo: "But who does not understand that all the parts, sick and slipping, of the state, were entrusted to you to heal and strengthen them by these arms?" (*Mil.* 68). The resolution of this paradox may lie in a change of meaning of the metaphor in the intervening years between the two speeches. Stone (1980:97–98) points out that this figure was the "official rhetoric" of Pompey as sole consul.[108] It had been co-opted for a political position antithetical to Cicero's cause; it symbolizes Pompey's authority to suppress thugs like Milo. Thus questions of violence in the Late Republic are tightly bound up with those of state power. When the Roman people had to take the bitter medicine of force, individuals would no longer be trusted to administer it. Despite Cicero's best efforts this had become the job of the state.

CHAPTER 5

Criminals Abroad

1. *DE REBUS REPETUNDIS*

The sources for the court of *res repetundae* ("recovery of property" from Roman officials) are a little different from those for the courts we have considered up to this point.[1] On the one hand, we have somewhat better sources for the enabling legislation, most notably extensive fragments of the so-called *Tabula Bembina* containing the inscribed text of a late-second-century law (*CIL* 1.2².583 = *FIRA* 1.7).[2] This text has many gaps and does not reproduce a state of the law under which extant cases were actually tried, but it is far more than we have for any other offense. On the other hand, the speeches dealing with this charge, while reasonably numerous, have a number of individual peculiarities which complicate their use in this study.

We have a total of ten speeches, including one prosecution.[3] The defenses range from the merely lacunose *pro Flacco* to the highly fragmentary *pro Scauro*, with *pro Fonteio* apparently in an intermediate degree of preservation. *Pro Rabirio* is essentially complete, but it argues a case apparently based on a different section of the law than the other three. We also have the accusation of Verres (in six separate speeches), but five of the speeches were never delivered to a jury and so are not strictly comparable. Instead of trying to give complete analyses of each speech, the sections of this chapter will consider individual topics in the argumentation for which comparative evidence exists. The remainder of this section will consider the history of legislation *de repetundis* and some questions it raises about the purpose of the court.

As was noted above, the court for *repetundae* was the first of the standing courts *(quaestiones perpetuae)*. It was established in 149 through the efforts of the tribune L. Calpurnius Piso Frugi (*Brut.* 106). The literary sources for his *lex Calpurnia* tell us little but the name of the court. References in the later law of the *Tabula Bembina* give us a few other clues. Part of that text reads, "because (under the *lex Calpurnia* or *lex Iunia*) there has been an action at law by oath regarding him" (23) [*quod de eo lege Calpu*]*rnia aut lege Iunia sacramento actum siet.*[4] This indicates that the *lex Calpurnia* mandated a procedural form known as the "action at law by oath" *(legis actio sacramento)*. Even in 149 this was an archaic part of the civil law, in which each side in a case swore competing oaths (selecting from a set of prescribed forms), and the jurors (*iudices*; or even a single *iudex* in some instances) decided who had told the truth. Later we will see that this procedural point may be relevant to the question of just who was meant to be protected under this law. The inscribed law also prescribed that money taken from provincials before its own passage would be subject to simple restitution, while money taken later must be repaid double (line 59). On this basis it is generally assumed that the *lex Calpurnia* also called for simple restitution. Both of these arguments apply as well to the *lex Iunia*, which is not otherwise known.

Since the inscribed law mentions only the *leges Calpurnia* and *Iunia*, it is itself most likely the next law on the topic in chronological sequence. It allows for any number of rehearings of the case until less than a third of the jurors vote *non liquet* (line 48), that is, until at least two-thirds of the jurors have made up their minds.[5] This corresponds to Cicero's description of the *lex Acilia de repetundis* (*Verr.* 2.1.26) but not to its immediate successors. Peculiarly, they required exactly two hearings (*actiones*) of each case. Under the inscribed law, senators may not serve as jurors (line 22). This is also the goal of legislation normally attributed to C. Gracchus (tr. pl. 123–22).[6] Cicero also mentions the employment of "strict" jurors under the *lex Acilia*: "The Roman people . . . employed the most severe jurors" (*Verr.* 1.51). In the context of trial of provincial governors, this presumably refers to the use of equestrian jurors rather than senators. The latter but not the former might one day find themselves tried on this very charge. We have already noted that the inscribed law does not contain any provision for the mandatory recess after the first hearing (the so-called *comperendinatio*). In fact, Sherwin-White (1972) has demonstrated that it shows no traces of any known post-Gracchan innovations, formal or substantive. Thus I would adapt his conclusion (affirmed by Lintott [1981:182–85]) that the law of the *tabula Bembina* is probably the *lex Acilia*, which was probably also the law effecting Gracchus' judicial reforms. Even if there were a distinct (and now lost) Gracchan law, two of the three (*lex Acilia*, hypothetical Gracchan law, and *tabula*) are almost certainly identical, and the third (probably the tablet) will be a somewhat later and largely tralatician measure, making unknown minor adjustments.[7] Henceforth I will refer to the inscribed law as the *lex Acilia*.

Although the text of the law is quite long, it is largely concerned with procedural matters.[8] The definition of the scope of the crime is itself quite short, taking up about two lines of perhaps 340 characters each (lines 2–3; cf. line 59).[9] If property above a fixed sum (now lost) is taken *(ablatum captum coactum conciliatum aversumve siet)*[10] from an ally or other foreigner[11] by a "dictator, consul, . . . [a list of other magistracies follows],"[12] or senator or the son of any of the above persons then this court has jurisdiction. The precise meanings of the verbs of taking have been studied by Venturini (1979:237–319) and Sherwin-White (1982:20). The purpose of the ensemble seems to be maximum breadth. The law covers appropriation of funds from provincials by whatever means. As mentioned above, this property was to be repaid twofold on conviction;[13] there is no evidence of any civic disability for the convicted except incidentally disqualification from this very jury in subsequent cases (line 23). There is certainly no sign of a capital penalty or even of exile.

The procedure under the *lex Acilia* was no longer the *legis actio sacramento* but the more modern *nominis delatio* (line 3). In this procedure anyone may bring *(deferre)* the name of the accused before the praetor.[14] There are two crucial points about this change. The first is the shift away from traditional civil procedure, designed for the use of an aggrieved party against the person who has done him injury, to the form characteristic of the later criminal *quaestiones*, which allowed anyone to prosecute without himself having any necessary connection to the crime.[15] The other difference is of more specific import. The *legis actio sacramento* (like all *legis actiones*) was available only to Roman citizens, whereas anyone could perform *nominis delatio*. Hence under the earlier laws it would have been necessary for provincials to obtain a Roman patron to initiate any action on their behalf. Under the *lex Acilia* they could start the process themselves (though they would be assigned patrons later if they wished [lines 9–12]). Under this, and later, *repetundae* laws, the precise amount of damages to be awarded was to be determined in a separate hearing before the same jurors *(litis aestimatio)* held after the determination of guilt (*l. Acil.* 58–59; *Rab. Post.* 8).

Next in the series of laws on the topic are the *lex Servilia Caepionis* of 106 and the *lex Servilia Glauciae* of 101 (or perhaps as early as 104). The former restored senators to the jury (at least partially) and the latter reversed this move.[16] The *lex Servilia Glauciae* is also responsible for the introduction of the mandatory division of the case into two hearings (*comperendinatio*; *Verr.* 1.34, 2.1.26; *Scaur.* 29–30; [Asconius] 230–31St.) and the introduction of the clause *quo ea pecunia pervenerit*, "where the money finally ended up" (*Rab. Post.* 9). This provision allowed illegally acquired funds to be recovered not only from the official on trial but from whomever he had passed them on to.[17]

One of the Servilian laws also introduced the important pretrial procedure known as *divinatio* (*Div. Caec.* 63). In this procedure, after a defendant's name had been brought to the praetor, other persons could present themselves as potential prosecutors. The full jury which would eventually try the case then selected the person they thought would be the best accuser. One consequence of this change was to lessen the control of provincials over the prosecution. The jurors would presumably be predisposed to take a Roman more seriously than a foreigner; hence, if there were a Roman who was willing to prosecute but who was not to the liking of the provincials, they might well not be able to prosecute by themselves.[18] The examples of *divinatio* at *Caec.* 63 show that this change was introduced in or before Glaucia's law. In fact, it must be attributed to the (earlier) law of Caepio if the traditional date for Glaucia's tribunate is accepted (Ferrary 1979:124).[19]

The next law *de repetundis* is Sulla's *lex Cornelia* (presumably of 81) about which we know almost nothing with certainty but its existence (*Rab. Post.* 9).[20] *Clu.* 103–4 shows that a senator could be tried *de repetundis* for accepting money *ob rem iudicandam*, "for making judgments," in the year 66 and hence under this law.[21] However, we do not know for sure that the provision originated in the *lex Cornelia*; see further below. Presumably the plaintiff in such an action could be a Roman acting in his own right.[22] This law was superseded by Caesar's during his consulship in 59. His *lex Iulia de repetundis* contains a number of provisions which have no known predecessors in the laws already discussed.[23] For instance, it restricted the circumstances under which provincial governors might levy money for a fleet and controlled the amount of support for themselves and their staff they might demand from provincials (*Pis.* 90; *Att.* 5.16.3).[24] It forbade them to leave their provinces or wage war (perhaps with some exception for emergencies)[25] without the approval of the senate (*Pis.* 50). It required them to respect various kinds of privileges granted by their predecessors and not to accept golden crowns (*Pis.* 90; Lintott 1981: 203, note 154). These are all features of the law that have more-or-less contemporary attestation. If we look at the title in the *Digest* for the *lex Iulia* (48.11) we find that it is almost completely concerned with official corruption. It lists a number of actions (e.g., posting a soldier, imprisoning someone [or not], giving a judgment) for which officials are not allowed to accept money at all. Contrast this to the simple limit of money acceptable under the *lex Acilia*.

The character of the *lex Iulia* is radically different from that of the *lex Acilia*. The historically central function of recovery of money extracted from provincials (as is indicated in the title of the court) has been expanded to forbid absolutely the receipt of funds under certain circumstances. The point of the regulation seems to be less the protection of the ruled from theft or extortion than the assurance (or at least the appearance) of uncorrupted administration. The other regulations are aimed even more clearly at the latter purpose. The *lex Iulia* is designed to reduce the power of individual provincial governors by giving specific definition to the scope of their powers; it is directed at the Roman power structure and not at Roman/alien interaction. Lintott (1981) has asked the crucial question of whether this represents a sudden reconceptualization at the time of Caesar or is the result of more gradual evolution over the course of the preceding fifty years or so. To answer this question he rightly tries to find traces of these regulatory provisions in earlier laws *de repetundis*. As I have suggested, there is only one certain example (the provision about judicial bribery in the *lex Cornelia*). We can consider now some more speculative possibilities, but little evidence of such a regulatory structure will appear.[26]

Dio tells us that P. Rutilius Rufus was charged for bribe-taking in 92 (*TLRR* 94).[27] We know for sure that the formal charge was *repetundae* (Livy *Per.* 70; Vel. Pat. 2.13.2). If bribery were in fact the basis of the accusation, then the relevant clause, which certainly appeared by the time of the *lex Cornelia* (*Clu.* 103–4), would date no later than one of the *leges Serviliae* in the late 100's (Lintott 1981:194–95). As noted above, this sort of charge could have served to bridge the gap between the "recovery" and "regulatory" functions of the court *de repetundis*. Unfortunately, we cannot tell from our sources whether bribery was actually the formal or effective basis of the charge or if it was simply introduced to make the mere acceptance of money (which might well have been in large enough quantity to trigger the recovery clause) seem more sordid. This would hardly have been the first instance of the introduction of marginally relevant material for the sake of character assassination in the history of Roman oratory. Venturini (1979:363) is inclined to include this function in the law we are here calling the *lex Acilia* (and *a fortiori* the *leges Serviliae*) on the grounds that the list of officials liable under the law is so extensive and particularly that it includes urban officials such as the aediles.[28] As we have seen, the wording of the law is quite broad, and there is no obvious textual reason that it could not be taken to include bribes taken by urban officials, even if that were not its main objective.

In a sense Venturini's theory flows a little too well from the wording of the *lex Acilia*. It is clear that the later laws had the actual words *ob rem iudicandam pecuniam accipere* (or something very similar), but there is no trace of the phrase in the preserved fragments of the *lex Acilia*; rather its effects would be brought about, under his theory, by an expansive interpretation of the main provision. If Venturini's reading is sound, the later amendment would be completely redundant. Furthermore, as Venturini (1979:364–65) himself points out, it would perhaps be odd that, if the *lex Acilia* really had judicial bribery as an object, only a sufficiently large bribe would trigger it. It would certainly be strange that the threshold level should happen to be precisely the same as for provincial extortion. Hence, I would be very hesitant to assume the existence of a general provision on bribe-taking before the *lex Cornelia*. However, we must keep in mind the possibility that some Romans might have entertained as broad a reading of the *lex Acilia* as Venturini's.

Cruelty on the part of the governor is also sometimes offered as a candidate for inclusion in early *repetundae* laws. This would certainly have been motivated by provincial complaints (see below) and may eventually have become part of the law (Lintott 1981:205), but was this the case before, say, the *lex Iulia*? There are a few references in historical texts that would suggest so (e.g., Sall. *Cat.* 49.2; Tac. *Ann.* 13.52), but here we encounter again the problem that we saw above in the case of Rutilius Rufus. To what extent did anyone at the time of the prosecutions see the claim of cruelty as the basis for an accusation, and to what extent are the later authors simply reading character attacks in the light of later law? Venturini (1979:337) points out a passage from the *Verrines* that might be taken to support the inclusion of cruelty in the *lex Cornelia* but that on closer reading tends to show the opposite. Toward the end of the first *Verrine* Cicero sums up his accusation against Verres as follows:

> *I assert that Verres, when he had already done many lustful things, many cruel things against Roman citizens and allies, many unspeakable things against gods and men, then on top of that he made off with 40,000,000 sesterces from Sicily in contravention of the laws.*

> (1 *Verr.* 56)

Dicimus C. Verrem, cum multa libidinose, multa crudeliter, in civis Romanos atque socios, multa in deos hominesque nefarie fecerit, tum praeterea quadringentiens sesterium ex Sicilia contra leges abstulisse.

Each of these four charges has its own characteristic mode described by an adverb or adverbial phrase (I have translated here by the corresponding adjective). These four are not interchangeable; consider, for instance, swapping "cruel" and "lustful." Thus it is significant that only the last action mentioned, the taking of the money, is described as being against the law. That action is also set apart from the other three syntactically in a different clause. And certainly sacrilege is not legally at issue. Even in prosecutorial mode (and as late as the year 70) Cicero gives *repetundae* the same narrow legal scope we saw in the legal text of the 120's.

A regulation mentioned by Cicero (2 *Verr.* 4.9) provides another possibility. He says that those who entered a province with *potestas* or in an official legation were not allowed to buy slaves there except to replace one who had died there.[29] Crawford (1982:81) points out that a fragment of Posidonius (265E-K) seems to show Scipio Aemilianus already observing this regulation (and even going it one better).[30] Now Scipio's embassy was to allied and foreign states, not provinces (Astin 1967:127). It is not at all clear that the rule would apply to him under these circumstances, but he may nonetheless have abided by its provisions as part of the ostentatious frugality of the mission (Val. Max. 4.3.13). However, aside from doubts about both the rule itself and the connection between it and the fragment of Posidonius, there is no reason to assume what is most crucial in the present context—a connection to legislation *de repetundis*.

This is brought out most clearly by another law cited by Lintott (1981:191– 92) as a parallel to the *lex Iulia*. An inscribed law (in Greek) found at Cnidos refers to a *lex Porcia* which, *inter alia*, forbade a governor to leave his province and ordered him to keep his staff in line as well (col. 3, lines 4–15).[31] Lintott (1976a:81) is probably right to identify this law as the *lex Porcia* cited in the *lex Antonia de Termessibus*, which restricted the provisions that officials could requisition from their subjects (*FIRA* 1.11.2.16). Thus the *lex Porcia* of 101 seems to have been a comprehensive law regulating the administration of provinces.[32] The point that Lintott does not confront is that the *lex Porcia* is not (as far as we can see) a law *de repetundis*. Similarly the slave-buying rule, if it existed, could have been part of the *lex Calpurnia* (or *lex Iunia*), but there is no reason to believe that it was not an independent law (or even a *senatus consultum*); the lack of any such restrictions in the *lex Acilia* might encourage us to believe that it was one of the latter. In short, while there is evidence for growing restrictions on the actions of provincial governors, there is little evidence before the *lex Iulia* that this was accomplished by means of *leges de repetundis*. Only the case of Rutilius Rufus seems to have any connection to this set of laws, and if we see the introduction of provisions against payment for services as the turning point in the definition of *repetundae*, then we would not expect to find other administrative or regulatory provisions until the *leges Serviliae* or, more likely, even later.

The other question of legal history to be considered here is the recent hypothesis of J. N. Richardson (1987) that the *lex Calpurnia*, the first law *de repetundis*, did not in fact allow suits by provincials but only by Roman citizens.[33]

On this view the law would originally have been designed to protect Roman citizens who happened to be in the provinces, out of reach of conventional legal safeguards. Both known pieces of direct evidence as to the scope of the early laws (*Caec.* 17–18; 2 *Verr* 2.15) controvert this claim, but those passages discuss a series of laws in general and arguably might not apply to a long-obsolete piece of legislation.[34] Hence Richardson offers a number of indirect arguments. The first has to do with motivation. The law as we know it does not seem to respond to the atrocities in the provinces which are generally taken to be the immediate political context for its passage. In the same year the law was passed (149) Ser. Sulpicius Galba, former governor of Spain, had escaped punishment for the sale and murder of a number of Lusitani there. A law *de repetundis* would not have addressed this problem.[35] However, other known provocative offenses, such as those prosecuted *ad hoc* and with mixed results in 171, were pecuniary (Livy 43.2). Thus, while we know of no single, immediate triggering event for passage of the *lex Calpurnia*, we cannot say there was no context for a law protecting the interests of subject peoples.

Another argument about political context is implied though never really asserted by Richardson. Can we really accuse the Romans of being so softhearted as to want to help provincials? Richardson's suggested motivation for his version of the law is that it would have been too hard for most Roman plaintiffs to win a normal civil action against a major figure such as any provincial governor must have been. Thus a new, more public option would have been in order. This kind of social leveling seems more alien to Roman legal practice than providing minimal assistance to foreigners would have been. The Roman tendency at this period is not (as later) to give explicit legal advantages to the upper classes but to legitimize their social advantages by a uniform code.[36] On the other hand, laws at least nominally protecting subject peoples would have had practical value. They allowed Rome to channel provincial grievances without explicitly disregarding or suppressing them; this should promote much-prized stability (as Richardson [1987:1] is aware).[37] They would also focus those grievances against individual governors, not Roman occupation in general. Finally, it seems unlikely that the Romans would later have allowed provincials double restitution under the *lex Acilia* while contenting themselves with simple repayment (on Richardson's reading) under the *leges Calpurnia* and *Iunia*.[38]

Richardson's second overt argument derives from the procedure of the *legis actio sacramento*. It was noted above that this action was normally available only to Roman citizens; Richardson reminds us that it was also a general principle that no *legis actio* could be entered into in another's name (*nemo alieno nomine lege agere potest*; Ulp. *D.* 50.17.123.pr, Gaius 4.82, Just. *Inst.* 4.10). Hence, he feels, the procedure would imply not merely Roman *patroni* but Roman plaintiffs. However, the general principle in question is far from absolute; there are several known *actiones populares*, that is, actions which are available to any citizen on behalf of the whole people, which by their very nature cannot be used in one's own name (Just. *Inst.* 4.10; cf. Gaius 4.82).[39] *Actiones populares* were created on an *ad hoc* basis for a variety of different fact situations (Mercer 1983:97–99). The *lex Calpurnia* could easily have created a parallel form for the circumstance it governed.[40] Another formal argument is based on two references by the jurist Paulus (*D.* 41.1.48.pr; 48.11.8) to provisions preventing the usucapion of property obtained in contravention of the *lex Iulia*. Richardson argues that this rule implies that, at least at some point, Romans would have been plaintiffs in suits for recovery. Admittedly, in the second Pauline passage the victim is supposed to have a legal heir and therefore must have been a Roman citizen.[41]

However, we should remember three points here. First, the *ob rem iudicandam* clause, clearly later than the *lex Calpurnia*, is the most likely statutory basis for the later case involving citizens. Second, Richardson is using a very late source as evidence for the earliest law, with no clear example in between. Third, Paulus is probably writing after the so-called *constitutio Antoniniana* (which granted citizenship to virtually all free inhabitants of the empire around A.D. 212).[42] The function of protecting noncitizens no longer made sense; if the *repetundae* laws still functioned at this point (as they clearly did), they must have applied to citizens. This need not, however, reflect anything other than the regulatory innovations of the original *lex Iulia* and beyond.

There is no compelling reason to accept Richardson's conjecture on the aims of the *lex Calpurnia*. The (traditional) function of laws *de repetundis* was always to give subject and allied peoples recourse against the depredations of Roman officials (cf. note 34). We have, however, noted evolution of the function of these laws in two respects. First is their increasing use to restrict the actions of provincial governors for reasons that have little to do with improving or worsening the condition of those subject to their authority. This change parallels the centralization of authority discussed in the previous chapter. The explicit prescriptions and proscriptions by which magistrates were bound are a different kind of example of the increased power of the state as a structure at the expense of individual office holders, who eventually became salaried employees of the state (Dio 53.15). Centralization of provincial authority perhaps predates the laws *de vi*, and its most dramatic manifestation, the *lex Iulia*, is seven years earlier than the *lex Pompeia de vi*. Nor did it require (quite) the same level of crisis for passage. This may perhaps be attributed to the fact that the centralization of authority is here not at the expense of the bulk of the citizens, but of only a small group of magistrates. The role of laws *de repetundis* in this process may have been comparatively minor until Caesar's legislation, though to some extent this is an argument *ex silentio* (especially with respect to the *lex Cornelia*). Hence it is hard to use the evolution of law itself to gauge the pace of evolution in conceptions of *repetundae*.

A final issue in the evolution of *repetundae* law is the effect of variations in procedure on control of prosecutions. At first, under the *leges Calpurnia* and *Iunia*, prosecutions could apparently not go forward at all without a Roman *patronus*.[43] The situation changed radically under the *lex Acilia*: provincials could carry through the prosecutions entirely on their own initiative. The praetor could assign them *patroni*, but they had the right to reject his choice.[44] The next change swung the pendulum back toward the original situation, though not all the way. The introduction of *divinatio* would privilege a Roman prosecutor with a personal grudge even if he did not have an intimate knowledge of the case. It is possible to overestimate the practical significance of both post-Calpurnian innovations. Surely at any period it would have been a disadvantage to a prosecution if no credible Roman could be found to argue a prominent case. In the *Verrines* there does not seem to be any question of the Sicilians representing themselves. Nonetheless we can read in this situation a concern with the degree of control the Romans would retain in dealing with complaints by their subjects and allies. Eventually the decision was to maintain strong control. This may suggest that the underlying concern was to maintain a healthy relationship with those allies and subjects, rather than an abstract respect for their rights. We will return to this question later.

2. THE *LOCUS DE TESTIBUS*[45]

A passage from Cicero's defense of M. Aemilius Scaurus in 54 sums up the basis of most surviving defenses before the *repetundae* court:

> *If you prove these charges with records I will pay close attention and look to what I must do in the defense (for the keeping of records has a certain sequence and follows the order of business). In fact, if you will rely on witnesses who are at least known quantities, if not actually good and upright men, I will consider how I must contend with each point.*

(*Scaur.* 18)[46]

Witnesses and tablets belong to the class of what rhetoric calls "extrinsic" proofs: that is, they "are not found by the orator, but brought to him by the case" (*de Or.* 2.116). Cicero the rhetorician points out that the orator's job is not finding such proofs but rather considering how to present them (*de tractandis argumentis,* §117). He eventually begs off describing exactly how to "treat" these topics: "for it would take a long time for me to explain how witnesses, records, and precedents ought to be supported or denied" (§119). Here we need only note that attacks on the reliability of witnesses or records were part of the arsenal of the practicing orator. It is in cases of *repetundae* that such extrinsic proofs are most prominent in preserved forensic oratory. That is, arguments about the value of various pieces of evidence take on a prominence of their own in these cases. Murders, for instance, usually have neither type of evidence, and almost no criminal cases are so dependent on accounting records as are *repetundae* trials. In this section I will treat the role of witnesses in *repetundae* trials.

Since Cicero normally pled for the defense, and since only the prosecution could compel the presence of witnesses, the most common argument we have is an attack on the credibility of the opposing witnesses.[47] One way to do this, always available in cases of this sort, is simply to attack the witnesses on the grounds that they are foreigners. Cicero does make this argument, and in a couple of different ways.[48] One, used only rarely, is simply to assert the superiority of domestic over foreign testimony: "Take care to seem to have trusted our witnesses more than aliens" (*Font.* 49).[49] Another version of this approach is more positive. Cicero twice claims a peculiar Roman reverence for the duty to give honest testimony.[50] For instance:

> *Recall, jurors, how hard you are wont to labor not only over what testimony you will give, but also over what words you will use, lest a single word seem to have been chosen immodestly or to have slipped out for some personal gain.*

> (*Font.* 28)

The same argument is made at greater length at *Flacc.* 10–12. In all these passages Cicero argues that the testimony of the aggrieved foreign parties is inherently suspect. Such arguments would be equally relevant in almost any trial *de repetundis.*[51]

Cicero's argumentation, however, is normally more complicated than this.

In all four defense speeches he presents specific arguments that the race *(gens)* of the opposing witnesses is particularly untrustworthy. For instance, he says of the Gauls:

> *Do you think that those very nations who are so different from the habits and nature of other races are moved in giving testimony by religious awe at their oath and fear of the immortal gods?*

> *(Font. 30)*[52]

Then he goes on to discuss ancient attacks by Celtic peoples on Delphi and the Capitoline (with its temple to Jupiter) and their practice of human sacrifice.[53] These attacks all have a specific force; the Gauls lack normal, not just Roman, reverence for the gods. Only slightly less specific is the contention that the Gauls bear grudges because of their recent military defeats at the hands of the Romans (*Font.* 13–14, 33–35, and 49).

Charges against other races in other speeches are similarly specific. In *pro Flacco* the Greeks are said to be notorious for being more interested in winning arguments than in telling the truth (§§10–11); thus Cicero turns their developed rhetorical heritage against them. Cicero's line in this speech is that the Greeks' unreliability is common knowledge: "Not that I myself am one of the main detractors of the trustworthiness of this people" (§9). To back up this position he produces a number of proverbial expressions, which supposedly testify to the broad contempt in which Greek honesty is held. For instance:

> *Where do we get that phrase "lend me your testimony"? Is it said by Gauls? Spaniards? Of course not. It belongs to the Greeks, so much so that even those who know not a word of Greek know that these words are habitually spoken by Greeks.*[54]

> *(Flacc. 10)*

Here the reason for the use of proverbs is made clear: it is meant to show that everyone knows that the Greeks are liars. Later, when he produces specific phrases for the different Asiatic groups represented, he need not repeat the whole explanation (§65).[55] The reference to the Gauls in the passage just quoted is ironic when read closely with *pro Fonteio*, but in its original context it again illustrates Cicero's reliance on ethically specific attacks against witness credibility. More briefly we may note that in *pro Rabirio Postumo*, Alexandria (whence the main opposing witnesses) is said to be the source of "all tricks, all deceits, all the plots of the mimes" (§35).[56] And in *pro Scauro*, the poor Sardinians are not only descendants of the Phoenicians (a "most deceitful stock," §42)[57] but rebels who have been repudiated by their own folk, "with many covenants violated and broken" (§42); they are too much even for their own kind. In all these cases the very ethnic group that has come to accuse Cicero's client just happens, on his account, to be the least credible people on the face of the earth.

The situation is more complicated still. In two, and perhaps three, of the defense speeches Cicero makes more or less elaborate distinctions of credibility among subgroups of the race he has just attacked.[58] In *pro Flacco*, after Cicero has attacked the Greeks as a whole, and then the individual towns that have sent delegations to testify, he turns around and claims that, *pace* what he had just said in sections 9–12, 23–6, and elsewhere, some Greeks are worth listening to after all. These are the natives of Greece proper and of the west; only the Asiatic Greeks are liars (§§61–66). Even among the Asiatic Greeks, there are the Apollonidenses who are "of all Asia the most frugal, most religious, farthest removed from the luxury and 'liteness' of the Greeks, patriarchs content with their own, ploughmen, rustics" (§71). And earlier he had remarked that there were many good and noble men in Tralles, but they had stayed out of this case in anger at Flaccus' treatment of the matter of money owed there to one Castricius (§§52–54). Hence the delegation sent by that town was unrepresentatively corrupt (and hostile). In *pro Fonteio* it is the people of Massilia and Narbo (admittedly the most Romanized areas) who are made the exceptions. The former is "a city of the strongest and most loyal allies," the latter the "mirror and guardpost of the Roman people" (§13).[59]

We have no example of a directly comparable distinction in the preserved parts of *pro Scauro*, but there may be a trace of one preserved in a fifth-century grammarian. When discussing various formations for ethnica, Pompeius (5.144K) records that in this speech Cicero distinguished between *Sardi* (the natives) and *Sardinienses* (immigrants). The likeliest context for this differentiation is that Cicero was making fine distinctions of credibility between various peoples, especially since the primary attack on Sardinian credibility is based on their ancestry (§42).[60]

In many instances there is an obvious immediate motivation for this division. In the case of the Trallienses Cicero is speaking of his family's own clients and must tread lightly, if not for their sake then for that of his own reputation (*Flacc.* 52–54). It is also the case that Cicero often has foreign witnesses testifying for his side, despite his lack of subpoena power. Naturally he will tend to phrase his arguments so as to protect those witnesses' credibility, and this could account for some of the other distinctions cited above. However, there is reason to suspect that these divisions are not made solely for such local, tactical reasons. On the one hand, Cicero does not need his witnesses nearly as much as the opposition does. If the defense lawyer can discredit all the (non-Roman) witnesses of either side at once, it will be greatly to his advantage. This is precisely the argument that Cicero makes at *Flacc.* 36–38. He begins:

> *[Asclepiades] said that the testimonial which was given to Flaccus by the Acmonenses was of no value. Our side would surely hope for the rejection of this testimonial. . . . For you are granting me what this cause clearly demands: that there is no gravity, no constancy, no firm counsel among Greek men, and no trustworthiness in their testimony.*

> (*Flacc.* 36)

Yet Cicero does not make this argument anywhere else, nor does he make reference to it later in *pro Flacco*. The main function of the argument here seems to be the local one of highlighting the (unusual) value of the laudatory decree of the Acmonenses. By "generously" offering to trade this genuine testimony for opposing testimony which is allegedly forged anyway (as shown by their respective seals: §37), Cicero wins acceptance for the presupposition of his offer: that his documents are genuine while those of the opposition are faked. What Cicero wants the jurors to remember and apply globally is the idea that some Greeks are worthy of a hearing. This is the point reiterated later in the speech (§100). Cicero does not normally surrender any argument absolutely, but it is not uncommon for him to do so conditionally. If discrediting all witnesses were a convincing argument, it would be advantageous for Cicero to use it. If it were advantageous, we might expect to see more of it, if only in the form "all foreign witnesses are bad, and even if some are not bad, the trustworthy ones are on my side." Perhaps Cicero is not simply making arbitrary distinctions to enhance the relative credibility of his own witnesses.

Another argument that Cicero does not perform ethnic division purely to protect his own witnesses lies in passages where he praises the integrity of persons who, as far as we can tell, are not testifying at all. In *pro Flacco* Cicero soft-pedaled his criticism of the people of Tralles because he was known to have personal connections there. Earlier he made an apology for his (apparently) well-known philhellenism. He says that he admires the learning and wit of the Greeks but not their integrity or religion (§9). This much may be taken as necessary to maintain his own integrity. But immediately before making that distinction he had said:

> *There are among their number many good, learned, and modest men who have not been brought before this court, and many shameful, ignorant, and frivolous folk, whom I see were suborned in various ways. But I am speaking here of the Greek race as a whole.*

> (*Flacc.* 9)

This is a gratuitous assertion of the credibility of persons who are by definition not present and so not testifying for Cicero's side. This is done in *pro Scauro* also. After he has attacked the descent of the Sardinians, he asks pardon from one personal friend and others who have been granted citizenship (his brother had connections in Sardinia as well; §39). These persons are both citizens and *laudatores* of Scaurus (§43). But then he goes on:

> *May the other good men of Sardinia pardon me—I certainly believe that there are some. I will not fail to make exceptions when I speak about the faults of a race, but I must speak about the whole race, among whom there may be some who have overcome the flaws of their descent and race by their own habits and humanity.*

> (*Scaur.* 43–44)

Here Cicero makes exception not only for persons who are not relevant to this case, but whom he does not even know.

A. Kurke (1989:175) has asked, "Why were [*ad gentem*] attacks found to be so effective? Surely Roman jurors, long accustomed to racial caricature at trials for extortion, could easily dismiss them as 'empty rhetoric.'"[61] First we must remember on the one hand that trials *de repetundis* were hardly everyday events and on the other that many of the "racial caricatures" had currency beyond the courtroom.[62] As a result these arguments are not as likely as Kurke implies to seem "empty" or *ad hoc*. We should also not be carried away by the fact that numerous arguments can be lumped together into a very broad rhetorical category. Much of Cicero's (or any surviving ancient orator's) material is topical. On the contrary what we should note is the care with which the topic is shaped specifically for each case. Criticism of the foreigner's credibility is directed at as small a group as possible.[63] Exceptions are pointed out (though often with the goal of protecting Cicero's own witnesses).

In many cases problems of credibility are connected to aspects of national character which are part of contemporary "common knowledge" and as such can be attributed to them "disinterestedly" (e.g., the recent hostility of the Gauls, the volubility and *levitas* of the Greeks[64]). The distinction is precisely that cruder forms of racial attacks *would* obviously have been "empty rhetoric." If such arguments were given compelling force, then there would be little point in having a *quaestio de repetundis*. The (Roman) defendant would always win in cases where provincials attempt to recover extorted funds. If *repetundae* had been popularly reconceptualized solely as a means of administrative control of provincial administrators, the care Cicero shows in framing his attacks on witnesses would be unnecessary. The court could perhaps get by without alien testimony. Instead, the court seems to retain its recovery function, and Cicero seems to allow that the jury will convict under some circumstances. Whatever the reasons for passing laws *de repetundis*, the courts apparently will enforce them, even at the expense of the occasional Roman citizen.[65]

Heretofore the discussion has concentrated on Cicero's attacks on the prosecution's foreign witnesses. It may be worthwhile to take a brief look at what he says on two other topics: the function of his own witnesses and the credibility of Roman testimony on the other side. Despite Cicero's hypotheses about the differences between the elite and the masses of Tralles (*Flacc.* 52–54), we have no case where there are clearly witnesses of the same foreign citizenship in court on both sides. Hence most of his witnesses have no direct knowledge of particular charges; they are character witnesses.

Finally, a few words are in order about the treatment of Roman witnesses. *Pro Flacco* is apparently the only surviving speech *de repetundis* in which Cicero had to deal with Roman witnesses on the opposing side.[66] We have already noted that one possible approach might have been simply to ignore them while carrying on sweeping *ad gentem* attacks on the mass of the other witnesses. But Cicero also takes on these Roman witnesses individually. The first is the witness and *subscriptor* Decianus. Cicero makes every attempt to assimilate him to the Greeks he is representing:

> *How long were you "away on business," given that you were born in that very place? You were in a forum for thirty years all right, but it was at Pergamum. Much later, chancing to wander, you come to Rome, bringing*

> *a new appearance, the old name, and Tyrian purple. . . . Leisure delights*
> *you; the courts, crowds, and praetor are hateful to you; you rejoice in Greek*
> *license.*
>
> (*Flacc.* 70–71)

Later, speaking of the absent Falcidius (whose letters have been read in court), he says: "But what a man! how unfriendly to his fellow citizens! who preferred to spend on Greek revels a quite substantial patrimony which he could have spent here with us" (§90). *Pro Rabirio Postumo* provides an interesting parallel to this identification of the plaintiffs' Roman witnesses with the plaintiffs themselves. Sections 22–29 of this speech are dedicated to defending Postumus on the charge of having adopted Greek title and dress.[67] Cicero produces *exempla* of such notable personages as Sulla, L. Scipio Asiaticus (or Asiagenus, *RE* 337), and P. Rutilius Rufus (§27) wearing Greek clothing in the east.[68] Compare this to Cicero's attack on Decianus' Tyrian purple (not only foreign but effeminate). Apparently one of the best ways to remove the advantage of Roman citizens on either side of these prosecutions (where the jurors' minds would naturally be sensitive to issues of nationality), was to try to de-Romanize them.[69]

3. CHARACTER IN *REPETUNDAE* TRIALS

Preceding chapters made a distinction between characterizations which were used for their own sake and those made because of their predictive value. What is the function of ethical argument in the *repetundae* speeches? There are passages in which an instrumental use of ethical argument is suggested. For instance: "And can a man be accused of greed when he avoided, not merely criminal accusation, but corner-cutting in rich circumstances, and insult in a slanderous city and a very tricky business?" (*Flacc.* 7). Later it is noted that Flaccus had given over the whole of an inheritance to a youth with whom he was co-heir, and "from this it should be understood that he did not accept money against the laws, who was generous in giving up a legacy" (*Flacc.* 89). The first passage makes an inference about general character (lack of *avaritia*) from specific actions.[70] The second then makes the inference back to (other) specific actions. Flaccus is not the sort of person who would resort for money to the crimes of which he is accused.

An independently preserved fragment of this speech (the so-called *fragmentum Mediolanense*) begins: "the external [facts] agree with his domestic life and nature." This seems also to demand that the crime be proven by bad character (which, in turn, would have to be proven by other crimes). We may also consider a passage in *pro Fonteio*:

> *He gave such an account of two magistracies, the triumvirate* [71] *and quaestorship (each of which is involved in acquiring and handling large sums of money), that no hint of theft and no suspicion of any wrongdoing has been found in those acts which were carried out before your very eyes, in contact with many, and recorded in public and private records.*

> *(Font.* 5)

Both magistracies were conveniently held in Rome and so under the public eye. Here we have no specific inferences, nor are any drawn in the extant portions of the speech (although there is a major lacuna shortly after this section). On the other hand we do have a fairly specific ethical narrative (as in the description of Chrysogonus' lifestyle in *pro Roscio*) rather than an analytic description of character. Fonteius had the opportunity for financial gain from an official position and did not take it. We should also note here that, if character *per se* were at issue, then there would be no reason for Cicero to introduce provincial witnesses at all: using Romans would have avoided the credibility problem. As it is, foreigners have the advantage of knowing what the defendant has done before in the peculiar set of circumstances at issue (and far away from Rome). Hence, something more specific than good versus bad is at stake.

Instrumental use of ethical argument is clear in *pro Flacco*, less so in *pro Fonteio*.[72] Its significance could have been obscured in *pro Fonteio* by the orator's expectation that the jurors would fill in the missing inferences themselves; it is, however, safer merely to note that such argument does appear, if only barely. Perhaps more informative for the nature of the connection of ethos and *repetundae* is the apparent prosecution strategy in these two cases. The fragment of *pro Flacco* referred to above reads in full:

> *. . . his life and nature, at home and abroad, are in agreement. Thus I will not permit, Laelius [the prosecutor], that you arrogate this to yourself and [prescribe?] this rule and condition* (legem condicionemque) *for others in the future and for us now. . . .* [73]

Given the contrast implied by "Thus I will not permit," Kurke (1989:123–24) has suggested that the "rule and condition" in question is that the *vita ante acta* be omitted from consideration, and further that Laelius in fact did not discuss past life in his prosecution.[74] When the text of the speech in the manuscripts resumes, Cicero says: "When you will have marked his youth and spread the stains of turpitude on the rest of his life, when you will have produced evil and wrongdoing" (§5, *fr. Med.* 1–2). This must be taken as ironic in any case, so it might well refer to failure by Laelius even to attempt such attacks. Kurke's view also receives some support from the fact that Cicero apparently launches into a defense of Flaccus' youth by saying: "As defender, then, I will hold to this course which the prosecutor avoided" (*ibid.*; *fr. Med.* 20–21). That is, Cicero will follow the normal pattern of discussing youth, earlier magistracies, and then the actual accusation.

The text, if not the situation, is clearer in *pro Fonteio*:

> *Fonteius has been accused twice and yet no objection has been raised which can show in him any trace of desire, impudence, cruelty, or audacity; not only have they not brought forth any criminal deed on his part, but they have not even attacked any word he has spoken.*

> (*Font.* 40)

This is an indication that the opposition in this case tried the same strategy of suppressing the *vita ante acta* in favor of tight concentration on the alleged crime. But as Kurke (1989:125, note 29) points out, the first three sections of the preserved part of the speech seem to respond to an attack on Fonteius' earlier career (his quaestorship). The charge may stem from an accounting trick which intentionally confuses notional and actual transfers of funds, or it may be based on improper reduction of debts owed by or to the state (§§1–2); in either case the excess funds would allegedly have ended up, at least in part, in Fonteius' hands (§3).[75] However, the precise circumstances are not clear. This section may belie the assertion that Fonteius' character was not attacked. On the other hand, we should consider exactly why the prosecution brought up this incident. The case of *publicani* from Africa and Gaul is offered as a parallel (§2), potential witnesses are described as "most alien men" (§3), and Cicero's complaint is essentially the normal summation of a case *de repetundis*.

> *We see that whenever men are accused of this offense, they are in the first place attacked by means of witnesses; for one who gave money to a magistrate can usually either be induced by hatred or be compelled by religion to*

speak; then if witnesses are deterred by personal influence, records at least
remain uncorrupted and intact.

(*Font.* 3)

While one might have suspected that the accusation described in this passage
would normally fall to the court *de peculatu* (theft of public funds), it is not
out of the question that it is actually a subsidiary accusation *de repetundis*. We
may recall here Alexander's (1982) contention that a Roman criminal trial was
meant to encompass all of the defendant's violations of the salient law before
the date of the trial. Even if this was not a legitimate charge for the *repetundae*
court, it has a clear and specific bearing on the charge of *repetundae*. Fonteius
had illegally accepted money before, therefore it is reasonable to assume that
he would have done it again. For the prosecution to omit or even limit its discussion of the *vita ante acta* is to permit precisely the claims of sterling character that Cicero makes.[76]

If this nonetheless happened in two of our preserved cases, and if Cicero felt
a need to introduce foreign witnesses for the defense, it confirms the impres-
sion given by claims (occasional but persistent and explicit) for the inferential
value of character evidence. Character is not at issue here for its own sake (at
least not solely for its own sake). The jurors are expected to use character as a
guide to whether the defendant would have committed specific acts. Earlier
chapters suggested that this emphasis is appropriate to crimes where those
specific acts are the point, rather than context (as for *vis*) or general pattern of
behavior (as for *ambitus*). The willingness of the prosecution to forego this
kind of ethical argument underscores its instrumental role: it exists to prove
another point (say, the taking of money from provincials). From this point of
view *repetundae* seems closer to homicide than to *vis* or *ambitus*. It is a crime
of *propria facta*.

4. *PRO RABIRIO POSTUMO* AND THE LONG ARM OF THE LAW

Several references have been made above to the peculiarity of the speech in defense of Rabirius.[77] It is unusual because Rabirius is accused of having received
money not from provincials but from the Roman official who had originally
obtained it illegally. It is also unusual because Cicero's case turns almost entirely on two legal issues specific to this different charge. The Roman governor
of Syria, Gabinius, had recently been convicted *de repetundis* for his actions in

Egypt.[78] He was unable to satisfy the judgment of the *litis aestimatio* either by giving sureties *(praedes)* or by the sale of his goods (*Rab. Post.* 9). In this situation Cicero tells us, "The *lex Iulia* commands seeking [damages] from those to whom the money which the condemned man had taken had finally come" (*ibid.*). He repeats essentially the same scenario at section 37: if Gabinius had been able to pay the judgment by himself or by giving *praedes*, then no action would stand against Rabirius. It seems that the law allows money to be recovered from the guilty man's associates only if (as was admittedly true in this case), it could not be recovered directly.[79]

Cicero claims first that Rabirius, an *eques*, was not subject to the *lex Iulia* (§§11, 12–19) and second that it was unusual (if not strictly illegal) to extract money under this clause from someone whose connection to the original crime was proven neither in the original trial nor in the *litis aestimatio* (§§9–11, 12, 37). I will concentrate on the former argument, since external evidence bearing on the latter is largely nonexistent (but see note 80).

In *Rab. Post.* 14 Cicero directs the jurors' attention to the opening words of the law as an indication of its scope:

> *When some proposed law was recited, Glaucia (a twisted, but clever man) used to warn the people to pay attention to the first line. If it read "dictator, consul, praetor, master of the horse," they need not worry; they knew it did not pertain to them; but if it were "whoever after this law is passed," they should see to it that they not be subject to some new court.*
>
> (*Rab.* 14)

If the *lex Acilia* is any indication, then the opening section of the *lex Iulia* would indeed have contained a restriction to magistrates and senators. However, the *lex Acilia* also suggests that the clause *quo ea pecunia pervenerit* was in an entirely different part of the bill from that restriction: the crime is defined at lines 1–3 while the procedures for recovery start at line 57. Does Cicero ever try to connect the two parts? In an earlier section he held an imaginary conversation with the jurors:

> *The juror's tablet is given to you. Under what law? The* lex Iulia de pecuniis repetundis. *Who is the defendant? A Roman knight. That order [the* equites] *is not bound by this law. He said, "But he is bound by that chapter:* quo ea pecunia pervenerit." *You heard nothing against Postumus when you were a juror trying Gabinius, nothing when you set the penalty after*

*Gabinius was condemned. "But now I'm hearing things." Then Postumus is
a defendant under a law from which not only he, but his whole order is free.*

(*Rab.* 12)

Cicero completely ducks the issue of Rabirius' possible involvement. This suggests that he cannot in any precise way apply the initial (senatorial) restriction of the law to the later *(quo ea pecunia)* clause.

Not only is there no positive evidence that the restriction of the law to senators applies to the *quo ea pecunia* clause, but there are reasons to expect that it would not have so applied. The proceedings after the *litis aestimatio* are not really criminal but administrative. Their purpose is to see that the victims' money is actually returned to them. Note that the form of the praetor's verdict in cases heard under this clause is not the formula "He seems (not) to have done it" *([non] fecisse videtur)* usually used in the public courts, but "I will (not) collect" (*[non] redigam, Fam.* 8.8.3, *Rab. Post.* 37); he does not announce that the defendant has (or has not) done anything, but whether he himself will extract the money.[80] The administrative function of this clause is also relevant to the question of its application to persons who had not been introduced in earlier hearings. Taken literally, this clause should apply to anyone who had money from the convicted official, even if that person had nothing to do with its initial extraction from the provincials.

If, as we have suggested, this clause serves an administrative function (rather than imputing a crime to the person *quo ea pecunia pervenerit*), then we need not doubt the literal reading: it does not matter from whom stolen property is recovered.[81] A letter of Pliny (3.9) suggests at least that the law eventually came to be interpreted in this way. After the posthumous conviction of Caecilius Classicus *de repetundis*, the sale of his goods did not cover the damages.[82] So the *consilium* sought further sources: "It is added that monies paid to his creditors be recalled" (§17). This looks a great deal like an application of the *quo ea pecunia* clause (or its descendant) without regard for the connection of the defendant to the original crime. The evidence for the text and function of the secondary recovery clause is very scattered, but it consistently indicates that the law is not designed to punish those against whom it is directed;[83] they are not even liable if the debts are paid otherwise. Rather the law-makers sought to ensure that the provincial victims would be able to recover their property wherever it had gone.

Why then does Cicero rely so heavily on arguments that Rabirius was neither technically liable under the *lex Iulia* nor implicated in Gabinius' original crimes? One reason is simple misdirection. This is essentially the same defense as that of *pro Cluentio* 143–60, where he emphasized the sections of the *lex Cornelia* which had limited applicability. In both cases different sections of the law apply to different classes of persons, and Cicero tries to generalize the provisions of the more restrictive clause. This repeated tactic gives rise to a couple of points. Both speeches seem to be clear cases of Cicero attempting to mislead the jurors as to what we may suspect would have been the ordinary reading of the law. The *lex Acilia* is quite long (some thirteen pages in *FIRA* even with substantial lacunae), and the *lex Iulia* must have been even longer. One might plausibly expect the jurors to have been familiar with (or to make themselves familiar with) the kinds of things prohibited or mandated by the law, but the detail and connections were perhaps beyond the immediate knowledge of most of them. We also see that this line of defense is much more prominent in *pro Rabirio* than in *pro Cluentio*. We may attribute this again to the administrative character of the clause *quo ea pecunia pervenerit*. Rabirius is (apparently) not accused of doing anything inherently requiring punishment, nothing inherently criminal. Cluentius was supposed to have caused someone's death. Even if the legal argument were sound, it would sound like "mere" legalities in Cluentius' case. Since Rabirius' case is inherently merely technical, such an argument is more appropriate.

Cicero does not distort the law in this case only by intentional conflation of different clauses. The senators/*equites* distinction he draws in both cases is an oversimplification. The abuse of process clause of the *lex Cornelia* applies to, among others, the military tribunes of the first four legions (*Clu.* 148). These twenty-four officials were generally of equestrian status.[84] There is no direct evidence for the *lex Iulia*, but the *lex Acilia* applies not only to those tribunes but to all sons of magistrates and senators; these would only sometimes be senators themselves.[85] Both laws were designed to protect against various abuses of official power. As was noted above, equestrians were not covered by the *lex Cornelia* because at the time of its composition they could not serve as jurors, i.e., quasi-magistrates. Thus the essential distinction both laws draw is not between the two orders but between office holders (and sons exploiting their fathers' offices) and private citizens. Since most of these office holders are in fact senators, and senators are (somewhat redundantly) specified in both laws, it is easy for Cicero to represent the distinction of jurisdiction as between the two *ordines*.[86]

Having defined the issue in these terms, Cicero could then appeal to the interests of the nonsenatorial jurors, who made up two-thirds of the jury: "While you can, while it is permitted, see to it that you do not impose a harsher condition on yourselves and your order than you can bear" (*Rab. Post.* 15). To justify a decision on these grounds he uses the *exemplum* of M. Livius Drusus' failed attempt to extend the judicial corruption law to equestrian jurors: [87]

> *The knights resisted openly. Why? Did they wish this bribery to be permitted? Not at all. Not only did they think this way of making money foul, but even unspeakable. Nonetheless they argued that only those who had of their own free will pursued that [senatorial] condition of life should be bound by those laws.*
>
> (*Rab.* 16)

Cicero explicitly says that the issue is not whether equestrians were doing anything wrong. More important is maintaining the balance of risks and rewards of pursuing a senatorial, political career as opposed to remaining among the *equites*. One might feel that this balance would be better maintained by matching responsibilities with specific offices, rather than the whole order, but Cicero's version is reasonable enough for the nonsenatorial jurors to use it as self-justification.

In any case, the story of Drusus' attempt at reform tells the jurors to subordinate the question of guilt to the question of how best to structure the Roman constitution. The "best" structure here is the one that suits the interests of the lower two-thirds of the jury. Thus the focus on legal structures serves two purposes. It allows Cicero to produce a quasi-legal, technical defense to what seems to be a technical charge; it gives the jury an excuse not to consider any of the actual facts of the case. It also allows Cicero to raise the political issues that lie behind the putative legal distinction. Similar strategies were used in *pro Cluentio* and *pro Murena*. In the former the stability of the political structure was made to depend on the reliability of official decisions; the jury must accept the *praeiudicia* which had purportedly already established Cluentius' innocence. One of the several arguments in *pro Murena* was that, whatever Murena's actions, the state needed him as consul at the beginning of the coming year. These two speeches as well as *pro Rabirio* introduce the suggestion that the jurors should vote on some basis other than the guilt or innocence of the defendant (however that may be defined in a given case). This leads us to the topic of the next section, Cicero's frequent reference to such external considerations in cases *de repetundis*.

5. POLITICS AND *RES REPETUNDAE*

The speech in which such external considerations are made most obvious is *pro Flacco*. Cicero opens this speech with an introduction (§§1–5) bemoaning the fate that could befall a good man (i.e., someone who aided him during the Catilinarian affair) in the criminal courts. It is much like the opening he would use in *pro Sestio* three years later. Unlike that speech, *pro Flacco* does not continue the theme throughout the body. Nor does Cicero appear to attempt anything here other than winning sympathy. (The text breaks off in the middle of section five; we may be missing some more specific point.)

However, the conspiracy makes a sudden reappearance toward the end of the speech, where Cicero dismisses various evidentiary arguments he had just been making to tell the jurors that they hold "the safety of us all, the fortunes of the city" on their shoulders (§94). And what does Cicero have to say about the health of the state? After rehearsing the horrors of the conspiracy and the glory of its suppression (§§94–97), he turns to a series of *exempla* of men acquitted in the criminal courts: M.' Aquilius, C. Piso, L. Murena, and A. Thermus (§98). All were defended by Cicero, and Piso, as Cicero would have it, had previously saved the state. Flaccus' story was the same on Cicero's account. More pointed are Cicero's comments on Murena:

> I, as consul, also defended L. Murena, the consul-designate. As the jurors listened to his noble accusers, none of them thought they should actually judge about ambitus, since they knew well what I had told them: in the war with Catiline there had to be two consuls on January first.

> (*Flacc.* 98)

The crime was not at issue. Not only could the jurors ignore the charge, but they had an obligation *(oportere)* to leave the election results intact. Most striking of all is the comment on Aquilius: "Our ancestors acquitted M.' Aquilius, despite convincing evidence of many crimes of greed, because he had forcibly waged the war against the fugitive slaves." Despite (purportedly) manifest guilt both of individual crimes and of bad character, he was acquitted on the strength of past service to the state. Cicero's hint to acquit Flaccus, without regard to guilt, is hard to miss.

However, for those who did miss the hint, Cicero spells the moral out in the next section:

When you are given the ballot, jurors, it will not only be about Flaccus, but about the leaders and movers of the salvation of the city, about all good citizens, about yourselves, about your children, life, country, and the common salvation.

(*Flacc.* 99)

In case his appeal to tradition and past service is not enough for the jurors, Cicero adds an argument about future benefit (§§104-6). Good men are few enough already in the state: few respect the "authority of every good and substantial man and order" (§104). If Flaccus, who has exemplified this path, is convicted, no one will follow his political example. Thus if jurors wish to support political conservatism, they must vote to acquit.[88] Speaking of Flaccus' own young son he says: "And if you preserve his father, you will show him what sort of citizen he ought to be; if you take him away, you will show that the *boni* offer no reward for good, constant, and serious counsel" (§106). So in *pro Flacco* the jurors are given not one but two criteria on which to judge. Both past and future benefit have nothing to do with guilt or innocence: they are told to give the benefit criteria priority over the question of guilt.

We noted above that the themes of the conspiracy and of Flaccus' service did not appear between the introduction and the conclusion. This description is literally true but can be nuanced. Kurke (1989:188-200) argues that the conspiracy theme resonates with Cicero's attacks on the witnesses. At the opening of the speech, he had questioned the motives of anyone who would prosecute a patriot like Flaccus; such a person would be a "critic of generosity" and an "enemy of virtue" (§2). He praises the character of the actual prosecutor Laelius but criticizes him for making "an accusation more suited to the hatred and madness of criminal citizens than to his own virtue and to his upbringing" (*Flacc.* 2). Kurke suggests that Cicero's meaning is, in part, that Laelius is pursuing this disreputable prosecution for personal gain, even though his background ("the best hope of the highest dignity") would have permitted him a more respectable approach to advancement. This interpretation is supported by Cicero's later suggestion that Laelius had undertaken the case "for the sake of glory" (§13).

In itself this motive was traditional, but Laelius might have gone too far in its pursuit. In his speech Cicero emphasizes the lengths to which Laelius went to procure Greek testimony (§§13-19, 57; *citati*, "stirred up, suborned," *passim*). This is the flip side of the frequent claim that Greeks speak whatever is needed at the moment, not the truth (e.g., §§36-38). Greeks are easily manipulated, and Laelius needs to manipulate them to create an accusation for his own personal advancement. It is not merely that a conviction will produce defections to the (ill-defined) antitraditionalist side, but that it would itself represent a victory for one of those very politicians who value unprincipled advancement over traditional values (cf. §104: "when they see that that path to office and all the other things they desire is easier").[89] Thus the supposedly "external" political situation, which would in itself justify an acquittal, is also the very reason for the prosecution and the reason not to trust any of the prosecution evidence on the underlying charge.

In *pro Fonteio* Cicero advances a pair of external considerations that militate in favor of Fonteius' acquittal. Instead of the appropriately submissive attitude that plaintiffs are expected to display, the Gauls are proud and even threatening (§33). The ancestors, says Cicero, would not have allowed themselves even to appear to cave in to threats:

> *If, jurors, Fonteius were at a loss for a defense, if he were brought into court tainted by a misspent youth . . . , if he were pressed by the testimony and records of Roman citizens, nonetheless you still would have to take great care lest you, apparently disturbed by their threats and terror, seem to have feared those whom you received from your fathers and ancestors so broken as to be contemptible.*

> (*Font.* 34)[90]

Here, as in *pro Flacco*, the clear import of the *exemplum* is that the jurors should vote to acquit regardless of guilt because of a more compelling interest: "lest this empire suffer some blot or ignominy, if the word will be brought into Gaul, that senators and Roman knights make judgments based not on the testimony of Gauls, but by their threats according to their desires" (*Font.* 36).[91] Rome's reputation is at stake, and it is more important than the facts of a particular case.

A curious turn of logic leads to the second external justification for Fonteius' acquittal. One might expect from the passages above that the threat following a conviction would be to make honest provincial governors subject to prosecution by any group with the audacity that the Gauls had displayed.[92] Or perhaps their administrations would be weak since, in anticipation of prosecution, they would go out of their way not to offend their subjects. This is not so. The other side had apparently suggested that an acquittal might lead to a renewed Gallic war: "Had I along with you, jurors, heard several times from the accusers themselves, when they asserted that you should beware lest a new Gallic war be stirred up by the absolution of this man" (§33). Cicero suggests this war will in fact be the consequence of a conviction (i.e., caving in to Gallic intimidation) and the resulting loss of respect for Roman authority. These are the words immediately following the passage from section 36 quoted above: "And so, if they try to make war again, we will have to raise Marius [and a list of other generals] from the dead" (*Font. 36*). Or, he goes on to suggest ironically, the prosecutor Plaetorius and his *subscriptor* M. Fabius will be able to soothe their new Gallic clients.

Why the need for necromancy? Cicero argues in sections 42–43 that the supply of experienced and talented generals (among whom we are expected to number Fonteius[93]) is not what it used to be and that they should be protected carefully by the court:

And if you pay close attention, jurors, you will prefer to retain for yourselves and your children a man unmoved by the labors of war, strong in the face of dangers, equipped by experience and doctrine, and blessed in fortune, rather than to hand him over to peoples most cruel and most hostile to the Roman people.

(*Font. 43*)

Cicero never explicitly privileges this question over that of guilt and innocence, but since the survival of the state is explicitly at stake, the hint is clear enough. Much as Murena was, Fonteius is too important to the preservation of the state to convict.

By contrast, Cicero's prosecution of Verres seems to be constructed so as to preempt precisely this line of defense. In the first *Verrine*, a speech which has very little to say about the purported victims, Cicero claims that Verres had divided the profits of this three-year governorship into three parts: one for himself, one for his future defense team, and one for bribes for the eventual jurors (§40). This leads him to the fantasy that provincials will petition to have the laws *de repetundis* repealed:

For they think that if there were no real courts each governor would only carry off what he thinks sufficient for himself and his children; now, because the courts are the way they are, each takes what will be enough for himself, his patrons, advocates, and the jurors; but this can go on without end; they think they can satisfy the cupidity of the greediest single man, but not the acquittal of the most guilty.

(1 *Verr.* 41)

He strikes precisely the plaintive and humble tone that he had demanded in *pro Fonteio*; it avoids giving the defense the hook that Cicero had apparently been handed there for threatening war (§34, quoted above). This war argument probably has something of the status of generic attacks on foreign witnesses (as opposed to the specific ones Cicero prefers). It can always be argued that convicting one provincial governor will lessen the *auctoritas* of all. If such arguments are admitted, what is the point of having a court *de repetundis*? Hence neither is frequently used, and the apparent (and perhaps real) integrity of the court is preserved.

The external arguments of *pro Fonteio* are even more interconnected with the treatment of witnesses than in *pro Flacco*. The Gauls are not to be trusted because of their irreligiosity and because they are but recently subdued, by Fonteius himself in some cases. These two factors, not guilt, led to the accusation. If the accusation succeeds, the Gauls will be encouraged to actual war. In fact, the accusation itself is already a "Gallic war": the Gallic witnesses have come "practically with battle flags" (§44), and the Romans of the province have come to Fonteius' defense "as they should in a Gallic war" (§46). In war one needs experienced and successful generals, and Fonteius' military skill is just what got him in this trouble in the first place. Finally, we have the introduction not of Fonteius' son, but of his sister, a Vestal Virgin (§§46–49). This is of course meant to be pathetic, but it also resonates with the theme of the Gauls' unnatural religious attitudes discussed above. The last words of the speech illustrate the indissoluble interweaving of the themes of credibility, war, and religion. I have quoted segments of this above, but I will reproduce the whole now:

Take care that you are seen to have trusted our witnesses more than foreign-born ones, to have been more concerned for the health of citizens than the desires of enemies, to have valued the prayers of her who presides over your sacred rites more than the audacity of those who wage war on the rites and shrines of all. Finally, look out, jurors (this is most relevant to the dignity of the Roman people), so that the prayers of a Vestal Virgin are seen to have had greater strength among you than the threats of Gauls.

(*Font.* 49)

To return to the general topic of external factors which are offered as induce-
ments to the jurors to vote a particular way, we may continue our consideration
of the first *Verrine*. One of the key arguments of the speech is that public con-
fidence in the court has evaporated because of the practical impossibility of
getting a conviction of a senator from an all-senatorial jury (§§1–3, 43–49):[94]

> *An opinion dangerous to both you and the republic has grown fixed in men's
> minds, one which is spread not only among our people, but among foreign
> nations: a rich man, however guilty, cannot be condemned by the current
> courts.*

> (1 *Verr.* 1)

Since Sulla's legislation a decade earlier, the juries had been entirely senatorial
(1 *Verr.* 38; Vel. Pat. 2.32.3). Cicero threatens that, unless Verres is convicted,
that order will surely lose control over the courts:

> *All agree that there has been no panel of this dignity and splendor since the
> establishment of the current jury system. If there is any problem here, all
> will not think that better men from the same order should be sought for the
> juries (which is impossible), but another order entirely.*

> (1 *Verr.* 49)

Here there is hardly any pretense of an argument based on the public interest;
rather there is a blatant appeal to the narrow political interests of the class that
made up the jury.[95] Here, however, the relation of the "external" motivation
and the case itself is different than in the previous speeches. Rather than pre-
empting the issue of guilt or innocence, *in Verrem* assumes the manifest guilt
of the defendant.

We may now briefly survey some of the generalizations that emerge from
this study of the exploitation of political factors external to the cases as means
to direct jurors to a particular verdict. One point has to do with the way in
which these "external" factors are tied to the rest of the case. In *pro Rabirio,
pro Flacco, pro Fonteio*, and (in a different way) *in Verrem*, Cicero creates a situation in which the factors which determine the question of guilt or innocence
are also the same which create the overriding "political" need to acquit (or
condemn).

To recall two examples: Cicero's close examination of the *lex Iulia* purportedly shows that Rabirius is not liable; it also sets up a conflict between the

orders who make up the jury, pitting the two lower classes (and so a majority) against the senators. Fonteius' military exploits are both the reason for his prosecution (the Gauls wanted revenge) and the reason he must be preserved (leaders are needed against the Gauls). One may describe this aspect of these speeches by saying that Cicero has created an extrinsic connection between his two implied judging paradigms.[96] This is unlike the situation in *pro Murena*, where the state-defense argument is simply tacked on. This simple juxtaposition was possible there because, as was argued in the second chapter, there was an intrinsic connection between a charge of *ambitus* and a policy-making approach to judging. *Repetundae* is a charge more like homicide than like *ambitus*. It is a question of a specific act (or set of acts) as is indicated by the emphasis on witnesses and Cicero's long refutations of specific charges (*Flacc.* 27–35, 40, 49–50, 55–59, 66–69, 76–80, 84–93; *Font.* 1–3, 17–20).[97] Hence the appeals to higher political values cannot stand alone but are grounded in the argument of the case proper.

To conclude this section we consider the nature of those values to which Cicero appeals. *Pro Rabirio, pro Flacco*, and *in Verrem* all advance (in discussing the composition of the juries) some argument about the best internal arrangement of the Roman state. In one speech Cicero goes so far as to say: "In this case you are not judging about foreign nations, nor our allies; you decide about yourselves and your own republic" (*Flacc.* 99). In *pro Fonteio* and *in Verrem*, however, the issue (supposedly that of rescinding the laws *de repetundis*) is Rome's reputation abroad. It is not surprising to find the first (internal) class of arguments in defense speeches, although it is interesting that Cicero openly sacrifices provincial interests to conflicts between the orders, with which they had no connection. One might have expected elision of the foreign issues. The second (external) class argues that what interest the Romans did have in the provincials' legal protection was instrumental; they wanted to channel their hostility through Roman institutions. What is most suggestive, however, though conclusions must remain speculative in the absence of more prosecutions, is the fact that *in Verrem* appeals to the same set of values as the defense speeches. This leads to a distinction between homicide and *repetundae*. Both are specific acts that are outlawed because of specific harms they cause. But the danger of murder to the Roman people is clear; the harm of any particular instance of *repetundae* is much harder to place. Furthermore, that harm is more remote (from the Roman point of view) and so is more easily turned aside by appeals to other values.

CHAPTER 6

The Iudicia Publica *in Roman State and Society*

1. SUMMARY OF CRIMES

In this final chapter I want to take a brief look at the broader situation of the *iudicia publica*. Given what we have learned about the substance of the individual offenses and the ways they are discussed, what can we then say about the ensemble? I want to draw two main conclusions. First, the purpose of the *iudicia publica* was to try persons for harms done to the community as a whole. By this I mean not offenses that merely happened to affect large numbers of individuals, but those which were understood as inherently detrimental to the community as such. This hypothesis will account both for the division of offenses between public and private courts and for the uncomfortable (to most modern audiences) coexistence of law and politics in the public courts. Second, I want to suggest that this category (i.e., offenses tried by the *iudicia publica*) was much less distinct in Roman culture than "crime" is for us. "Crime" is not only the object of a branch of our courts but is also the subject of academic scrutiny, political outcry, and representation both fictional and nonfictional.

For the Romans, public offenses were part of a much larger ethical category of wrongdoing, and not sharply distinct from wrongs done, on the one hand to individuals (and perhaps families?) and on the other to the gods. Thus while our sources speak from time to time of individual events which we may reasonably label crimes from a modern perspective, those same sources show little interest in any overarching phenomenon we could call crime. Nor do they show any interest in the collective object of repression of the *iudicia publica*. For the sake of English expression I will continue to use the word "crime" both for the various offenses and for instances thereof, but the reader should keep in mind that this category will eventually be called into question.

To begin, however, let us briefly summarize the conclusions of the chapters on individual crimes. In the second chapter we considered the crime of *ambi-*

tus in the context of Roman campaign practices and of a more general distinction between gift- and market-exchange in an aristocratic society. There was no very clear distinction between *ambitus* and legitimate campaigning; the difference is largely one of perspective. Both involve requesting votes in return for more or less reciprocal favors. *Ambitus* is campaigning which too clearly reveals this reciprocal relationship between the candidate and the voter. The prototypical case of *ambitus* is the exchange of a specified amount of cash for a specified vote. To the extent that a specific instance deviates from the prototype either in terms of the item exchanged (e.g., food, public games, political favors) or in explicitness of the *quid pro quo* (e.g., passing money on to underlings) it looks less like *ambitus*, but the line will be different when established from different points of view.

The prototypical case involves a simple matter of fact, so on these issues Cicero issues a denial and tries to establish a high burden of proof for the other side. However, it is also necessary to deal with more peripheral cases. Hence Cicero argues that Plancius is a true friend and patron to his people: he is so tightly integrated into a local community (where favors are freely and frequently exchanged) that his distributions near election time could not possibly be taken as *quid pro quo*. The *lex Tullia de ambitu* has been praised for finally defining the crime in a precise fashion by providing a list of specific offenses.[1] We may think this a virtue now, but it might not have been a productive approach at the time. Such an attempt would almost necessarily fail because it would be able neither to foresee innovative types of "bribes" nor to allow for jurors' preexisting sensitivity to the contextual (in)appropriateness of particular exchanges. *Ambitus* is defined by prototype, not by exhaustive list. The fact that further electoral legislation *(lex Licinia de sodaliciis, lex Pompeia de ambitu)* followed so soon afterward suggests that Cicero's legislation was not in fact a compelling practical success.[2] Rather the boundaries of *ambitus* continued to be renegotiated in each trial.

The third chapter began with an examination of the place of parricide in the homicide legislation and an examination of the precise charges which might have been laid against Cluentius under the *lex Cornelia de sicariis et veneficiis*. The general conclusion was that, at least by our period, there had been an attempt to bring the various types of murder (assassination, parricide, poisoning, abuse of process) under a single and fairly uniform statute, and in particular to assimilate them all to simple murder. The idea seems to be that killing someone, whatever the circumstances, is simply too dangerous not to come within the cognizance of the state. Correspondingly, the arguments in the murder cases seem to center around the factual issue of whether the defendant was responsible for the victim's death: did anyone see him do it? did he have motive or opportunity? Naturally Cicero again tries to set a high standard of proof for the opposition in these cases.

We should also note what was described as the "instrumental" use of ethical argument. Explicit inferences are drawn from the *vita ante acta* as to what kind of actions the defendant is likely to have taken and, from there, how likely he is to have committed the particular crime(s) at issue. When character is regarded as a stable determinant of behavior this kind of inference can be a compelling, if circumstantial, argument about the facts that underlie the defendant's guilt or innocence. In contrast the defendant's character is simply displayed in the *ambitus* speeches, not argued from. The issue there is not clearly enough defined to allow the same kind of inferences, since the difference between the honest and the corrupt candidate is one of degree and context, not of kind. Also discussed was the opposition between *iudicia* and *invidia* constructed in *pro Cluentio*. Cicero argued that the case, in effect, had already been decided. (Hence the elaborate argument that past judgments favorable to Cluentius happen to "count" as sound judgments and that those against him do not.) In any event, says Cicero, it is politically necessary to acquit Cluentius or the legitimate institutions of government lose their meaning. This argument is tied to issues of rank, rather than to the facts of the case, but it is not argued that social rank justifies murder or that Cluentius' status makes it inconceivable that he would have committed a murder.[3] In short, political issues, though relevant to the jurors' votes of *condemno* or *absolvo*, are not related to the issue of whether Cluentius committed murder, and hence are not made directly relevant to the definition of the crime. Murder, for the Romans as for us, was conceived of largely as a matter of simple historical fact.

In the fourth chapter, adopting Andrew Lintott's formulation, we noted that *vis* (much like *ambitus*) had a two-part definition under the law of the 70's through the 50's: it required both violence (hence the name) and an impact which was against the interests of the general public *(contra rem publicam)*. Examination of Cicero's defense strategies shows that this two-part definition is valid. It also shows a difference from *ambitus*: both conditions must be met completely for the crime to have been committed. The main argument of *pro Sulla* is that Sulla was not involved in the Catilinarian conspiracy; if he had been, then Cicero, the chief investigator at the time, would have heard of it. By contrast Cicero as much as admits Sestius' use of force and instead defends him on the grounds that his good violence countered Clodius' seditious violence. Thus Sestius is innocent because—at the risk of oversimplifying—he is politically aligned with the optimates.

Even more interesting is the subtle but persistent suggestion in *pro Sulla* that it is incoherent to claim that one of the *boni* could commit *vis*. In turn we can refine Lintott's formulation; the *contra rem publicam* element depends not so much on public safety (which would suggest outlawing all use of violence) as on political motivation. In light of this fact we considered the probability that Cicero added an argument from political motivation to his defense of Milo only in the later, published version. This addition is linked to a change in popular attitudes toward violence, soon to be mirrored in legislation, which would leave the sole right to legitimate violence in the hands of the state. This in turn is connected with the rise of the imperial state itself.

The fifth chapter turned to the *repetundae* court. The original function of the law was to penalize Roman officials in the provinces for extracting (too much) money from their subjects (the "recovery function"). The law attempted to define "too much" and "extract" very precisely. Despite arguments that over time the focus of laws *de repetundis* shifted from protecting provincials to regulating provincial administrators in a more general way (the "regulatory function"), there is no evidence that the recovery and regulatory laws were united before the *lex Iulia* of 59. Some evidence, though, suggests that they evolved independently. In examination of the speeches it becomes clear that most cases turn on the kinds of facts that were actually defined by the law; unlike *ambitus*, the conception of *repetundae* seems to have been more amenable to precise definition. This emphasis on specific actions is illustrated by the heavy use of arguments directed at the credibility of opposing witnesses. Political arguments are also advanced for voting in a particular way, but as in the murder cases and in contrast to the *vis* cases, these arguments are not held to be intrinsically connected to the charge; *repetundae* itself retains a factual character.

Both the question of witness credibility and the several political issues tended to depend on the fact that the plaintiffs in these cases are (inevitably) not themselves Romans. However, these arguments are phrased so as to be as specific to the case at hand as possible. Apparently it was not productive for the defense to turn one of these trials into a simple conflict of Roman and non-Roman; rather, the court's integrity (or at least the appearance of integrity) had to be maintained. Finally we noted that the technical defense of Rabirius, which was probably flawed, depended on the gap between what he had actually been accused of and the central notion of what constituted *repetundae*. All the cases we have seen indicate that the recovery function (i.e., restoration of money to provincials) remained central to the notion of *repetundae* and may even have been the sole defining feature of the popular notion even after Caesar's legislation broadened its legal scope. The treatment of witnesses and the extrinsic use of political arguments confirm that the precise factual character of *repetundae* implied by the earlier legislation accurately reflect this popular conception.

Important here is the contrast between Cicero's treatments of *ambitus* and *repetundae*. Each charge is more-or-less the mirror image of the other. Money ordinarily passes between a single noble and a number of members of lower classes. In neither case is there a body or "smoking gun" which proves the existence of a crime (much less the identity of the criminal). Arguments about *ambitus* differ from those about homicide because of the inherently unclear (and narrowly political) character of the former. A number of points (e.g., the "factual" treatment of judicial bribery in *pro Cluentio*) suggest that this definitional difference, not the distinction in the evidence potentially available, produced the differences in argumentation. The strongest evidence, however, is the contrast between *ambitus* and *repetundae* cases. Despite the lack of a "body in question," *repetundae* speeches focus on evidentiary questions and the factual issues they underlie, at least to the extent that the crime, however defined, is put at issue. This is in marked contrast to the focus on interpersonal relations in the *ambitus* cases.[4] Thus the "fuzzy" or prototype definition of *ambitus* is not merely sufficient, but necessary to account for the argumentative strategies Cicero uses.

Finally, now that we have examined a number of specific cases in detail, we may return to the general question of the interrelationships among Ciceronian oratory, contemporary law, and popular conceptions of criminal offenses. On the one hand, Cicero's arguments on a given charge (especially outside of *vis*) show relatively little variety at the basic level. That is, they seem to appeal to similar understandings of the offense in question. On the other hand, there is considerably more variation in the treatment of differing offenses. As was just noted, these differences cannot be explained solely by the different evidentiary situations. And although both the differences (between offenses) and the similarities (regarding a given offense) can be described in terms of ancient rhetorical theory, it will be argued in the next section that rhetorical theory nonetheless fails to *explain* why a particular traditional approach was taken in any given case, as against other equally traditional approaches that were available.

Indeed, while I hope the patterns I have traced within Cicero's oratory may be treated as fact, any explanation of those patterns must remain hypothetical to some degree. Nonetheless, it is not mere fantasy or circular reasoning to see in those patterns reflections of the public's understanding of the offenses tried before the various courts.[5] First, the external evidence presented in the introduction suggested that trials were not a front or farce but actually revolved around the crimes which were their nominal object. The definition of these crimes could conceivably have been reconstructed for the occasion by advocates or by the state (the latter is certainly the case today), yet what we know about the workings of the Roman courts suggests otherwise. Nothing about the institution would have lead jurors to substitute someone else's understanding of *vis, ambitus*, and the like for their own. Second, variety is normally a hallmark of Cicero's oratory. He can often be found on both sides of the same issue as immediate circumstances demand (see chapter 4, note 45), and, as we have just noted, he argues different charges differently. When Cicero restricts himself to certain arguments in a given context, we may suspect that he is exploiting some feature of that context. In this instance, the most obvious such feature is a broadly shared (at least among the limited audience) conception of the offense that lies before the jurors.

What, then, if anything, do these popular models have to do with the law? In most cases the same general concerns were the focus both of Cicero's speeches and of the legal history of the various offenses. The unification of the homicide court (in Cicero's lifetime) suggested the recent development of a broad conception covering any intentional killing, whatever the means or the method or the status of the parties. Cicero thus offers extensive (if flawed) chains of inference to show that his client didn't do it. The complex series of *ambitus* statutes suggested a more complex negotiation of appropriate campaign behavior. Cicero accordingly switches to testimonial and narrative which do not serve to establish his clients' actions (or inaction) but to characterize and contextualize them. This general similarity is hardly surprising. After all, both laws and oratory arise from the same small segment of the same society. On the other hand, the two do not move in total lock-step.[6]

On the present interpretation of *pro Milone* practical judgment in *vis* cases may have begun to "anticipate" future expansions in the legal definition. Conversely, *pro Rabirio* may have attempted to exploit Caesar's recent expansion of *repetundae* beyond its conventional bounds to make a specious technical legal argument more palatable. Again, this is not particularly surprising. The cumbersome Roman law-making process would have made precise calibration of statutes unlikely, even if we leave aside the extent to which these legal issues became entwined with personal political motives.[7] In general the situation is such as to justify the assertion (at the beginning of this study) that, while legal theory and legal practice were never completely divorced, they were distinct enough to demand some study as separate entities. They are not merely better and worse kinds of evidence for "the law." One feature of the speeches that would probably not have been predicted on the basis of any statutory evidence is the frequent intrusion of "political" concerns. It is to the apparent tension between the "legal" and "political" aspects of the courts that I now return in the final section.

2. THE *IUDICIA PUBLICA* IN ROMAN STATE AND SOCIETY

Now that we have in place an analysis of several of the major offenses tried by the *iudicia publica*, we can turn to the broader question—what was the function of these courts as a whole? I want to approach this question by looking back at the issue (already considered in the first chapter) of how "political" the Roman courts were. External evidence suggested that they were not in fact very political, at least in some important senses of that word. However, while trials cannot be considered trials of popularity or authority (whether personal or factional), the possibility remained open that they might have been political in another sense. That is, they might have been used to settle substantive disputes over policy or ideology.

We have seen enough political arguments in the last four chapters to make this suggestion very attractive. We noted that cases which were related to tax collection might raise conflicts between the different orders on the juries. Other issues that might produce such a division include the composition of the courts and liability to prosecution. Cicero attempts to exploit precisely these issues in *in Verrem* and in *pro Cluentio* and *pro Rabirio Postumo*, respectively. In the ordinary case of our period, however, a primarily nonsenatorial jury sits in judgment on a senator. There are no real class differences and the issue of equestrian vulnerability to prosecution would not arise. Thus the advocate will only occasionally find purchase for this particular kind of political argument. But there are also the several cases where Cicero suggests the outcome should depend on what are to us external political considerations, as in *pro Murena, pro Flacco*, and *pro Fonteio*. These are not particularly numerous, but when this argument is made, it is done quite openly (especially in *pro Flacco*).

Nonetheless, I want now to recall the suggestion made on this point in the introduction. Roman criminal trials were political not because they were co-opted by the politicians; politics is in a strong sense at the very heart of the definitions of the offenses tried in the *iudicia publica*. At Rome there were no crimes that were not political crimes. The courts existed not for the sake of justice in the abstract (which serves no one in particular) but for the good of the Roman people as a whole. The private courts are the courts where individuals protect themselves, their property, and their rights. The public courts are those where the community protects itself, its property, and its rights. This idea, if not always in the front of the minds of the jurors, is one they can be led to accept. Hence a higher political good may on occasion be used to preempt the issue of guilt or innocence.[8]

One argument for the interpretation advanced here of the function of the criminal courts is provided by a look at the choice of what acts do or do not merit a standing *quaestio*.[9] Many of them are on their faces "political." The crime of diminishing the majesty of the Roman people *(maiestas diminuta)* is by its very definition political; it is a catchall category for miscellaneous injuries to the community. A similar claim holds for *vis*, if it is defined as violence *contra rem publicam*. From here it is but a short step to the indications we saw in chapter 4 that the idea of *vis* could be tied closely to political alignment.[10] *Peculatus* (theft of state funds) speaks for itself as well.[11] *Repetundae* involves danger to Rome's reputation as well as (possible) misuse of state power by officials. *Ambitus* corrupts the election of government officials and so distorts the relationship between government and society as a whole.

It is also important to note what offenses were *not* tried before a standing *quaestio*. The crucial cases are the ways the Romans partitioned murder and various pecuniary offenses. The original "homicide" courts covered (separately) poisoning, parricide, and racketeering. The last is dangerously close to sedition in that it creates a locus of loyalty and armed power distinct from the state and state apparatus. Parricide has a religious dimension and it is thus of state interest to see the pollution removed from its midst. Poisoning is a less obvious fit for this scheme. However, the key may be found in the difficulty of detecting and tracing poison. The uncertainty caused by the possibility of poisoning creates a level of instability even where no poison is actually present.[12] This interpretation is supported by the fact that simple and aggravated theft *(furtum* and *rapina)* are private delicts, while *falsum* (forgery and counterfeiting) warranted a public *quaestio*. Theft is easily recognized, but the possibility of *falsum* makes all one's property uncertain. Finally, *adulterium* produces the same instability born of uncertainty (here uncertainty of paternity) and so becomes the subject of a public court under Augustus (Treggiari 1991:277–90).[13] (Augustus also introduced a prosecution for hoarding grain or otherwise tampering with its supply and price [*D.* 48.12], but it is not clear that this charge was ever heard before a *quaestio*.)

Thus the offenses covered by the *iudicia publica* fall into two broad categories—offenses directly against the community as entity (e.g., *maiestas, sicarii, ambitus*)[14] and those which are directed at individuals but whose substance produces insecurity in the entire community (e.g., *falsum, venenum*).

In either case, however, the *iudicia publica* do not merely cover crimes in which the Roman state happened to take an interest, as some would have it.[15] These courts cover all and only the offenses which were understood to affect the state or society as a whole. Simple theft, murder, and assault have a more individualized effect and so are left to private courts, at least until changing views of violence bring many or all cases of the latter two before the criminal courts.

Some may object again to this line of argument on the ground that it is based too heavily on defense speeches. Perhaps there is a "natural" tendency for the defense to try to broaden any case, even if this is in some sense "illegitimate." There is no specific evidence for this view, and it would not in any case apply to some of the above points (for instance, the distinction between *furtum* and *peculatus*). Nonetheless, it may be worth considering the question further. Our only direct evidence, the first speech against Verres, tells to the contrary since it was as political a speech as Cicero ever gave. His defense of Fonteius strongly suggests that the prosecution in that case made foreign policy claims about the possible consequences of an acquittal.

This evidence is admittedly somewhat sparse, so it is fortunate that we can also find external confirmation for our view of the courts in certain arguments of philosophy and of rhetorical theory. These arguments hold that it is right (and perhaps necessary) to defend a friend, even a guilty one, so long as he is in general a good man (*Off.* 2.51; *IO* 12.1.33–45, 7.4–7). The American system, nominally directed at justice in a fairly narrow sense, does not officially require the proviso about the defendant's character. A fair adversarial process is needed to ensure the discovery of the truth of a particular situation, and so it is always the advocate's duty to offer his client the best representation possible. For Cicero and Quintilian it is acceptable to defend a good man, for he is of value to the society regardless of his particular guilt. This does not mean that guilt or innocence is an irrelevant issue. The courts are still deciding whether the defendant has done the community certain wrongs. Nonetheless, the defense advocate can justify his behavior by claiming that acquittal of a truly good man, even if guilty, will on balance promote the interests of the state. The same argument which provides the advocate's self-justification may also provide his argument in court.

In either case there is a play on the intent behind the establishment of the courts. The first-order intent, recalling the discussion of the first chapter, is the detection and punishment of certain activities detrimental to the interests of the state as a whole. But the second-order intent behind the creation of such an institution must be the protection of those common interests. That protection may not in every single case be best advanced by condemnation of the guilty. Here is the best opportunity for oratorical manipulation. Where there is an ambiguity of values, even (especially?) at different levels of abstraction, the skill of the advocate comes into play.[16] It clearly required considerable rhetorical effort (especially with favorable outside circumstances) to privilege the second-order intent over the first, but it was possible.

It may be useful to contrast the views expressed here on this point with two alternative models. The first is that of Wolfgang Kunkel, whom I have followed in most other respects, and the second is a currently functioning system, American presidential impeachment. Kunkel's (1962) monograph attempts to replace Mommsen's (1899) evolutionary account of the pre-Sullan "criminal" courts with one more sensitive to the vagaries of actual social change.[17] Kunkel argues that originally there were two jurisdictions at Rome. The first, that of trials before the assembly, included only "political" offenses, also several times described as offenses "against the community *(Gemeinwesen)* as such." At first this category included only *perduellio* and, perhaps, some severe religious errors; later *ambitus* and *peculatus* came to be included. The other jurisdiction, which included all trials for murder and theft, was not significantly distinct from the rest of the "private law" of property and obligations. These trials were held before a nonprofessional *iudex* (or *iudices*) appointed by the praetor.

Relatively early on (perhaps by 413[18]) an alternative to clumsy comitial trials was developed to try "political" crimes.[19] This new mechanism was investigation *(quaestio)* by a magistrate, normally the praetor, and judgment by his *ad hoc* advisory panel *(consilium)*.[20] This procedure was authorized, until Gracchus' *lex Sempronia* of 123, by a vote of either senate or assembly (usually the former), thereafter only by vote of the people.[21] The first standing *repetundae* courts (established by the *lex Calpurnia* of 149 and later the *lex Iunia*) were not extensions of the *quaestio* process but rather a routinization of civil procedures for the recovery of property.[22] They did, however, provide a precedent for the formation of standing courts (and in particular for yearly jury panels), which were soon taken up by the public courts, and thus the *quaestiones perpetuae* were born. Over time the extraordinary, and later the standing, *quaestiones* also extended their reach beyond the "political" to establish a level of "police-justice" (Kunkel 1962:133). The prime examples of this new range Kunkel (1962:91–92) gives are the various courts *de veneficiis* and *de sicariis*.

All of this is certainly plausible given Kunkel's static understanding of the categories of the political and the nonpolitical. While there is nothing wrong in principle with picking one definition and seeing what it yields, in this case it misses a significant generalization. Kunkel (1962:133) himself comes close to this realization when he notes that one reason that extraordinary *quaestiones* were first turned to deal with "general" (i.e., nonpolitical) offenses was that their targets "were seen as a political danger."[23] But if something is "seen as" a political issue, it is *eo ipso* a political issue. Kunkel argues that there is a procedural shift, so that once the *quaestiones* (especially the standing ones) had proved their usefulness, they absorbed parts of the original "private" jurisdiction. This is not inherently implausible; the standing *quaestio* does present advantages of equity (Kunkel 1962:96).[24] However, in this particular case it is easier to claim that there is a category shift. Actions move from private to public procedure because they have (only recently) become public actions. What, under Kunkel's hypothesis, would be the rather haphazard extension of public procedure, is better described as an expansion of what counts as activity "against the community as such."

Under the United States Constitution (Art. II, §4) the president or other "civil officers" may be removed from office for "treason, bribery, or other high crimes and misdemeanors." In principle they are also subject to ordinary criminal prosecution for the same underlying actions, if those actions happen to constitute criminal offenses (Art. I, §3).[25] It is generally agreed that "high crimes and misdemeanors" is meant to encompass acts which, whether or not otherwise criminal, pose a grave threat to good political order.[26] For example, abuse of power or official funds, corruption, and interference with separation of powers have historically been sufficient grounds. Superficially, the Roman *iudicia publica* show some similarities to the impeachment system as opposed to the ordinary American criminal law. The former two systems include treason and bribery. Both have vague catchall categories (Roman *maiestas* and American high crimes and misdemeanors) so that legal technicalities will not allow escape in a moment of constitutional crisis.[27] Both are largely restricted to a small segment of the political class, both for their defendants and their jurors. Closer inspection, however, reveals crucial distinctions. First, impeachment depends very heavily on the catchall category of "high crimes and misdemeanors." There is little attempt to enumerate specific offenses that expose someone to impeachment, especially in the light of the narrow constitutional definition of "treason" in American law (Art. III, §3). By contrast, the Roman system offers six fairly well fleshed-out offenses in addition to the residual category of *maiestas*. Second, while rare, prosecutions of ordinary citizens in the *iudicia publica* were technically possible and did occur.[28] Third, conviction following on impeachment results only in loss of and disqualification from office (Art. I, §3). The punishment, like the offense, is purely political. (Fines and/or imprisonment can result only from a separate criminal conviction.) *Ambitus* was punished similarly, but other offenses carried other penalties which might be thought more appropriate to the "criminal" realm—fines and exile. American law makes a sharp distinction between criminal trials and political ones. Roman law collapses them onto one level; the *iudicia publica* were simultaneously about specific offenses and the general political order. This is what gives them the dual character discussed above.

This duality gives a more specific sense to the claim, made at the beginning of the book, that the public courts were a less "legal" institution than, say, the private courts. It also shows that recognition of this fact, not in itself a novel observation, does not require us to fall back to a view of the public courts as either slightly dressed up aristocratic dueling or ritual expulsion along the lines of ostracism. Here in the standing *quaestiones* the Roman people (or rather the elite fraction that so often stood in for the whole) enforced their collective legal rights. Some may feel that this duality of roles is a flaw; that, if definition and enforcement of acceptable behavior are not better separated institutionally, both functions may be corrupted. There may well be some truth to this, but the situation was not merely accepted *faute de mieux*. After all, the Romans had the model of their own more carefully articulated private law before them. Yet see how Cicero describes the different ways an orator must prepare to argue before the different types of court:

> *I don't need to talk at length about why I think an orator should know both public law (publica iura)—after all it is key to state and empire—and records of past deeds and tales of antiquity. Just as private cases often demand a speech drawn from the civil law (and, thus, as I've already remarked, the orator must have a knowledge of civil law), so in public matters before the courts, the people, or the senate all this recollection of times past and all the authority of the public law and the whole science of governing the republic should serve as raw material for those orators who are involved in public affairs.*

(*de Or.* 1.201)

Here he celebrates the connection of the public courts to public affairs at the same time that he respects the relative autonomy of the civil law.[29] Some offenses (*vis* and *ambitus*) were too close to live political issues to be entrusted to the jurists. More important, though, all public offenses were too *important* for them. If a jurist or *iudex* erred in a civil matter, an individual or at most a set of individuals were harmed. But by definition the interests of the entire community were at stake in the public law. Hence, all the citizens, or at least all the "best" ones, had to be allowed their voice.

The above provides some partial answers to a question that could be raised regarding the first chapter. If the *iudicia publica* are meant to discover the "truth," we can and should ask, "The truth about what?" Is it anything more specific than, as suggested above, injury to the community as a whole in the form of the various statutory offenses? I want to suggest not. We may keep in mind here that what we have been calling "criminal courts" are not *iudicia criminalia* in Latin, but *iudicia publica*.[30] Republican Latin has a variety of words for "wrongdoing" in general—*crimen, scelus, maleficium, facinus*—but none specific to the offenses tried by these courts.[31] In answering a similar question Foucault (1977) and Leps (1992), particularly the latter, examined a variety of discourses that surround what we would be inclined to call crime and penal practice. This examination lead to a characterization of the object(s) constituted by these discourses. These scholars had available *(inter alia)* statutes, journalism (particularly the subgenre of crime reporting), academic criminological studies, and even detective fiction. The last two of these are historically recent developments, and journalism is not that much older, so it comes as no surprise that we have no resort to such evidence.[32] Yet it is still striking that Rome seems to have had no parallel discourses of its own which were specifically attached either to the *iudicia publica* or to the acts they are supposed to investigate. We might then wonder whether, for the Romans, there was such a thing as "crime."[33] This claim is naturally based on silence, but we may claim that it is a principled silence, not (as so often with the ancient world) an accident of transmission. To support this claim we must look at several places where we might expect discussion of crime or criminality.

"Crime" was not, so far as we can tell, a major part of the political landscape. We do not know of "law and order" candidates for office who promised to crack down on criminals. This perhaps only makes sense. The behavior the courts address themselves to is quite restricted, whether because of the narrow applicability of some charges (e.g., *repetundae*) or because of the extreme level of antisocial behavior involved in others (e.g., homicide).[34] The scope of the courts is also restricted chronologically. The first standing court was created, according to Cicero (*Brut.* 106), in 149; we have already noted that the full form of the standing *quaestio* (of the sort Cicero actually participated in) cannot be dated before 123 (Kunkel 1962:61–62). The date of the second is not clear, but it may not predate 116.[35] They are superseded over the first two centuries of the empire. The transfer of jurisdiction seems to vary for different charges, and there is some dispute over whether any *quaestio* actually survived into the Severan period (late second/early third century A.D.).[36]

Nonetheless, the underlying legislation continued to be enforced by a different institution—the so-called *cognitio extraordinaria*.[37] This is a more inquisitorial procedure conducted by the emperor himself or by various delegates (most notably the urban and praetorian prefects and provincial governors). Though not required to do so, imperial *cognitio* continued to organize crimes largely in terms of the original Republican and Augustan legislation authorizing *quaestiones*; witness the retention of those categories by jurists after the courts themselves had disappeared, even down to the *Digest*. Penalties were different, and the presiding magistrates used their discretion to expand *(inter alia)* the scope of some charges (notably *maiestas*) drastically, but it is clear that the decline in the *iudicia publica* produced no formal jurisdictional gap (Pugliese 1982:750–63).[38]

Only one of the fifty books of Justinian's *Digest* of juristic writings is devoted to the *iudicia publica*. Criminal law is entirely absent from Gaius' mid–second century textbook, the *Institutes*, and so from Justinian's later one as well.[39] If we concentrate on the Republican period, we find that jurists pay, if anything, less attention than at later periods.[40] Among the testimonia collected in Bremer 1896 and Huschke et al. 1908 we have precisely one reference by a Republican jurist to the *iudicia publica* and/or to their individual functions.[41] Alfenus, probably quoting Sulpicius Rufus, considered the jurisdictional question of whether a freed slave was subject to criminal trial for something he had done while a slave (*D.* 44.7.20). Beyond this the earliest citation is of the Augustan figure Ateius Capito (Gell. *NA* 4.14.1, 10.6.4).[42] Q. Aelius Tubero, a somewhat younger contemporary of Cicero, is described in the *Digest* (Pomponius *D.* 1.2.2.46) as "most learned in both private and public law." We have only two fragments, of which one fits into the public category:

> For in book 8[43] [Capito] says that Tubero says that no decree of the senate may be made without a division of the house, because in all decrees of the senate, even those which are made by asking individual opinions, the division is necessary.

> (Gell. *NA* 14.7.13)

From the remains of other Republican jurists (especially Tuditanus' book on magistracies and Gracchanus' on "powers"[44]) we may assume that the surviving fragment of Tubero is representative, and that Pomponius' mention of *ius publicum* need not have had anything to do with the *iudicia publica*.[45] By contrast we have references to jurisprudence on delicts such as *furtum* as early as Sex. Aelius Catus (cos. 198; *Fam.* 7.22). The tradition on *furtum* is well attested thereafter to the end of the Republic (*Fam.* 7.22; *NA* 6.15.1–2, 17.7.3; Gaius 3.183; Pomponius *D.* 47.2.77.1). Juristic comment on *iniuria* and *damnum iniuria datum* is not clearly attested before Ser. Sulpicius Rufus (cos. 51, but contemporary with Cicero; Ulp. *D.* 47.10.15.32, Alfenus *D.* 19.2.30.2) but may well go back at least as far as P. Mucius Scaevola (cos. 133; *ad Her.* 2.13.19). Since *furtum* is at the latest a creation of the Twelve Tables, not the edict, it is not surprising that it comes up first. Thus criminal law was either ignored completely or at most treated as a small corner of public law by Republican legal scholars.[46]

Teachers of rhetoric could have provided analysis or at least examples, yet their interest, insofar as it is in the real world at all, seems to lie for the most part outside the realm of the *iudicia publica*. The criminal offenses they do bother with are rarely treated in terms of actually existing statutes. The only general treatments of the *iudicia publica* in Cicero's rhetorical works are quite brief: *de Or.* 2.105–9 and *Part. Or.* 104–6 (both in the context of discussions of rhetorical *status*), nor are there many passages that discuss, even in passing, the appropriate response to various criminal charges (*Inv.* 2.52–55, 58; *de Or.* 2.201; cf. *ad Her.* 1.21, 2.43). Within the latter group there is considerable redundancy, especially concerning the notoriously unclear definition of *maiestas*, hence there is really even less discussion than appears at first sight to take place. Finally, and most important, even when criminal offenses are discussed, they are not treated as a unit. For instance, consider a rare passage from Quintilian that mentions three different criminal offenses (4.2.10):

> *Although I feel that these reasons sometimes suggest omitting the narration, nonetheless I disagree with those who think that there should never be a narration when the defendant simply denies the charge. Cornelius Celsus believes this; he thinks that most murder cases and all charges of* ambitus *and* repetundae *fall under this heading.*

The heading under which both Quintilian and his source discuss these charges is not "criminal cases" but "narrative." Even at that lower level, only three offenses are included, and one of them only under certain circumstances. And even though Quintilian does not mention it, cases which require simple denial could clearly include civil as well as criminal cases—"I never injured your horse" or "We never even discussed the sale of that farm." Hence, nothing in the argument presupposes a category made up of all and only the offenses tried in the criminal courts.

One particular aspect of rhetorical theory needs to be singled out for special treatment here. The doctrine of status sets out the various bases on which a case may be argued.[47] There are numerous minor variations of the theory, but the basic idea is that the speaker asks himself whether the question is one of fact ("did he do it?"), or one of definition ("how should we call what he did?"), or, usually as a last resort, one of "quality" ("was what he did a bad thing?"). This way of categorizing arguments could perhaps be said to offer a set of judging paradigms. Two points, however, show that it is not in itself a way of talking about crime. First, it is equally applicable to private law matters. For instance, someone accused of underpaying a hired laborer might argue, "we never had a contract," "read properly, the contract supports my claim as to the wage," or "he did such a poor job that the lower wage is only fair."[48] As with other rhetorical theory, status can be used to talk about *inter alia* particular crimes, but it tells us (and the Romans) nothing about crime in general. Second, the theory of status is in fact more descriptive than prescriptive. That is, there are no substantive guidelines which determine what the relevant status is. It depends on an ultimately intuitive judgment of (depending on the particular rhetorical sect) the defense's most general proposition, the main propositions of both defense and prosecution, or the clash arising from those two.[49] To attribute the use of any particular argument used by Cicero (or anyone else) to status theory begs the question. The choice depends on the particular circumstances of the case, and in particular the substance and definition of the offense charged. All of this could equally well be said about other parts of ancient rhetorical theory, e.g., the standard topoi deployed to discredit witnesses or rumors.[50] They are of applicability beyond criminal cases, and in any case little instruction is given for their use. Hence none constitute or even assume any particular theory of crime.

The situation in declamation is very similar. Let me begin with one specific example which has been proposed as a link between rhetorical and juristic argument. Numerous declamations were argued over whether someone provided the "cause of death" *(causa mortis)* for someone else. Nörr (1986:101–15) has linked this tradition to a similar provision allegedly contained in the *lex Cornelia de sicariis et veneficiis*.[51] Even if we were to accept this questionable reconstruction of the *lex Cornelia* (cf. chapter 3, note 15), it still does little to establish a category of crime. The notion of *causa mortis* was clearly part of private law jurisprudence under the *lex Aquilia*, probably by the time of Labeo at the latest.[52] Hence, not only were declaimers on this topic not talking about "crime" as a category, they were not even clearly talking about a criminal offense at all. In general, criminal offenses are rarely discussed, and even then not *qua* criminal offenses. For instance, it is interesting that among the six Senecan *Controversiae* in which a poisoning is alleged (3.7, 6.4, 6.6, 7.3, 9.5, 9.6), only two are actually cases on that issue (6.4, 6.6). Declamation is also notoriously casual about the precise procedural status of individual causes for action. Recognizable public offenses such as *veneficium* and *maiestas* are treated as *actiones*, private actions, in the works of Seneca and Calpurnius Flaccus.[53] Rather than specific charges, declamation favors very general rubrics like *iniuria*, *mores*, and *mala tractatio* (the latter two invented for the purpose). The object is to cover misbehavior in general without worrying too much about the specific legal details. The deliberate confusion of public and private law is of a piece with this strategy. Divisions within the broad category of "wrongdoing" are unimportant; "crime" as such is of no particular interest.

Finally, we may return to Cicero and consider works written in a more reflective mode. After all, he wrote and thought about many different aspects of his society, especially those with clear political ramifications. Might he have written elsewhere about crime or the criminal courts? There is a brief but revealing mention in *de Officiis* (3.73) where Cicero explains why he has taken up only very delicate ethical questions:

> *Nor is there any need to treat here assassins* (sicarii), *poisoners, forgers of wills, or thieves of private or public funds, men who are to be checked not by words or the arguments of philosophers, but by chains and prison. We consider here those things which are done by those who are considered to be "good" men* (boni).
>
> (*Off.* 3.73)

We may note two things here. First, Cicero lumps together four public offenses with one delict (theft), which was subject to punishment, but by private suit. His interest (such as it was) was thus in a somewhat broader category than the *iudicia publica* treated. Second, he does not find much intellectual interest in explaining either the "problem" of crime (anyone can see that these acts are wrong), or its solution *(vinclis et carcere)*, or its causes (which are not even mentioned).

We might also logically look to his *de Legibus*, but even there we will find little more. None of the three extant books of this work are devoted to the *iu-dicia publica*, but we know from a citation preserved in Macrobius (*Sat.* 6.4.8) that there were at least two more books originally. Although it is sometimes suggested that one of these books was at least in part about the criminal courts, there is good reason to doubt this.[54] Book three (on the structure of the government) already has regulations that correspond to laws on *vis, ambitus, repetundae*, and (perhaps) *peculatus* (3.11):[55]

> *Let there be no* vis *among the people. . . . Those who transact public business are to observe the auspices, obey the public augur, publish their acts and file them at the treasury, deal with one matter at a time, explain the matter to the people, and allow public comment by the magistrates and private citizens. . . . Let no one receive or give a gift while seeking office, or during or afterward.*[56]

This quotation and that in note 56 are all that Cicero has to say on the subject in the preserved portions of the work. The praetor has previously (3.8) been charged with presiding over private matters *(privata)*, but public ones are not mentioned.[57] By contrast the topics selected for popular vote in the assembly include "trials by the people," *iudicia populi* (3.10). In other respects — such as the revival of the temporary dictator and master of horse (3.9), the lack of the secret ballot (3.10) — Cicero's constitution is deliberately archaizing. He seems also to have returned to the days before the standing *quaestiones*, even exaggerating the role of comitial trials to make this point.[58] We might also remark in passing that the "criminal laws" cited above are separated by considerable material of other sorts, only a sample of which has been quoted. Cicero here shows precisely the same organization we have already attributed to the jurists. The criminal law is a small and not particularly distinct part of the "public" law.

In any of these individual cases one could imagine specific reasons for the absence of discussions of crime and criminal law. The striking fact, however, is that the only Republican discourses (of which we are aware) which deal systematically with crime or the criminal courts are legislation (which also has many other topics) and forensic oratory — the main sources for the body of this study. This lack is not due to problems of transmission but is a feature of the culture which demands comment in its own right. There are two related points I want to make here. The first is that the targets of the public courts, however we wish to label them collectively, are hardly visible as an independent category in the Roman world. We have suggested that the *iudicia publica* existed to punish injuries to the community at large. Thus they were situated at the intersection of two very general categories, injury and the "public," rather than existing in their own right.

An illustration of this situation can be drawn from the ethical arguments we have been following throughout this book. Perhaps it is not surprising that Cicero, in a passage we have already seen, so casually mixes a number of accusations against Verres together with the sole charge which, as he himself admits, constituted a violation of the law:

> *I assert that Verres, when he had already done many lustful things, many cruel things against Roman citizens and allies, many unspeakable things against gods and men, then on top of that he made off with 40,000,000 sesterces from Sicily in contravention of the laws.*

(1 *Verr.* 56)

Perhaps this could be written off as just the character assassination which we expect a prosecutor to engage in. That "just," however, seems to me to beg the question at hand.

It is harder to ignore the equally scattershot nature of character defense in Cicero's other speeches. Flaccus gave up an inheritance to a co-heir (*Flacc.* 89); Roscius didn't like parties (*Rosc.* 39); Murena had not, contrary to some reports, been caught dancing inappropriately (*Mur.* 13). In fact, despite rules in the rhetorical handbooks for doing so, Cicero virtually never admits to any wrong on his client's part.[59] While we can see this very broad character defense in most of the speeches, we should note especially here the "instrumental" ethical argument, whereby a defendant's other good behavior (of whatever sort) can be adduced as evidence that he was not the sort to commit the crime at issue. Any instance of good behavior is evidence for any other, just as any wrongdoing is evidence for any other. The absence of ethical distinction is due to the lack of conceptual distinction; the "crimes" tried by the *iudicia publica* were not an entity unto themselves.

In a famous article Mary Beard (1986:46) has argued that the primary point of Cicero's *de Divinatione* was not to take a position for or against divination but to establish divination (and religion more generally) as a "subject of Roman discourse." That is, it was to become (as it had not been before) a matter on which there were positions to be taken and argued for, not just another part of the background of habitual action that makes up much of one's life. Cicero's dialogue was an effect (and subsequently a cause) of a period in which "'religion,' as an activity and a subject, became clearly defined out of the traditional, undifferentiated, politico-religious amalgam of Roman public life." Thus it was only relatively late in Roman history that a mass of long-standing "religious" activity became visible and unified "Religion." What I have been suggesting here is that "Crime," in the Roman Republic at least, never had its Cicero nor its *de Divinatione*. It never became a distinctly articulated topic of discourse or area of action.

The second, more specific point is that the courts were not about the "repression of crime."[60] This is true insofar as the courts do not depend conceptually on any of the notions which today define the "criminal": social pathology, social contract, protection of citizens (as opposed to the collective citizenry). No trace of any such notions has been found here. It is also true in a practical sense, especially for Republican times, in that the system is not designed to handle most of the activity which we would today label crime. Theft in the broadest sense (including robbery, embezzlement, blackmail, and so forth) and crimes against the person short of homicide are normally left to the private courts. Republican Rome was, it must be remembered, a state essentially without a police force. Even if we accept the most expansive interpretations of the police powers and responsibilities of the *tresviri capitales* and other magistrates, they simply did not have the manpower to repress crime in a city the size of Rome.[61]

As Nippel (1995:22–26) has pointed out, these expansive interpretations assume that control of crime is a natural function of larger states and then seek to locate a police function whose existence they simply presuppose. Yet, he goes on, comparative evidence shows that this presupposition need not be true. It is particularly suspicious in a society (such as Rome's) in which the law-writing class is largely insulated from ordinary crime by private security. While direct evidence for the presence or absence of some ordinary criminal jurisdiction is not decisive, this interpretation of the court system provides another piece of evidence for its absence. It is of course possible that lurking somewhere in the culture is an idea that corresponds more-or-less to that of "crime," but I hope to have shown that such an idea has no place in the areas where one might have expected it.

Absent such a concept, we have one less reason to presume a significant police function for the Roman state. Conversely, the lack of an institutional response to "crime," or even of any institution that presupposed the existence of crime as an identifiable phenomenon, must have made the development of such an idea less likely. No one would ever have been confronted by Crime in his or her daily life (even if he or she encountered the occasional criminal act). This is the environment—both practical and ideological—in which the jurors of the *iudicia publica* could exercise their commonsense judgments of whether defendants had done some wrong to their community.

APPENDIX A

Summary of Cicero's Criminal Cases

Pro Murena (TLRR 224)

Date: 63

Defendant: L. Licinius Murena

Prosecutor(s): Servius Sulpicius Rufus (assisted by Cato the Younger and two others)

Co-counsel: Hortensius, Crassus

Result: acquittal

Rufus, whom Cicero had supported in the consular elections of 63, lost to Murena and prosecuted him for *ambitus* during that campaign. He was assisted by Cato, who had promised to prosecute the winners (whoever they were) because of the flagrant bribery allegedly used on all sides. Cicero turned around and defended his friend's old rival, apparently out of a desire to maintain political stability amidst the threat from Catiline's forces.

Pro Plancio (TLRR 293)

Date: 54

Defendant: Gn. Plancius

Prosecutor(s): M. Iuventius Laterensis (aided by L. Cassius Longinus)

Co-counsel: Hortensius

Result: acquittal

Plancius defeated Laterensis (a man of much more elevated birth) in elections for a lower magistracy (the aedileship). Laterensis prosecuted on the grounds that Plancius had won by using illegal organizational techniques. Cicero's speech deals at length with Plancius' efforts to protect Cicero when the latter was in exile in 58–7.

CHAPTER 3: MURDER

Pro Roscio Amerino (TLRR 129)

Date: 80
Defendant: Sex. Roscius
Prosecutor(s): C. Erucius (aided by T. Roscius Magnus)
Co-counsel: none
Result: apparently acquittal

Sex. Roscius was accused of arranging the murder of his father, also Sex. Roscius. Cicero hints (and it may be true) that the prosecution was actually mounted by the efforts of one Chrysogonus, a freedman of Sulla who had perhaps profited from the elder Roscius' estate (which was apparently sold, rightly or wrongly, as part of the program of Sullan proscriptions). The presence of Roscii on the other side during the trial suggests that some ongoing property dispute was probably involved, but it is not clear (despite Cicero's assumption) that either side had anything to do with the father's death.

Pro Cluentio (TLRR 198)

Date: 66
Defendant: A. Cluentius Habitus
Prosecutor(s): Statius Albius Oppianicus (aided by T. Attius)
Co-counsel: none
Result: acquittal

Cluentius was accused of a series of poisonings and perhaps also of bribery leading to the judicial condemnation (several years earlier) of the present prosecutor's father. This case is almost certainly tied to long-standing family quarrels over property, whose rather confusing tale Cicero recounts at great length.

CHAPTER 4: *VIS*

Pro Sulla (TLRR 234)

Date: 62
Defendant: P. Cornelius Sulla
Prosecutor(s): L. Manlius Torquatus (and one other)
Co-counsel: Hortensius

Result: acquittal

Sulla was tried on the grounds of his alleged complicity in the Catilinarian conspiracy (fomenting sedition in Rome and Spain). He had previously been prosecuted (successfully) by Torquati for *ambitus*.

Pro Sestio (TLRR 271)

Date: 56
Defendant: P. Sestius
Prosecutor(s): P. Albinovanus (and two others)
Co-counsel: Sestius and three others
Result: acquittal

Sestius was accused of organizing and participating in a number of violent acts during his tribunate in 57, many undertaken in opposition to P. Clodius.

Pro Caelio (TLRR 275)

Date: 56
Defendant: M. Caelius Rufus
Prosecutor(s): L. Sempronius Atratinus (and three others)
Co-counsel: Caelius, Crassus
Result: acquittal

The prosecution seems to have been launched, at least in part, in revenge for Caelius' prosecution (on two occasions) of the present prosecutor's father. Caelius was accused of a number of acts of sedition surrounding an Alexandrian embassy to Rome (sent to discuss the settlement of the Egyptian throne) and perhaps also a plot against the life of Clodia, sister of P. Clodius. Cicero's speech emphasizes the connection of the Clodii to the prosecution.

Pro Milone (TLRR 309)

Date: 52
Defendant: T. Annius Milo
Prosecutor(s): Ap. Claudius Pulcher (and three others)
Co-counsel: M. Claudius Marcellus
Result: conviction

The rival gangs of Milo and Clodius met (apparently accidentally) outside Rome, and Clodius was killed in the ensuing fight. Milo was tried for this under a special statute of Pompey, which put considerable restriction on the scope of the trial.

CHAPTER 5: *REPETUNDAE*

Pro Fonteio (TLRR 186)

Date: 69?
Defendant: M. Fonteius
Prosecutor(s): M. Plaetorius Cestianus (aided by M. Fabius)
Co-counsel: none?
Result: acquittal?
Fonteius was tried for financial misconduct (its nature somewhat unclear), primarily as governor of Gaul in the late 70's.

In Verrem (TLRR 177)

Date: 70
Defendant: C. Verres
Prosecutor(s): Cicero
Defense counsel: Q. Hortensius and two others
Result: Verres gave up and fled to exile between the two hearings of the case.
Verres was tried for extortion against the inhabitants of Sicily, where he had been governor in 73–1. Cicero's 1 *Verr.* was the speech he actually delivered in the first hearing. 2 *Verr.* is a much expanded version of what he would have said in the second hearing. Also attached to the case is *Div. Caec.*, by which Cicero first convinced the jurors that he would be the most energetic prosecutor of the case.

Pro Scauro (TLRR 295)

Date: 54
Defendant: M. Aemilius Scaurus
Prosecutor(s): P. Valerius Triarius (and three others)
Co-counsel: Scaurus, Clodius, and four others (all of the highest rank)
Result: acquittal
Scaurus was tried for some kind of extortion (or other misconduct) as governor of Sardinia in 55.

Pro Flacco (TLRR 247)

Date: 59
Defendant: L. Valerius Flaccus
Prosecutor(s): D. Laelius and four others
Co-counsel: Hortensius
Result: acquittal
Flaccus was accused of a number of schemes to gain illegal profit while governor of Asia in 62.

Pro Rabiro Postumo (TLRR 305)

Date: 54/3
Defendant: C. Rabirius Postumus
Prosecutor(s): C. Memmius
Co-counsel: none
Result: acquittal?
Rabirius was a minor figure causght up in the much more important trial of Gabinius (governor of Syria, 57–4) for *repetundae* in Egypt. When Gabinius was convicted but could not pay the entire fine, attempts were made to extract the money from his alleged henchmen.

APPENDIX B

Published vs. Delivered Speeches

The introduction noted that published speeches were suitable evidence for this study simply by virtue of the fact that they could be offered as representations of court proceedings, even if they did not represent what was actually said in any particular trial. If, however, we can establish that the speeches were directed primarily at the judicial audience, then we can draw even more specific conclusions about institutional practice.[1] This brings us to the long disputed issue of the relationship between what Cicero actually said in court and what he eventually published as *orationes*.[2]

Let us begin by looking at the few cases where we know something about the divergence or correspondence of delivered and published versions of extant speeches. In the case of the fragmentary *pro Cornelio* we have ancient (apparently eyewitness) testimony that the published version was a nearly verbatim transcript:

> *For Cornelius Nepos says that the speech for Cornelius (the seditious tribune) was delivered in his presence in almost the same words (*iisdem paene verbis*) in which it was published.*

> (Jerome 23.365M = Cornelius Nepos, *Vita Ciceronis* fr. 2 Peter)[3]

In a letter to Atticus (13.20.2) Cicero rejects the former's suggestion of including a discussion of Tubero's wife in the published *pro Ligario*. This implies correspondence of the two versions (at least on this point) but of course also leaves open the possibility of such additions in other instances. We also have three fairly clear cases of divergence: the *actio secunda* of *in Verrem*, *pro Milone* (as we have it), and the second *Philippic*. These are more numerous than the examples of correspondence, but they are all pathological: in two cases (*Ver-*

rines and second *Philippic*) the "original" was not reproduced because it was never delivered.[4] Cicero did make a defense of Milo, but its delivery was apparently hampered by external factors (Asc. 41.24–42.2C).[5] None of this evidence appears decisive for Cicero's general practice of publication. As a result we will have to try some more indirect approaches.

One possibility is to look at the types of attested divergence which are suggested and consider whether they are significant. First, even though there is little specific evidence, we may presume a certain amount of stylistic tinkering (for examples see *Att.* 1.13.5 and *Att.* 15.1a.2).[6] Antitheses will have been made to balance, tricola to rise smoothly, offensive rhythms will have been removed.[7] Points of fact were also corrected (*Att.* 1.13.5, 13.44.3). This detailed work would not affect the structure of the argument. Second, Ochs (1982) and Enos (1984; 1988) have noted that the *dispositio* of the *actio secunda* of the *Verrines* is significantly different from that prescribed in the rhetorical handbooks and followed (more-or-less) in the *actio prima* and other early speeches. Each individual speech contains only a few of the conventional parts (e.g., *exordium, narratio*). The force of arguments can be subtly affected by their arrangement, but again the basic argumentative repertoire is not changed. Furthermore, in the *Verrines* it is largely nonargumentative material which is displaced. Third, there is some evidence that the published speeches may have been more extensive than the delivered versions. The *actio secunda* and the second *Philippic* could be conceived of as extreme examples under this rubric. More to the point are *pro Milone* and *pro Ligario*. The latter, as noted above, was not expanded, but might have been. It is broadly accepted that the former was significantly expanded for publication (see full discussion in chapter four). We may also cite here two other letters of Cicero. In one (*Att.* 1.13.5) he describes additions he has made to two speeches, though it is not clear what kind of speeches these are:

> *I have included, as you have asked, the description of Misenum and Puteoli in my speech . . . and now it seems much more "Attic" to me because you have approved. I have added certain things into the oration against Metellus.*[8]

In the other (*Fam.* 9.12.2) he mentions that he has not yet "pruned" or "cleaned up"[9] *pro rege Deiotaro*. But this need not refer to anything more than the stylistic polishing referred to above. In all the cases where anything useful can be said, the difference between the delivered and published versions is the addition of new (and in the one clear case ornamental) loci rather than the elimination or replacement of old ones. Thus the arguments Cicero made to the jurors will have been preserved. Even if we assume, however, that speeches were potentially expanded, it is striking that, despite the suspicions of varying strength that can or have been directed at certain passages in the speeches, there are not demonstrable anachronisms of fact.[10]

The nature of divergences between versions is not, however, crucial if we can find reason to believe that such divergences are small or rare. We have seen that there is a little direct evidence to this effect, but there are a number of pieces of indirect evidence. The first is the presence of *tituli* in the manuscripts at *Mur.* 57 and *Font.* 20 (and perhaps *Cael.* 19[11]) marking places where arguments have been omitted. These lacunae are significant for the interpretation of the individual speeches, but they do not argue for a general program of reduction. In fact the scrupulousness with which they are marked should make us more confident that such excisions have not been made elsewhere. It would not have been hard to rewrite so as to eliminate all trace of these arguments. In this connection we should note that the *titulus* of *Font.* 20 (*de crimine vinario, de bello Vocontiorum, de dispositione Hibernorum*) mentions arguments whose omission could not have been inferred from anything in the text. In his letter 1.20, Pliny cites the *titulus* of *Mur.* 57 and one from the now lost *pro Vareno* (§7) to support the contention that speeches were normally trimmed down for publication. He makes it clear that this is his own inference, not an illustration of a fact of which he has independent knowledge. Similarly he argues that *pro Cluentio* and *pro Cornelio*, as published, are not long enough to record Cicero's entire delivered speech. Here again we have Pliny's own inference, directly contradicted by ancient evidence in the case of *pro Cornelio* (Cornelius Nepos *ad* Jerome 23.365M = *Vita Ciceronis* fr. 2 Peter). Thus Pliny's letter does not advance our knowledge of the subject.[12]

Another type of evidence is the close verbal repetition common within many of Cicero's speeches. The best-known examples are *Cael.* 28/41–3 and 35, 38/48–50, but we have seen others above. Heinze (1925:239–45), Humbert (1925), and others have used this repetition as the basis of arguments that some or all of Cicero's speeches are composites of different versions or of different parts of the *actio*. They misunderstand. This repetition is typical of oral discourse (of any era); it is for the benefit of an audience which cannot refer back to a point already made on a previous page. These repetitions share an important feature with the *tituli* discussed above. One can imagine that an author who was completely recomposing an originally oral work for written publication might still add rhetorical questions, *dubitatio*, or the like to establish verisimilitude. It is far less plausible that repetition or labeled omissions would be so used. This is particularly relevant for the repetitions. If Cicero was trying to maintain an oral style, it would be easiest simply to reproduce the original.

Two circumstantial points arise from *argumenta ex silentio*. Cicero did not generally write his speeches out in full before their delivery, but he did write out outline notes—*commentarii*.[13] Both Asconius (87.10–12C) and Quintilian (4.1.69; 10.7.30) claim to have had access to these *commentarii*, and neither notes any divergences between them and the published speeches. This is particularly important in the case of Quintilian, whom we know to have been interested in the relationship of written and delivered orations (12.10.49–57). While far from conclusive, it is interesting that neither notes any additions or omissions in the published texts. The other point is that, if it was conventional to distinguish delivered and published versions, it is surprising that we have no cases where such a distinction is invoked whether truthfully or not. Contrast the tactical appeal to the distinction between an orator's words and his beliefs (*Clu.* 138–42) or the (essentially false) claim of forgery at *Att.* 3.12.2.

Thus there are a number of reasons to believe that the published versions of Cicero's speeches correspond closely, at least in outline, with those that he originally delivered. But is this too much to hope for? Much recent progress has been made in the study of Cicero on the basis of the recognition that he did not write with the intention of being a dispassionate source of "facts" about the Late Roman Republic for later scholars. It is right to be suspicious on these general grounds of the historicity of anything in Cicero, but instead of simply giving up we should rather examine the circumstances of the composition and publication of particular texts (or sets of texts) and judge their value for various historical questions individually. The remainder of this section will suggest that Cicero's reasons for publishing his speeches, while not historiographical *per se*,[14] may have made it advantageous to him to reproduce his delivered orations more-or-less exactly.

First, a pragmatic consideration may have motivated Cicero. One was that his main, perhaps nearly sole, political and professional asset was his skill as an orator. He presumably wanted to extend his reputation beyond those who actually heard him in court. The character of the reputation which he hoped to extend may be suggested by his selection of speeches to publish. In particular one may note the appearance of such technical pieces as *pro Quinctio*, *pro Caecina*, and *pro Tullio*. The program that lies behind this choice seems to emphasize the practical skill of the advocate rather than the abstract aesthetic value of the rhetoric. Cicero need not have published all his speeches for the same reason, but at least one motive seems to have been the reproduction (likely in idealized form) of his actual courtroom triumphs.

In the absence of mass media, Romans must have relied on personal communications for much of their knowledge of each others' doings. Much of Cicero's correspondence is an exchange of news with friends when one or the other is out of town. What Cicero has to report is often a speech he has given, and in some cases (*Att.* 2.1.3: "You will see from the same books both what I did and what I said"; cf. *Fam.* 9.12.2) he explicitly states that he is enclosing the text. Sending these speeches (and requesting them from your friends) seems to have been one of the duties of *amicitia*, "friendship, alliance," (*Att.* 1.13.5, 2.1.3, 2.7.1, 4.5.1; *Fam.* 1.9.23, 9.12.2; *Q. fr.* 3.1.11). Sending the speech more-or-less as delivered would accomplish the informational goal, and significant changes would require some effort but would be of no obvious benefit. There would then be no reason to edit. This inference is supported by the following passage from a letter to Dolabella:

> *I have with me the little speech for Deiotarus which you requested, although I had not pruned it. I am sending it as is; I hope that you will read it in this spirit: a small and meager cause, not worthy of great writing.*

Cicero sends the authentic version despite its inadequacies as a display piece.[15]

Other letters indicate that this distribution of speeches to friends constituted a stage in their publication or even the publication itself. In *Att.* 13.44.3 Cicero tells Atticus to have his staff correct an error in *pro Ligario* (which Brutus had noted), and in *Att.* 13.20.2 he says that it is too late to make certain minor changes Atticus had wanted in *pro Ligario* since it had already been *pervulgata*.[16] At *Att.* 2.7.1 he suggests that he had not sent Atticus a copy of a particular (unknown) speech because it contained a sentiment that he did not actually support ("lest I praise him whom I do not love"). Atticus would surely have known this (or could at least have been informed in a cover letter); Cicero must be worried about broader circulation. Most significant is *Att.* 2.1.3, referred to above. It announces the publication (for Atticus' benefit and that of the general population) of Cicero's collected consular speeches. This published corpus is the same set of texts that is supposed to inform Cicero's close friend and ally. This is a second (and potentially very large) class of published speeches which are liable to be representative of the delivered versions: those speeches that diffused more-or-less directly through his immediate circle of friends.

In writing about the consular orations Cicero makes reference to the "interest of the youth," *adulescentorum studiis*, which also motivates his publication (Stroh 1975:52–54). This leads us to a third possible motive for publication: education. He makes similar remarks at *Q. fr.* 3.1.11 to the effect that the youth have learned his speech against Calventus Marus by heart. Cicero's *philosophica* were educational tools (*TD* 1.1; *Div.* 2.4). He repeatedly makes it clear that the later philosophical treatises are also to be taken as stand-ins for his speeches: they are both means by which he will accomplish his political ends (*Div.* 2.7). There is also some evidence for the reverse: Cicero came to see the publication of his speeches as part of an educational project. We have already cited two passages (*Q. fr.* 3.1.11 and *Att.* 2.1.3) where this seems to have been their use in practice. Cicero also makes the connection programmatically.

Div. 2.4 makes the point that the educational value of the *philosophica* lies in providing examples of philosophical writings in Latin. The beginning of the *Tusculan Disputations* puts the speeches in the same context:

> *Greek learning overcame us in every area of letters, though it was easy to conquer those who were not fighting back. But we quickly embraced the orator. Philosophy has lain silent until now.*

> (*TD* 1.3, 5, 6)

TD explicitly makes the publication of the speeches and the treatises different phases of the same program:

> *Although we realize that many will be eager to say otherwise [than that there is a value to writing this philosophy], which we could not avoid unless we did not write at all. For if our speeches, which we wished to be approved by the judgment of the many—for that is an ability that deals with the people and the end of eloquence is the approval of the listeners—... what do we think would happen, since we apparently cannot rely on the support here of the same populace as before?*

> (*TD* 2.3)

Particularly interesting here is the reference to the difference in style between the two genres. We noted above that the purpose of the philosophical part of the program was exemplary; this is typical of ancient educational practice.[17] This explains the style of the published orations. The best (and easiest to produce) examples for teaching how to write courtroom orations would be actual courtroom orations. This motivation is strongly consistent with the traces of oral style which we have already noted in Cicero's published speeches.

To summarize, it is not crucial to the arguments above that the published orations closely follow the delivered versions. After all, as Zetzel (1993:450) emphasizes, Cicero put these speeches forth as if they were things he would say in court.[18] But close reproduction does give them a sharper focus. The direct evidence for relationship between the delivered and published versions of Cicero's speeches is weak. What there is suggests that most of the changes consist of small-scale stylistic polishing and occasional brief additions. There is little or no evidence for changes in the substance of any of Cicero's arguments. Stylistic details of the published speeches are characteristic of oral discourse; the simplest explanation for this is that they derive directly from the original. A study of Cicero's implicit and explicit motivations for promulgating his speeches (advertising, information, and education) shows that it would have been to his advantage to reproduce fairly closely the texts of the speeches as he delivered them in court.

APPENDIX C

Some Nontrials

Here I collect trials that, on certain published accounts, would be relevant to the arguments about *vis* and *maiestas* in chapter 4 but which can be shown on closer examination not to bear on the issues discussed there.

Vis: In two of these trials (*TLRR* 184 [defendant unknown] and 316 [Dolabella]) there is simply no evidence for either the charge or its alleged factual basis. *TLRR* 334 (Sempronius Rufus) cannot be a *vis* trial. Rufus later made a counteraccusation of *vis* against his prosecutor, to delay the start of his own trial; *vis* accusations received special, accelerated hearing (*extra ordinem*) before the courts (*Fam.* 8.8.1). If he had been cited for *vis* in the first place, this strategy would have made no sense.[19] Tuccius, the original prosecutor, was accused of *vis* (*TLRR* 335), but we do not know the alleged basis, and the accusation was apparently unsubstantiated in any case.

Gruen (1974:227) suggests that the trials of Camurtius and Caesernius illustrate that *vis*, as a criminal offense, need not have been *contra rem publicam* under the *lex Plautia*. That was apparently the position of Caelius' prosecutors, but we do not have enough evidence to decide between their view and Cicero's suggestion that the defendants were convicted primarily on the strength of general moral turpitude. It is also unclear whether the allegedly missing factor in their cases was political or whether it was actual violence. In any case we do not know enough about the trials to make much of them.[20]

Maiestas: The case of the tribune Manilius (*TLRR* 210) was actually a double trial like that of Cornelius. Manilius was originally tried for *repetundae* (*TLRR* 205), but the proceedings were never completed. Some have argued that the second trial was for *maiestas*. However, since Philips' (1970:603–5) arguments from the relevant text of Asconius and from the prosopography show that the Bobbio scholiast (the only source for the latter charge) is probably mistaken,[21] we may suspect a continuation of the *maiestas* charge. And so this trial too is not relevant. The charge in the trial in 59 of Cicero's former consular colleague Antonius (*TLRR* 241) is not known with certainty. A few references in Cicero such as *pro Caelio* 15 (Caelius had been Antonius' prosecutor) suggest that Antonius was accused of complicity in the Catilinarian conspiracy:

> *Not only if he [Caelius] had been in on the conspiracy, but even if he had not been resolute in opposition to that crime, he would never have tried to ornament his own youth by prosecution of the conspiracy.*

> (*Cael.* 15)

However, as Gruen (1973) points out, this is an unlikely accusation against the official conqueror of Catiline; rather we should accept other sources which tie this trial to Antonius' stint as governor of Macedonia.[22]

Cicero's emphasis on Antonius' known Catilinarian connections (undoubtedly used to impugn his character whatever the actual charge) is probably caused by a combination of Catilinarian accusations against Cicero's client and Cicero's own obsession with those events.[23] Some have suggested that the charge was *maiestas*, based on military failures in Macedonia.[24] If this is the case, our hypothesis that the charge of *maiestas* will come to be restricted to nonviolent offenses will be confirmed. However, the only specific charge cited in the ancient sources is *repetundae* (*SB* 94St.), and this fits at least equally well with the established connection to his term as governor.[25] In this, the most likely case, Antonius' trial has no bearing on the question of *maiestas* and *vis*.

Notes

1. Obviously, I am farther still from more traditional jurisprudential studies of Roman law. To the extent that this study focuses on actual practice in individual legal situations, it aspires to some similarity to Champlin 1991.

2. Evidence for the precise wording of individual statutes, where it exists, is collected in Crawford 1996.

3. Unlike the *iudices* in a civil trial, criminal jurors voted immediately and without consultation with an expert *concilium* or even with each other.

4. Cf. Foucault 1977.

5. One might argue that laws are only significant for social practice insofar as they influence the evaluation, official or unofficial, by individual agents of their own actions (or potential actions) or those of others. This is one of the central contentions of Cohen (1991), who considers modern theories of social order. A similarly sceptical conception of the relationship of law and social practice seems to underlie the (more judgmental) formulations of Hor. *Carm.* 3.24.35–36: *leges sine moribus vanae*; Tac. *Germ.* 19: *plus ibi boni mores valent quam alibi bonae leges*; and Plaut. *Trin.* 1037–40. However, the ancient authors are not interested in the point that laws and norms can produce effects other than simple compliance (cf. Cohen [1991:22–23] on traditional sociological accounts).

6. The common translation "embezzlement" is misleading; see chapter 6, note 11.

7. For instance, Perelman and Olbrechts-Tyteca 1958:31–33; a representative remark is: "The important thing in argumentation is not knowing what the orator himself considers true or probative, but what are the opinions of those to whom the argument is addressed." Of course it is the emphasis, not the idea, that is modern.

8. And more concisely at *Tusc.* 2.3: "The aim of oratory is to win the approval of one's audience." Judging by the criminal trials in *TLRR*, in general about 46 percent of defendants were acquitted, while Cicero was successful in about 81 percent of his defenses (and in two of two prosecutions). We should keep in mind, however, both the uncertainty that attaches to the outcome of many individual prosecutions and our ignorance of how representative our sample is. These figures also do not take into ac-

count the many trials we know of that were resolved without a formal verdict. These provisos should be kept in mind when considering all statistics that will be derived below from *TLRR*.

9. On this point cf. the similar observations of Vasaly (1993 : 209 – 16).

10. Gotoff (1986) gives an account of the potential difficulties.

11. See Robinson 1995 : 16, 44 – 45.

12. See Robinson 1995 : 19 – 20. Most, though not all, of the evidence she cites deals with delicts, not the offenses tried by the *iudicia publica* (but see Claud. Sat. *D.* 48.19.16 pr).

13. I treat this subject at slightly greater length in Riggsby 1997.

14. Rhetorical figures: Craig 1993; self-reference: May 1988; ambiance: Geffcken 1973 and Axer 1989. None of these scholars necessarily adopts either of the more extreme views of the courts described in the remainder of this paragraph.

15. Zetzel 1993 : 451, 450.

16. Swarney 1993 : 155. Cf. "The judges were asked, then, to judge the truth of competing portraits, not the validity of evidence" (153).

17. Thus it is notions of "evidence" and of "murder," "extortion," and the like that have been wrongly imported into our study of the Roman courts, rather than the idea of "court" itself.

18. Cf. *Acad.* 2.146 and Frier 1985 : 203 – 4. It should be admitted, however, that the passage in *de Officiis* seems to envision a civil rather than a criminal trial. One might argue that its validity should not be extended.

19. *[Iudicatum] religiosum est quod iurati legibus iudicarunt.*

20. Cf. *ad Her.* 4.47: *officium est.... testis dicere quae sciat aut audierit.* The remark is part of an exemplary oratorical sample.

21. The fervency of these disputes is particularly notable in light of current estimations of the lack of real class distinctions between the two orders. See, for example, Nicolet 1966 : 285 – 315, Hopkins 1983 : 110 – 11, and Brunt 1988 : 144 – 93.

22. There are, of course, numerous cases in which an advocate claims that a specific prosecution was mounted purely out of personal animosity.

23. In addition to the letters cited below see *Fam.* 3.11.2 and 5.17.2.

24. On the influence of politics and bribery on the outcome of cases see Kelly 1966 : 31 – 68, Nicolet 1980 : 336 – 41, and Perelli 1994 : 245 – 80, though all underestimate the fuzziness (equally obscured by tendentious ancient advocates) of the line that separates undue use of social status and "legitimate" inference from character in a Roman court.

25. I accept in the last sentence of the passage Shackleton Bailey's reading of *lacrimans* for the manuscripts' *criminans* and the concomitant interpretation that Clodius was the defense advocate.

26. This kind of generalization is recommended as a deliberate strategy by Cicero at *Or.* 45 – 46 and criticized at *Cael.* 29.

27. There is more that could be said about the role of jurors even given the above. Should they merely arbitrate between the parties' formal presentations or take various, more activist, steps to produce their own account? See Frier 1985:215–20.

28. The historical tradition almost unanimously attests to Rutilius' innocence, but that tradition is heavily influenced both by Rutilius' own account in his published memoirs and by Cicero's personal ties to him. However, traces of another tradition can be discerned in Tac. *Ann.* 3.66. See Hendrickson 1933:153–75 and Kallet-Marx 1990:122–24.

29. Shackleton Bailey in his commentary on the letters to Atticus *ad loc.* suggests that Cicero refers here to the three books of *de Oratore*, but no certain conclusion is possible.

30. The Latin reads: *Catilina, si iudicatum erit meridie non lucere, certus erit competitor.*

31. Also cited by Rufinianus 42.17–20 Halm. A suspiciously similar remark is attributed to Cicero in the context of his defense of Munatius (*TLRR* 325) at Plut. *Cic.* 25.1.

32. Rufinianus claims that the trick lay in giving the jurors many issues to decide, instead of just one; however, the late rhetorician's authority is suspect (and see Alexander 1982 on the particulars of the case). Further literature includes Humbert 1938 and Stroh 1975:232, with their bibliography.

33. By "facts" I mean here the facts as understood by the individual advocate.

34. Gotoff 1986:123. *Brut.* 184–201 explicitly advocates such a results-oriented approach. *De Or.* 2.178 goes so far as to suggest that jurors are better swayed by emotion than reason. This passage does not, however, claim that this is best done by appealing overtly to those emotions rather than reason. In fact, at *de Or.* 2.310 Cicero claims that when making rational arguments, the speaker should only appear to be doing that, while weaving ethical and pathetic elements into the fabric of the speech unnoticed: *Una ex tribus his rebus* [sc. *docere, conciliare, permovere*] *res prae nobis est ferenda, ut nihil aliud nisi docere velle videamur.*

35. A somewhat similar critique of Gotoff can be found in Rose 1995:384–85. Alexander (1993b) establishes that the announced audiences (the *iudices* in most of the cases we have, but potentially the entire *populus* in a comitial trial) are the primary audience of judicial speeches. This, of course, does not mean that other audiences would not appreciate the same oratory. Cicero (*Brut.* 290) claims that you can always tell a great orator at a distance, even without hearing him, by watching the reactions of the officials, jurors, and corona (all apparently acting as one). Nowhere in this passage, however, does he suggest that pleasing these other audiences should be a goal for the orator, much less one which should be indulged at the expense of persuading the jurors. And in a very similar passage (*Brut.* 200) he makes nearly the same point about being able to see the effects of good oratory, but mentions only jurors.

36. It has been suggested (e.g., Landgraf 1914: *ad* §32 *patrem meum*) that Sex.

Roscius could have claimed to have killed his father legally as part of the proscriptions. Even if this was factually and legally sound, Cicero's rejection of the strategy in *pro Roscio* seems wise.

37. The idea of truth as "trope" is, of course, inspired by Hayden White's writings (esp. 1978:1–25, 101–20), but his preferred tropes (metaphor, metonymy, synecdoche, and irony) are too broad to be of much analytical use here. See White 1978:114 and Scott 1990:208, 222 on the objectivity effect.

38. Thus Byron de la Beckwith's defense never raised the claim that Medgar Evers was an "uppity" black man who needed to be dealt with (or any other overtly racist argument), even if we believe that was what the jurors had in mind when they voted to acquit. On the contrary, a successful defense required the claim that de la Beckwith was not even present at the time of the crime, i.e., a claim that was salient to a charge of murder as defined in court (Massengil 1994:180–209, esp. 208). Even decades later, while patrons in a cafe in Jackson, Mississippi, could express sympathy with de la Beckwith's supposed motive in the killing, a juror who voted to acquit still felt compelled to explain his vote in terms of alleged "contradictions" in the evidence (Nossiter 1994:3, 132–34).

39. A similar distinction is made by Alexander (1993a:239–40).

40. If such actually existed. The current orthodoxy is reasonably skeptical of the significance of faction: Beard and Crawford 1985:67–86, Brunt 1988:443–502, North 1990, and Harris 1990.

41. For an extensive discussion of the varying, often overlapping, and sometimes even contradictory motivations for prosecution see David 1992:297–589. In addition to persons who accused for reasons specific to individual cases, David (1992:533–35) notes a few persons who seem to have made a career of prosecution. Also useful is Epstein 1987:110–26, but his main distinction (between *inimicitia* and faction) is neutralized in the present context.

42. It is necessary to note that he did not, in fact, prosecute his brother-in-law D. Iunius Silanus, and that Cicero claims to have prosecuted Verres *gratia patrocinii, not causa rei publicae* (*Off.* 2.50). Cicero, however, may have been interested more in advertising the existence of his clientela than in justifying his prosecution.

43. E.g., C. Norbanus (*TLRR* 86), Q. Servilius Caepio (*TLRR* 88), M. Lucullus (*TLRR* 204), C. Rabirius (*TLRR* 220–21), A. Licinius Archias (*TLRR* 235), L. Calpurnius Bestia (*TLRR* 268–69), and P. Sestius (*TLRR* 270–71).

44. E.g., L. Marcius Philippus, M. Aemilius Scaurus, and Q. Servilius Caepio (*TLRR* 95–97) and C. Norbanus (*TLRR* 86). Cf. Epstein 1987:116–19.

45. In fact, even the prosecution may not have expected a conviction. Eric Orlin suggests to me *per litteras* that such delayed prosecution may have been staged for the sake of display as, essentially, a form of invective. If so, the point here is unaffected.

46. Cicero simplifies the situation here. The secret ballot for most trials was introduced in 137 but only extended to *perduellio* trials in 106 (*Leg.* 3.36).

47. There were 2,400 or perhaps 1,800 knights with the *equus publicus*; see Nicolet 1966:113–23. There is no real way to estimate the numbers of the *tribuni aerarii*, but if they are a lesser set of quasi-officials of equestrian census then we might expect roughly as many again as the true knights. If they are a separate census class, then their number could be much higher.

48. *Contra* Kunkel (1962), to be discussed in the final chapter.

49. The first two examples are from an illuminating discussion in Scheppele 1991: 54–59. At pp. 62–65 she explains how even in our more juristically oriented culture some rhetorical effort must be expended to enforce the technical definitions of such terms. The phenomenon certainly occurs in Roman private law; see Watson 1974:127, 184 and Gaius' (quite typical) definition of *iniuria* (3.220).

50. On the terms see Cody 1973.

51. So *Clu.* 74–76; see Greenidge 1901:497-98 and Strachan-Davidson 1912:129–36. This may not have been true at a very early period: the *lex Acilia* (*FIRA* 1.7.46–49) seems to suggest that those who voted *non liquet* were removed before the final decision, but that need not affect our period. Cloud (1994:530) notes that there is no clear reference to a *non liquet* vote being allowed after the *lex Aurelia* of 70 and therefore that that law may have abolished the possibility of voting thus; on the other hand, Jones (1972:73) notes the possibility of *non liquet* votes in Clodius' extraordinary trial for *incestum* in 61.

52. Greenidge 1901:416. *Lex Acilia* 58–59, *Rab. Post.* 8–9.

53. The topic is covered by *D.* 22.3, which deals entirely (except perhaps for Marcellus *D.* 22.3.10 on the preemptive value of public records) with civil matters. Widely differing views have been expressed in the secondary literature, such as those of Pugliese (1956; 1960) and Longo (1960). Even on the expansive view of Pugliese (1960: 393–98), which I am inclined to accept, theory of proof was regarded as the domain of orators, not jurists, during the Republic, and was in any case primarily a development of the private law (cf. Lemosse 1944:159). Trajan's dictum that it was better that a guilty man escape than that an innocent one be condemned (preserved in Ulp. *D.* 48.19.5 pr) is a philosophical justification for a particular decision on trials *in absentia*, not a general legal rule.

54. Greenidge 1901:428–33 and Jones 1972:58–59. The cover term for the presiding officer, regardless of his political rank, is *quaesitor* (Greenidge 1901:417).

55. For opportunities for influence in the pretrial proceedings, see Kunkel 1963: 753, 755–56. *I Verr.* 32 suggests that the presiding officer counted the votes.

56. Mommsen (1899:422), Greenidge (1901:481, 495), and Strachan-Davidson (1912:125) comment on the absence of rules of evidence. No one, however, would have been in a good position to prevent the *quaesitor* from making informal comments on the proceedings. Cf. *ad Her.* 4.47.

57. Strachan-Davidson 1912:128; for an explicit statement of this principle see *Clu.* 159. Cf. Lemosse (1944:158–80) on the comparable freedom of private *iudices*.

58. Asc. 45.23–26C; cf. Rosc. 84, [Asc.] 141St.

59. On *quaestiones extraordinariae* see Strachan-Davidson 1912:225–45 and Kunkel 1963:732–33.

60. *I Verr.* 20, *II Verr.* 3.137, 146. Interestingly, Asconius (see note 52) suggests that his severity consisted precisely in his application of the *cui bono* maxim.

61. See Garnsey (1966:177–80), *contra* Kunkel (1963:733).

62. This procedure is incorrectly explained by Greenidge (1901:465–66). My discussion of the *inscriptio* is largely based on the extensive treatment of Alexander (1982); I will not attempt to cite him systematically. See also Jones 1972:64.

63. For the attribution see Girard 1913:344–51.

64. See *Inv.* 2.58 on procedure and above on penalty.

65. For a similar view see Mommsen 1899:385.

66. Nor, if *Inv.* 2.58 is any indication, could the defense advocate expect any aid from the presiding officer in these matters.

67. For references and further examples, see chapter 4, note 11, Bauman 1967: 85–87, and Jones 1972:79–80. Jones, however, gives too much weight to dual trials caused by Pompey's very limited *ad hoc* legislation in 52 and to the theoretical possibility that early laws (such as the *lex Lutatia de vi*) were not, as usually assumed, superseded by later legislation on the same topics.

68. The *tribuni aerarii* were originally minor treasury officials, perhaps military paymasters (Varro *LL* 5.181, fr. 224 [= Gellius *NA* 6.10.2]). Eventually the name came to refer to a property class, apparently immediately below the *equites*. For the suggestion that it may refer to persons of equestrian census, but who had not been awarded the public horse, see chapter 5, notes 84, 86. This division of the juries is the result of the *lex Aurelia* of 70; see Asc. 17.5–7C, 67.11–14C, 78.29–30C; *SB* 94.24–26St. This holds for all the cases discussed in this study except those of Sex. Roscius of Ameria (in 81) and of Verres (70, but before the change [*I Verr.* 1])—there the jury would have been entirely senatorial.

69. For the broad extent of formal rhetorical training in Cicero's day, see *de Or.* 1.16; this passage may involve a certain amount of overstatement, but there is no reason for him to misrepresent the lines of the situation. The availability of rhetorical education outside the main political and intellectual centers (*Caecil.* 39) also suggests that such training extended well beyond the senatorial nobility. In addition, the public nature of trials (and *contiones*) would have given many people some general familiarity with rhetorical technique. For rhetorical education in this period see more generally Bonner 1977:68–74 and Suet. *Rhet. et Gram.* (though the former takes *de Or.* too literally as a source for the views of the interlocutors). For the role of apprenticeship in the orator's education (the *tirocinium fori*) see Bonner 1977:84–85.

70. Conley and O'Barr 1990:78–81, 109–11.

71. And, in fact, the jurors in a given trial were selected from a fairly small list (the praetor's *album*) made up at the beginning of each year (*Clu.* 121), then perhaps further subdivided in advance for the particular courts. Hence the juror could know be-

forehand what kind of trial he was likely to serve in. See Kunkel 1963:749–55, esp. 753. Prosecution was also sufficiently likely during the lifetime of (at least) a senator to draw his attention to the courts; see Alexander 1993a.

72. For present purposes the distinction between trial before a *unus iudex* and multiple *recuperatores* is not particularly important. By contrast Roman jurors are in a far stronger position than American ones (see Lakoff 1990:91–92, 96–99). Criminal jurors may also benefit from extraneous "knowledge" of notorious cases that civil jurors would not ordinarily have.

73. The arguments at *de Or.* 1.165–200, 234–50, and *Part. Or.* 99–100 assume that, for better or for worse, the level of legal knowledge among advocates is low.

74. On *altercatio* see Kennedy 1972:15, 277, 507, 530 and Frier 1985:208–9.

75. Note that on the (very rare) occasions when Cicero makes a statutory argument in a criminal case he appeals either to the "obvious" meaning of the law (*Clu.* 143: *lex ipsa renuntiavit*) or to broad, practical experience of the law (*Rab. Post.* 9).

76. Ziegenmueller and Dause 1990:153–55.

77. On the use of the published speeches as representative of what Cicero said in the courtroom, see Appendix B.

78. I have derived this sense from the use of the word in the theory of competitive academic debate, though its use there tends to be normative rather than descriptive. See Zarefsky 1987 and Zeigenmueller and Dause 1990; I thank Joe Bellon for bringing this literature to my attention.

79. Or, more dramatically, he sometimes attempts to shift the entire "communicative situation" from courtroom to something else, e.g., theater. Then the implicit judging paradigm calls on the jurors to act not as jurors but, e.g., theatrical spectators. See Axer 1989 and below.

CHAPTER 2

1. The standard handbook discussions of *ambitus* and related matters are Zumpt 1869:217–34, 250–63, 367–91, and Mommsen 1899:865–75. Recent work on *ambitus* in the Late Republic includes Linderski 1985, Deniaux 1987, Lintott 1990, and Yakobson 1992. For a more historical perspective and particularly the possible relationships between *ambitus* and (respectively) *repetundae* and sumptuary legislation, see Fascione 1984 and Chenoll Alfaro 1984.

2. The other offenses said to demand simple denial are *res repetundae*, homicide, and *peculatus*.

3. At *Off.* 2.52–64 the distinction between *largitio* and *liberalitas* is even less clear.

4. Fascione's (1984:28–31, 44–47) reconstruction is highly speculative and provides an implausible dating for the first permanent court (cf. note 5 below). We will consider the earliest (fifth and fourth century) laws below.

5. A very probable *terminus ante quem* is established by the series of trials in 115 (Plut. *Mar.* 5). The *terminus post quem* is the *lex Calpurnia de repetundis* which set up

the first *quaestio perpetua* in 149 (*Off.* 2.75; *Brut.* 106). It is just possible that *Off* 2.75 is only referring to the first court *de repetundis*, but *Brut.* 106 ("L. enim Piso") is unambiguous on the absolute priority of this court (*contra* Fascione [1984:56–59]).

6. Cicero's own *lex Tullia* of 63 seems to have been a fine-tuning of the previous law, adding exile to the penalty (*Mur.* 47, 89; *Planc.* 89; *SB* 78–79St.) and forbidding gladiatorial shows by candidates within two years before the election (*Vat.* 37 and the equivalent passage of *pro Sestio* [§133]; *SB* 140St.; Dio 37.29.1 [who limits the exile to ten years]). See also Crawford 1996:761–62.

7. Taylor (1949:67 and note 98) argues that the *lex Calpurnia* extended penalties for *ambitus* to the *divisores* (bribery agents), basing her case on Asconius 75.24–76.2C, which describes their violent resistance to the law. Only a little before, however, Asconius has quoted Cicero as saying in *pro Cornelio* that Cornelius' proposal, rather than Calpurnius', was aimed at *divisores* (Asc. 74.21–75.1C). Dio (36.38) also records a conflict between the *ambitus* laws proposed by Cornelius and by Calpurnius. I would suggest that the extent to which the *lex Calpurnia* attacked the *divisores* is open to question (though something about the law apparently disturbed them).

8. Cited in reduced form at §72: *At spectacula sunt tributim data et ad prandium volgo vocati.*

9. A similar comparison has been suggested by Leeman (1982:219), and, in the reverse direction, by Nicolet (1980:304). Although the authenticity of the work is subject to question (cf. Henderson 1950, Nisbet 1961), the balance of current argument tends, rightly, to support it: see Balsdon 1963, Richardson 1971, Ramsey 1980b, David et al. 1973, Nardo 1970: esp. 3–28, 129–37, and Fedeli 1987:14–18.

10. Rotondi (1912:368) and Perelli (1994:80) have tried to connect the *lex Antia* of ca. 68 to this aspect of *ambitus* legislation. That law forbade (among other things) that magistrates or magistrates elect *(capturi magistratus) go to* dinners unless hosted by certain persons. However, the other provisions of the law were apparently more traditional sumptuary restrictions. It is easier to imagine that the *lex Antia* was intended to prevent the use of the banquets to influence magistrates, since it is far from clear how it would have discouraged *ambitus* in any form.

11. The best Roman parallel is *Q. fr.* 1.1, which advises Quintus Cicero at some length on governing a province where he has already been in charge for two years. In general, see Stowers 1986:91–94.

12. Note also the use of *sodalis* as a clearly positive term at *Sull.* 7, *Mur.* 56, and even *Planc.* 29. However, the change in the legal usage seems to be reflected at *Planc.* 29: *quos tu si sodalis vocas, officiosam amicitiam nomine inquinas criminoso.* Linderski (1961:113) rightly points out that the difference between "legitimate" (religious?) and "illegitimate" (political) *sodalitates* and *collegia* must have been more a matter of perspective than of fact.

13. Thus Taylor (1949:210) and Treggiari (1969:169–77), both following in part DeRobertis (1938:110ff.) (repeated in DeRobertis [1971:117–26]). Linderski's (1961) rebuttal of DeRobertis deserves attention but is not conclusive. In any case it still pre-

serves a significant role for the suppression of Clodius' gangs. On Clodius' political style, see Benner 1987. I mean "populist" here in the sense of one who plays heavily to a relatively broad electorate, not necessarily one who has their interests at heart. See further at chapter 4, note 32.

14. On *beneficium* in the context of gift-exchange see Dixon 1993.

15. On this distinction see Sahlins 1972:185–230 and Gregory 1982:41–69. I use "market exchange" for the more conventional "commodity exchange"; "commodity" is better used as a cover term for both gift and market items (cf. note 20 below). The characterization that follows is drawn largely from Gregory 1982. What will be sketched here as an either/or distinction is in fact better thought of as a continuum with pure gift and pure market exchange serving as the extremes.

16. See Appadurai's (1986b:13) definition of the "commodity situation" in the "life" of an object. "Situation" is the right way to look at the question, but I focus here on the gift situation.

17. On the characterization and analysis of the Pompeiian electoral posters see also Franklin 1980 and Jongman 1988:284–89.

18. For another possible example of open-ended exchange of favors in an electoral context, see Crawford 1994:146.

19. Of course, Quintus may merely have been representing the voters to themselves in an idealized manner, just as he was presenting his brother's candidacy in an idealized fashion.

20. For some exceptions to this generalization see the essays in Parry and Bloch 1989, and, in a more theoretical vein, Appadurai 1986a and Ferguson 1989. Their response to the approach of Gregory (1982) is sound, but there is less conflict than they suggest, especially if we keep in mind the caveats of notes 15, 16 above and the attached paragraph. Another case which shows Romans attaching market value (as usual) to money is to be found in the development of Roman contract law as discussed by Watson (1985:10, 25).

21. As Linderski (1985:89–90) observes, "If you do not immediately control the voters, you must pay for their support. This can be done in two ways: by means of legislation appealing to special interest groups or directly by handing out money and gifts." There are, in fact, devices intermediate between these two.

22. Quintus recommends, moreover, that Cicero promise everything he could possibly do, and perhaps more, especially when he did not have to meet a specific deadline (*CP* 45–48). The strategy remains popular today.

23. Livy gives as the motive protection of plebeians from overzealous patrician candidates, but this is probably an inference from the fact of the law and the presumed context of the "conflict of the orders." It is possible that the law itself is a fabrication on the basis of a much more ambiguous notice in the Fasti such as *album proscriptum*, perhaps referring to the roll of citizens or senators (see Ogilvie 1965:574–75). Nonetheless, such a reconstruction would show that Livy (or a source) thought general limitations on campaigning (not just cash) were plausible.

24. Linderski (1985:90) registers some doubts about the authenticity of the law because it is a tribunician law predating the *lex Hortensia*, but the level of detail and the surface discrepancy from the subject of later *ambitus* laws suggests an essentially trustworthy report. See also the general comments of Mitchell (1990:186–206) on the role of early tribunes in legislation, though he goes too far in denying any legislative initiative to the regular magistrates.

25. Linderski (1985:90): "Electoral *largitio* was always an instrument of wresting electoral *clientelae* from their inherited allegiances." See also perceptive remarks by Gruen (1991:255–57). But simple cash payments do not exhaust the means for this. Legislation against *ambitus* would ideally check all these means. Conversely, the trial of Plancius will suggest that generosity in maintaining this *clientela* was not so clearly objectionable.

26. This is precisely what Earl (1960:240–41; 1967:32–33) finds for the meaning of *ambitio* in Plautus; cf. note 34 below on the relationship between *ambitio* and *ambitus*.

27. Mommsen (1899:865) observes: "The search for electoral support . . . is in republican society a necessary element, but also a necessary evil."

28. In the opening section of *pro Cluentio*, Cicero claims that he will take on an expanded burden *ut omnes intellegant nihil me nec subterfugere voluisse reticendo nec obscurare dicendo*. That a jury would accept this shows that irrelevancy is a legitimate defense, though it does not necessarily show what counts as "irrelevant." Hence *Clu.* 1 is a clear, if somewhat different, example of the use of paradigm-setting for ethical advantage.

29. The offer (§§47–48) to review the voting of every tribe singulatim, which clearly cannot be taken seriously, is another example of such a bluff.

30. Cf. *Planc.* 47.

31. Cf. *Mur.* 70.

32. Here I follow Beck's bracketing of *passim* as an intrusive gloss (note also the lack of a conjunction). As Cicero cites the law above only the word *volgo* appears in either clause (*Mur.* 67). Since *passim* would, if anything, strengthen the definition he is about to make he would have included it there too if it were part of the text. Also the violation of the form of the preceding answers detracts considerably from the rhetorical force of the passage.

33. Cf. Adamietz (1989:223–24): "[T]he incidents criticized as violations of the law proved in reality to be in accordance with social and political norms." See also his note at 71c.

34. For a discussion of *ambitus/ambitio* see Hellegouarc'h 1972:208–11. There is no way to distinguish the meanings etymologically, and usages overlap considerably, but in general *ambitus* is more likely to retain the concrete sense of "walking around" instead of the more abstract sense of "seeking political power." In the abstract sense either word can potentially refer to corrupt electioneering (cf. *OLD* s.vv.), especially in Plautus and Sallust. *Ambitus*, however, is unexceptioned in naming laws and courts.

Pro Sulla 1 appears to use *ambitio* as a euphemism for *ambitus*. See also Adamietz (1989) at 72c.

35. Leeman (1982:221) recognizes (without demonstration; he appears not to have seen Craig 1979) this change of status and notes that it is even foreshadowed in the parenthetical remark *sive ambitio . . . sive liberalitas* of the previous section. There, however, it is firmly subordinated to a denial and hence to the *constitutio coniecturalis*.

36. As Classen (1985:161) points out, the defendant Murena is also incidentally aligned with the *innocentes, impotentes, calamitosi,* and *cives in periculo . . . et in pernicie* (§59) when Cicero explicitly draws out the "moral" of his tales.

37. Craig (1979:149), however, has doubts as to whether the guilt of Cotta and Galba is actually meant to come into play at this point.

38. For Cotta see Val. Max. 8.1.11. For Galba see *Brut.* 89–90 and *de Or.* 1.228.

39. For the term and a commentary on the passage see Bürge 1974.

40. On the trivializing familiar language of §§23–28 see Laurand 1931:279–81.

41. Though such language might serve to preserve the exclusivity of juristic activity, which is, at this period, still near the peak of its prestige. See Kunkel 1967:38–61 and esp. *Off.* 2.65.

42. This case is similar to the famed *causa Curiana (TLRR* 93 and Vaughn 1985 for references); there the two opposed paradigms (based on *scriptum* and *voluntas*) were explicitly at the center of the case.

43. For the notion of "resonance" see Craig 1979:3–4 (and *passim*) and A. Kurke 1989:5 (and *passim*). It refers to the repetition of themes or motifs which produces a familiarity and resulting credibility for the audience.

44. In a somewhat similar argument at *Planc.* 37–44 Cicero uses this same authority to argue not for *mos* as opposed to *lex*, but for a particular interpretation of the *lex Licinia*. Note that in this section Cicero attributes the passage of the law entirely to Sulpicius, conveniently suppressing the fact that he himself sponsored the legislation. Cf. also Classen 1985:156.

45. Of course, at the global level this disassociation helps Cicero with his continuing ethical dilemma of being both author of the *lex Tullia* and advocate of one charged under that law.

46. Here and throughout I use "ethos" and "ethical" to refer, respectively, to the depiction of character and to things having to do with that depiction, whether the character in question is that of an advocate, the defendant, or otherwise. This sense of the terms is nearer to Aristotle's (*Rhet.* 1356a4–6) or Cicero's (*de Or.* 2.183–85) than to Quintilian's (6.2), though somewhat broader than any of the three.

47. This distinction between ethical arguments with and without behavioral inferences can be maintained despite the strong Roman notion of the immutability of *ingenium* (see May 1988:6 and notes 26–29 and Adamietz 1989:104), since it is a tactical issue whether an advocate chooses to mention or emphasize the inferences that he could legitimately draw. Berry (1996a:275) brings together arguments suggesting that the notion of fixed character was not widely held and was adopted only when it was

tactically convenient. If it were not widely held, it is hard to see how it would ever give significant tactical advantage (I hope to discuss this point at greater length elsewhere).

48. Adamietz (1989:104): "In Roman practice (as emerges from Cicero's speeches) the investigation of the *vita ante acta* was not limited to the question of whether there already existed some identical or similar offense, but the whole person was evaluated in an all-embracing form, without anyone's sense that this part was *extra causam.*" As a description, this is broadly correct, but it implies (I think falsely) that there is no difference between the specific and general inquiries.

49. Cicero's ethos is the main topic of May 1988.

50. See also May 1988:62–64, 118, 120–21). It is interesting to note that in both cases Cicero praises the opponent's *nobilitas*, only to claim later that the respective noble ancestors are from so long ago that no one even remembers them (*Planc.* 58; *Mur.* 16).

51. The summary following in the text represents (at least in outline) the positions of Craig (1979:145–46; 1986:229), Leeman (1982:223–25), and Kennedy (1972:185). Adamietz (1989:93: "The argument that two consuls must take office at the new year was the basis for Cicero's success in this case") takes a similar position, but it should be noted that he later (p. 231) implies that *ambitus* cases are inevitably political. Classen (1985) intentionally considers only local effects (p. 13).

52. The audience is, however, prepared for this line of argument by the brief mention of the need for two consuls in §4 and by the more extensive discussion of the Cataline problem in another context at §§48–53. Cf. Adamietz 1989:93, 188.

53. Also, and to a lesser extent, at *pro Sulla* 79: "Strengthen the common citadel of the good, block the escape of the evil."

54. And recall that the essential point of *Planc.* 8 and 14 was to request that the jurors *not* make policy, as if this were a real danger.

55. See Ludwig 1982:232–36 and Michel 1960:158–73. This use of the phrase *in utramque partem* is postclassical, but it appears in the literature above, and in a strictly oratorical context there is little danger of confusion with the original definition of "arguing both sides of the same dispute."

56. Craig 1979, 1985; Ludwig 1982.

57. And if we take the *constitutio definitiva* of §73 seriously, it is the third line of defense. According to Craig (1985:136) such a tripartite structure is a Ciceronian innovation (at least in extant speeches), and even among his work only once structures an entire speech *(pro Quinctio)*.

58. *Contra* Leeman (1982:207).

59. Leeman 1982:213; May 1988:63–64.

60. Craig (1979:110–11) points out that much of the *contentio dignitatis* is actually devoted to questions of popularity (though they are inextricably linked to other issues).

61. For instance Adamietz 1989:111 (and at §15) and Craig 1990:80. Contested already by Gotoff (1993:297–99).

62. Brunt (1965:15) can cite a total of eleven speeches (including these two) in which Cicero claims that an opposing attorney was an *amicus*.

63. Craig 1979:110–11.

64. Cf. Adamietz (1989) on §§15–53.

65. Cf. the distinction made in *Planc.* 60 between the roughly eight hundred men who had been consuls (apparently deservedly) and the 10 percent *(vix decimam partem)* who were truly worthy of glory.

66. Cf. Adamietz (1989:28–29): "The task of the juror was clearly seen as the determination of whether the accused could be tolerated as a member of the citizenry or not, and his general character was relevant to this issue."

67. For yet another version of the master virtue *(iustitia)* see *Off.* 3.28 with Atkins 1990.

68. For *beneficium* in this context, see *Red. Pop.* 22–23, *benefici* (bis), *beneficiis*.

69. This claim, too, appears immediately on his return from exile: *Red. Sen.* 2, *Red Pop.* 5.

70. Note particularly: *L. vero Apuleio hunc tanti facit ut morem illum maiorum qui praescribit in parentum loco quaestoribus suis praetores esse oportere officiis benivolentiaque superarit (Planc.* 28).

71. For Mommsen (1899:872) the precise relationship between the *lex Licinia* and previous *ambitus* legislation was unclear, and the situation has not substantially improved since then (despite Nicolet's [1980:310] assertion—plausible, but unsupported—that the *lex Licinia* subsumed the earlier laws). As a result it is hard to tell whether Cicero's complaint is valid or even reasonable. At *Planc.* 47 even he seems to mix simple bribery with *sodalicia*.

72. Under the *lex Licinia* the prosecution could choose four tribes from which jurors would be picked, then the defense rejected one of the four *(Planc.* 36; *SB* 152St.).

73. Also §§42, 46.

74. Compare the praise of Alfius as *quaesitor: quem tandem potius quam hunc C. Alfium quem habet, cui notissimus esse debet, vicinum, tribulem, gravissimum hominem iustissimumque edidisset?* (§43).

75. Cf. §39.

76. For similar attacks on the value of accusations without an identifiable source, see *Cael.* 3 and *Mur.* 13.

77. Cf. also Classen's (1985:125) comments on aligning the jurors' verdict with the will of the voters.

78. See, for instance, Rosch et al. 1975:104–9 and Allan 1986:1.99–109 (and *passim*). Prototypes are generated by a variety of different cognitive structures; see Jackendoff 1983:135–40 and Lakoff 1987.

79. Individuals will also have room for a certain amount of self-justificatory rhetoric, whether or not they personally believe that they have done anything wrong. Fascione (1984:125) and Perelli (1994:74) both note the lack of a clear line between licit and illicit in cases of *ambitus*. The latter attributes this to the presence of certain

practices which were conventionally allowed but hard to exclude from any formal definition.

CHAPTER 3

1. For the spelling *sicariis* I follow Cloud (1968). However, it should be pointed out that the one inscription he cites (*CIL* 6.1283) has somewhat unusual orthography in other respects. Purported *"veneficiis"* (as well as "viis" = "roads") are spelled there "veneficIs" and "vIs." The tall-I conventionally represents a long vowel (Gordon 1983:14) not a double one. For the contraction, which would explain the single long vowels, see Kent 1946:§§224, 240. For handbook discussions of the law see Zumpt 1869:19–38 and Mommsen 1899:612–51. The most recent reconstruction (and a nearly comprehensive survey of the evidence) is found in Ferrary 1991, followed closely in the same author's contribution to Crawford 1996 (749–53). Also useful are Ewins 1960 and Cloud 1969.

2. Throughout I will use "murder" as a synonym for the ordinarily more general "homicide," as, I think, nontechnical English usage allows. Roman law does not have a notion comparable to "malice aforethought" which would distinguish murder from other forms of homicide. In this context stylistic variation between the terms will be harmless.

3. The inscription cited in note 2 shows that the office of *iudex quaestionis* of the court was held by one Claudius Pulcher; his tenure can almost certainly be dated to 98–96 (between his aedileship and praetorship) and probably to 98 (the year immediately following his aedileship). For the evidence see *MRR* 2.4.

4. Even under the composite law there were at least occasionally separate *iudices quaestionis* for the courts *de sicariis* and *de veneficiis* (*Clu.* 126, 147), and so presumably two courts did (or at least could) sit separately. Thus it is impossible to show on the present evidence that the unification of the two under a single statute did not pre-date the *lex Cornelia*.

5. The phrase *cuiusve dolo malo id factum erit* occurs three or four times in the *Digest* (Scaevola, 48.4.4 pr, Marcianus 48.9.1 pr, and Paulus 48.10.2 pr; and compare the following note); Ulpian (*Coll.* 1.3.1) has the Wackernagelian order *cuiusve id dolo malo*.

6. I would follow Wacke's suggestion (for which see Ferrary 1991:425) to emend D. 48.8.1 pr from *qui hominem occiderit, cuiusve dolo malo incendium factum erit* to *q. h. o., c. d. m. id f. e.* Arson, which was doubtless part of the law, nonetheless fits awkwardly here and seems to have been imported (perhaps by reading *id* as an abbreviation).

7. This understanding of the term *sicarius* somewhat undercuts Shaw's (1984: 19–23) contention that bandits were outside the normal workings of the law in theory as well as in practice.

8. In the context of a Republican criminal trial, a "capital" sentence involved loss of

civil rights, not life. In practice, the penalty apparently consisted of permanent exile along with confiscation of property.

9. *Mil.* 11; Ulp. *Coll.* 1.3.1; and Marc. *D.* 48.8.1. For discussion see Cloud 1969: 260–67 and Ferrary 1991: 420–22; I follow the reconstruction of the latter (p. 424). In *Mil.* 11 I would read *quae* [sc. *lex*] *non modo hominem occidi, sed esse cum telo hominis occidendi causa vetat*, accepting *non modo* with ETδ, instead of (as Clark) *non* alone (BH). The construction *non modo . . . sed*, without *etiam* or *et* is quite common (*pace* Kunkel [1962: 65, note 244]); e.g., *Quinct.* 18, 72, 77; *Rosc.* 44, 48, 81. Either version makes perfect sense in the context of Cicero's argument (for which see below).

10. See Cloud 1971, Thomas 1981, and Magdelain 1984.

11. However, Thomas (1981: 679–82) points out that nearly all specific instances (real or literary) involve the killing of a real or metaphorical parent, normally a father.

12. The date of the *lex Pompeia* is variously given as 81 (Radin 1920: 121), 70 (*OCD*), and 55/52 (Rotondi 1912: 406); there is no clear evidence for any date. The identity of the eponymous Pompeius is similarly uncertain, though Pompeius Magnus is widely assumed.

13. On the origin and reliability of the *Collatio* and the *Pauli Sententiae*, see Robinson 1997: 63–65, 113. For a much more skeptical view of *PS*, see Liebs 1989.

14. *Apocol.* 14.1: [*Aeacus*] *lege Cornelia quae de sicariis lata est, quaerebat . . . edit subscriptionem: occisos senatores XXXV* [more victims follow].

15. The first chapter heading is based on Marc. *D.* 48.8.3, the second is an inference from this heading and from the order of items in his *D.* 48.8.1. We will consider the "first" chapter of the law *(esse cum telo)* again in the next chapter. Classen (1985: 23) and Ferrary (1991: 426, 432) supply similar restorations. Ferrary (1991: 432–34) rightly rejects an additional clause targeting a person *qui . . . mortisve causam praestiterit* (*PS* 5.23.1).

16. *Quive, cum magistratus esset publicove iudicio praeesset, operam dedisset, quo quis falsum iudicium profiteretur, ut quis innocens conveniretur condemnaretur.*

17. No source for the text of the *lex Cornelia* specifically mentions a penalty for the giving of bribes (though this may have been outlawed by another statute).

18. See, for example, Zumpt 1869: 32–33; Fausset (1887: xiii–xx); Hoenigswald 1962; Classen 1972, 1985: 107–19; and Alexander 1982: 162–63. Further sources at Stroh 1975: 312.

19. We should, however, keep in mind the caveats in the original article (and reiterated by Alexander [1990: xii]) about the generality of the results.

20. Hence the point of *Clu.* 49: *simplex in iudicium causa, certa res, unum crimen adhibitum est.*

21. Given the arguments above, there are not linguistic or historical reasons to think chapter six of the *lex Cornelia* would be applicable.

22. Cicero does not question the propriety of charging Roscius for a crime on the

grounds that he allegedly masterminded it rather than committing it himself. This suggests that the legal extension of liability to persons by whose *dolus malus* a crime was committed was popularly accepted.

23. Cloud suggests a gradual change first clearly visible in Seneca the Elder (*Ben.* 3.6.2, 5.14.2) and completed by the time of Hadrian (Marc. *D.* 48.8.1.3).

24. Thus Kunkel's compelling interpretation of the laws *de sicariis* undermines his own claim (1962:70, 135) that the composite law was not only purely tralatician (perhaps literally true) but clumsily so (false). The practical reconceptualization of the law against *sicarii* made a composite homicide law attractive.

25. In this context it may be useful to note that the killing of a slave (by someone other than his master, who had specific legal authorization) was apparently covered under this statute, and not merely by a private law action for damages; see Marc. *D.* 48.8.1.2, Ulp. *Coll.* 1.3.2; Robinson 1981:222–23.

26. This "power of life and death" was part of *patria potestas* and was thus only possessed by men without living ascendants in the male line. It also did not apply against daughters who were married in the *manus* of their husbands. See Harris 1986 and below.

27. I take it that Marcianus' judgment does not follow precisely from the rescript he claims to follow, since the latter explicitly mentions only acquittal, not reduced punishment. On intent, see Robinson (1995:44–45). The *SC Silianum* many not exactly, however, constitute an "exception" to the requirement for intent, for it is perhaps a separate matter from the *lex Cornelia*.

28. That is, the only question of intent ever raised is whether the defendant understood what he was doing, not whether he had a motivation that mitigated his offense.

29. Later in the speech Cicero sarcastically adopts a similar burden of proving his counteraccusation: "Until, jurors, you understand that there is no duty, no right so sacred and inviolable that his crime and treachery have not violated and diminished it, may ye judge him the best of men." The sarcasm apparent here seems to support the notion that the other adoptions of heavy burdens are purely rhetorical posturing.

30. As well as *accusatoris, oportere, peccata, maleficium,* and *scelus,* which could be regarded as demanded by the sense. Note the variety of interchangeable words for "offense" or "crime."

31. See also *Rosc.* 88, 89.

32. Similar arguments about who had the better motive appear also to have been at the core of the defense of Varenus *de sicariis* a few years later. For the defense see *IO* 7.2.36 and *pro Vareno* fr. 6 Cr.; for the charge see *IO* 7.1.9.

33. Vasaly in fact refers specifically (and plausibly) to theatrical "masks" and characters. Axer (1989) points out the possibility of using any broadly recognizable situation to remodel the "communicative situation" away from a judicial model. Thus one may wish to take an agnostic view as to whether theatrical character types are primary categories or are merely particular instantiations of more culturally pervasive types.

34. See Afzelius 1942:214 and Vasaly 1985:17–19 on the truth in this issue.

35. There is a clever implied dilemma here. The Roman heroic type is probably almost as distinct from a Gorgias as it is from a Knemon, but given only a choice between only the two, the audience must opt for the positive member of the pair.

36. For the use of key words such as *avaritia*, *audacia*, and *sicarius* in characterization, see Vasaly 1985:14–16 and May 1988:26, 29–31.

37. This form is only used when the commanded action is to be at some temporal remove from the command (as shown by, e.g., temporal adverbs or future perfect conditionals). One of the most common such circumstances is in the instruction of audiences in criminal and civil trials as well as deliberative assemblies. Michael Alexander suggests *per litteras* that the future imperative is "legalese." I do not think that the two explanations are contradictory.

38. Cicero says, "They say that not many years ago there was a man, not unknown, . . ." (§64). The case may or may not have been previously known to the jurors, but neither the event nor the person seems to have any historical significance. Wiseman (1967) confirms the spelling of the name Cloelius and speculates on his family and story (cf. also Cloud 1971:46).

39. The story is made more generic by the fact that Cicero does not actually name Orestes.

40. Gruen (1968:268), following Gabba, suggests that this passage is heavily ironic and was added after Sulla's death. Kinsey (1975) shows that this is an unnecessary hypothesis. In general, one should be hesitant to see flattery in ancient texts as ironically fulsome, and especially hesitant to find that passages could *only* be read in this way.

41. For the use of the theatrical reference in the more general project of establishing the rural and urban character types, see Vasaly 1985:7–8.

42. In what follows I do not restrict dilemma to the strict sense of a pair of alternatives, either of which leads to a conclusion that is beneficial to the same side. Rather I include all cases of paired alternatives whether one is rejected or both are beneficial. See Craig (1989; 1993) and Dyer (1990:23–24) for general remarks on the effect of dilemma.

43. Also more briefly at *Rosc.* 78.

44. Of course one of the major uses of dilemma is to silently eliminate dangerous propositions by appearing to cover all cases. See *Rosc.* 39 for a particularly egregious example of such a strategy in this speech.

45. It is certain not merely that a particular act was committed (a killing), but that a criminal act (murder) occurred. This is an important distinction because in *pro Plancio* there is also a clear fact (the money seized in the Circus Flaminius) which is brushed over with little notice, much less the extensive counterargumentation characteristic of *pro Roscio* (and *pro Cluentio*). On the basis of the definition of *ambitus* in the previous chapter, we may suggest that this is because there is no specific act which can itself require an *ambitus* conviction, that being more a matter of general circumstance.

46. If, as will be argued, this counteraccusation is a natural part of the defense, then why does Cicero frequently apologize for his behavior? There are several possibilities.

The political implications of this case may make more direct accusation dangerous. The defense attorney normally maintains a generally submissive posture. And in any case Cicero goes through the whole charade (if that is what it is) again in *pro Cluentio*, calling his accuracy into question. *IO* 7.2.9–10 gives two examples of reciprocal accusation, and both are homicides.

47. Murder (in most societies) is a crime unique in being proved normally on circumstantial grounds. The victim is, by definition, not available to provide testimony, and it is only recently that forensic technology has become of real use.

48. See Wirszubski 1961 on the implications of the word *audacia*.

49. Also *Rosc.* 127.

50. There is considerable disagreement on whether this is an accurate characterization. Gruen (1968:268–71) holds that Roscius' case represented a test by the nobility of the return to normality and the actual implementation of the Sullan program. Kinsey (1980) questions whether it had any real political significance. See Afzelius 1942:213–17 and Gruen 1968:271, note 69 on the political consequences of the trial for Cicero.

51. This assumption is also implicit in the opinion that Cicero attributes to the opposition (that Sulla's influence will be taken to back their position because of Chrysogonus' position). Since this is practically put in the mouths of the opposition, he can take it as a given for his own argument without difficulty.

52. Parricide's penalty of the sack is the one apparent exception to the general rule that capital penalties were not actually carried out. However, in Cicero's encomium of the ancestors who established that penalty, he never explicitly says that that penalty was still in use (*Rosc.* 70–72). Since we do not know the precise date of the *lex Pompeia* and its assimilation of parricide to general homicide, we do not know whether it was in use in 80. As a result we cannot be sure that Roscius actually faced execution.

53. Such arguments are not lacking in the *ambitus* cases (e.g., *Planc.* 44–45, 47, *Mur.* 70–72), but they are the only type found in the homicide cases. One might question whether, if a killing were admitted, one could realistically imagine a political justification. I offer *pro Milone* and Cicero's treatment of the Catilinarian conspirators as examples of precisely this in Roman society.

54. Cicero had been able to use this trial as a rhetorical example in 70 at *I Verr.* 29, *II Verr.* 1.157.

55. Also *Clu.* 164.

56. When Cicero says "Then show that Oppianicus was a good man," he seems to be suggesting that he can do as much for his own client.

57. One might also consider in this light the technical argument about applicability of the law at §§143–60.

58. On the use of the term *praeiudicium* (and its relationship to *invidia*) see the next section.

59. Given the inherent problems of the story (there is no clear correct position), Cic-

ero cannot and does not offer it as an explicit *exemplum*. As a result, he cannot attach a tag or moral (as he does in, say, the Africanus story of §134) to control interpretation.

60. Cf. also *Rosc.* 81–83.

61. Most of Oppianicus' alleged murders, Sassia's infidelities, and the other incidental details are never connected to the crime, despite all Cicero's protests about the appropriately narrow scope of the trial.

62. Sisenna died the year before this trial, and so his translation (Ov. *Tr.* 2.443) was presumably available by then. For the genre see Plut. *Crass.* 32 and passing references at Apul. *AA* 1.1, 4.32, [Lucian] *Am.* 1. Cicero's story is not, as Milesian tales ordinarily were, overtly erotic, but the mention of a pregnant woman is perhaps not irrelevant; he may hint at the prequel.

63. For somewhat different perspectives on *invidia* see Pöschl 1961 and Dunbabin and Dickie 1983.

64. One may perhaps see here some similarity to the Stoic *sapiens* who never deceives and (more to the point) is never deceived and never needs to change his mind. See *SVF* 3.216 (Stobaeus) and 3.548–56 (esp. 548 [Stobaeus *Ecl.* 2.111.18W] and 549 [Diog. Laert. 7.121]).

65. Compare also the opposition of the censors' authority to that of other magistrates in §126.

66. There is also a similar evolutionary account of the Roman constitution (emphasizing the borrowing and reshaping of foreign influences) at *Rep.* 2.30. Both of these passages take a diachronic view of collective knowledge, but the principle should hold synchronically as well (Wood 1988:70–78).

67. Cf. *Clu.* 120: "Our ancestors wished that no one be a juror not only about anyone's reputation, but not even about the least amount of money, unless there were a meeting of adversaries."

68. Also passing references at §§88, 94, 96.

69. Wagenvoort (1947:113–16) and Hellegouarc'h (1972:279) point out that the word retains physical connotations throughout its history. See Lakoff 1990:226–29 for rhetorical correlates of *gravitas* and its opposite *levitas*, which she aptly terms "liteness," although Laughton (1942) rightly points out that the full periodic style is not so predominant as Lakoff might suggest.

70. Cf. *ad Her.* 4.36: *O virtutis comes, Invidia, quae bonos sequeris plerumque atque adeo insectaris.*

71. Cf. §§112, 136. And *invidia* is excluded from senatorial judgments: *illa iudicia senatoria non falsa invidia sed vera atque insigni turpitudine* (§61).

72. Cicero also depicts this mob volatility directly. See §137 for the sudden evaporation of public hostility (conveniently ignored in the rest of the speech).

73. Needless to say, this argument is not made possible by Cicero's personal convictions (though one might suspect that he did believe it), but by the fact that he is addressing the usual elite jury.

74. Accounts of politics in the narrowest sense are also relevant to *ambitus* cases to show motive (or lack thereof) for bribing voters.

75. For all his self-promotion, Cicero is of course willing to play the fool occasionally, as at *Planc.* 64–65 (cf. Gotoff 1993:312–13). However, all other things being equal, the orator will prefer to preserve his dignity both out of self-interest and to maximize his own *auctoritas* in the interests of his client (cf. Kennedy 1968:428–29).

76. The repeated phrase in the law *occidendi hominis causa* requires that the criminal be aware of what he was doing. This defense is a question of knowledge, not of attitude.

77. Note, however, that Cicero does not avoid this argument on the grounds that the refutation is too obvious. The character argument which he does claim to have made is that Scamander was approved of by his patron. This is the textbook argument to make under normal circumstances, but in this case the patron is *ex hypothesi* the mastermind of the crime with which the freedman is charged, and so not disinterested. Nonetheless he represents himself as having made the flawed defense.

CHAPTER 4

1. For treatments of *vis* laws see the handbooks of Mommsen (1899:652–66) and Zumpt (1868:266–81), the articles of Hough (1930), Lintott (1968:107–24), and Cloud (1988; 1989), and the dissertation of Vitzthum (1966).

2. Cloud (1988) argues plausibly that *vis publica* and *privata* were not legal categories until centuries after the period discussed here. Hence, (1) there was probably at most a single *lex Iulia* under Caesar and Augustus, and (2) I do not use *vis publica* in the title as a technical term.

3. Of course there is civil legislation on injury dating back at least to the Twelve Tables (Tab. 8 *apud* Gellius *NA* 20.1.14); the praetor's edict included interdicts featuring exceptions for *vis* by 161 (Ulp. *D.* 43.17.1; an allusion at Ter. *Eun.* 319–20 provides the *terminus ante quem*); and similar language is incorporated in a *lex agraria* of 111 (*FIRA* 1.8.18). In general see Lintott 1968:125–31, Labruna 1971, and Frier 1985.

4. This was the year of Catulus' (*MRR* 2.85) consulship. The following discussion of the history of *vis* legislation depends heavily on Lintott (1968), who subtly modifies the views of Zumpt (1868) and Hough (1930).

5. Sall. *BC* 31.4; *SB* 84, 149St.; [Sall.] *in Cic.* 2.3. The name is also spelled *Plotia* in some traditions.

6. The date of the *lex Plautia* is obscure. Labruna's (1975:98–106) argument for 70 is compelling so long as it is assumed that the Plautius in question is otherwise known as the author of the *lex Plautia de reditu Lepidanorum* probably of that year (see *MRR* 2.128, 130 note 4). Any date between 78 *(lex Lutatia)* and 63 (accusations against the Catilinarians) is possible.

7. Labruna (1975:113) has made the more radical (but still plausible) suggestion that, despite the example of the Sullan standing courts, the *lex Lutatia* created a

quaestio extraordinaria. In that case the *lex Plautia* simply established a standing *vis* court. In either case Lintott's characterization of *vis* under the *lex Plautia* will hold.

8. For an accurate summary of other positions expressed in the secondary literature see Vitzthum (1966:38–45). Unfortunately, most of his own evaluation is based on either questionable prosopographical assumptions or a too literal reading of *Cael.* 70.

9. *Vis* in civil contexts is a different matter; see Frier 1985:171–83.

10. For this sense of *orator*, see *OLD*, s.v. 1, but it is not exampled elsewhere in the *Digest.* Cloud (1989:433), following Vitzthum, raises some doubt as to the text of this passage.

11. See Bauman 1967:50, 53–54. As noted in the introduction, the same act could in principle lead to criminal liability under several different statutes. Many cases of *vis* would also potentially fall under the *esse cum telo occidendi hominis causa* clause of the *lex Cornelia de sicariis et veneficiis.* Cicero describes Piso's acts as governor of Macedonia as things *quae cum plurimae leges veteres, tum lex Cornelia maiestatis, Iulia de pecuniis repetundis planissime vetat (Pis.* 50). See also below on Gabinius.

12. It is widely agreed that the phrase *maiestatem minuere* was left deliberately undefined. However, Bauman (1967:54, 75) argues that the law only applied in certain (additionally defined) fact-situations. He has little or no direct evidence for this, and if the case of Cornelius (discussed below) is any indication, those fact-situations would have been defined almost as vaguely.

13. Asc. 58.14–20C. The consul was threatened in an ensuing riot, but the charge almost certainly stems from the reading (Asc. 60.21–61.5, and Cicero *ad* Asc. 71.17–72.7C). The first trial was disrupted and never completed (Asc. 60.2–7C).

14. App. *BC* 2.24: ὅτι χωρὶς ψηφίσματος ἐς Αἴγυπτον μετὰ στρατιᾶς ἐσέβαλεν.

15. On the details of the mechanism see Watson 1968:21–60.

16. I take *contra* and *adversus rem publicam* to be equivalent expressions. A search of the PHI Latin database reveals only two authors who use both: Cicero and Ulpian. The Ulpian passage (*D.* 48.4.1.1, to be discussed below) uses both within a few sentences, and they are clearly synonymous. The distinction seems to be one of individual style.

17. Prospective: Sallust *BC* 51.43; Cic. *Phil.* 8.33, *Fam.* 8.8.6, *Att.* 2.24.3, *Har. Resp.* 15; Livy 25.4.7. Retrospective: Sallust *BC* 50.4; Cic. *Mil.* 13, 14, 31, *Att.* 1.16.13, *Q. fr.* 2.1.2; Livy 3.21.2.

18. Asc. 55, *Cael.* 70; Lintott (1968:114–15, 119). Bauman (1967:69) rejects this kind of reconstruction in suggesting that Roman criminal law is not tralatician, but Cloud (1989:442) and Gruen (1965:59–60) have shown examples of tralatician legislation *de vi* and *de maiestate*; Cicero (*Rab. Post.* 9) implies that the same holds for laws *de repetundis.* Presumably the situation varies from law to law, but there seems to be no general resistance to recycling legislation.

19. I follow *IO* 5.11.42 and the manuscripts of Cicero, not (as Peterson in the OCT) Asconius 70.3, 22C in the title of this speech.

20. In this function it is similar to the (apparently) more *ad hoc* decree, cited at *Mur.* 67, that certain campaign practices violated the *lex Calpurnia*. If it is really the case, as Cicero implies, that responsibility was not assigned by this decree, it makes his tendentious reading of the *contra rem publicam* declaration slightly less implausible. Bauman (1967:53) also finds the same role for public interest in the construction of *maiestas* in the case of Caepio (*ad Her.* 1.21).

21. A similar contrast elsewhere (e.g., *I Verr.* 31; Ter. *Heaut.* 356; Cato *apud* Gellius *NA* 13.25[24].15) is motivated in part by alliteration. The fact that these two passages are several sections apart suggests that their opposition here is not so motivated.

22. This is not to assert the historicity of the "first Catilinarian conspiracy" of 66/5. See Seager 1964 and Gruen 1969. It should, however, be noted that the so-called first conspiracy was not created from whole cloth; the fabrication lies in the piecing together of (probably) unrelated incidents of sedition and civil disturbance and attaching them to Catiline. Berry (1996a:34) rightly points out that the *vis* charge should not be strictly limited to participation in the Catilinarian conspiracy (nor would we expect it to cover mere Catilinarian sympathies).

23. An abortive coup attempt in 66/5, probably a later fiction (see previous note). Cicero elsewhere is much less reticent about discussing these events; see Berry 1996a: 150–51, 153–54 for an account of the discrepancy.

24. The famous coup in 63, detected prematurely by Cicero and put down in the field by his colleague Antonius.

25. Note also the strictly factual character of the arguments at §§14–17, 36–39, and 51–68. Cicero here specifies several forms of conspiracy in which Sulla did not participate. §§1–10, 18–35, and 40–50 are a defense of Cicero's decision to take this case. The purpose of this defense is probably exactly what Cicero says it is (§35)—a defense of consular *auctoritas* (both his and Hortensius') which is essential as the basis of the factual defense. For a discussion of the consular ethos in this speech see May 1988:69–79.

26. The story behind this assertion is told at §§56 and 58: Sittius had Sulla sell off the family estates for him to pay off his debts, even though he could have paid them off out of debts owed to himself after only a slight delay.

27. *Cael.* 17, 30. The only reference to this topos is the phrase *non libidine sed negoti gerendi studio* (§58).

28. See also *Cat.* 2.4 (*bis*), 8, 19, 20, 21. The same kind of argument is made also about the followers of other so-called *popularis* opponents of Cicero such as Clodius (e.g., *Sest.* 38). Contrast Catiline's letter in Sallust *BC* 35.3. The temptation to hold onto property seems to have been very great in Cicero's scheme, for at *Sest.* 97 and 99 he categorically denies the status of optimate to anyone who is too encumbered by personal debt. Nor is this construction of debt purely Ciceronian; see Shaw 1975 on debt in Sallust.

29. "Political" here again in the narrow sense of overt struggles of power and policy; in broader senses of the term all ethical arguments could probably be considered political.

30. Essentially the same claim more briefly at *Sull.* 77.

31. Hellegouarc'h (1972: 484–93, 528–30) discusses the use of *bonus* and *improbus*. He points out (p. 528) that when contrasted with *improbus*, *bonus* takes on a particularly "political" (in the conventional modern sense) color, while *probus* and *malus* are more generally "moral" characterizations.

32. By "conservatives" I mean to imply primarily a stylistic opposition to those "populists" (see chapter 2, note 13 above) whom Cicero calls (depending on the demands of the occasion) *populares* or false *populares*. The conservatives value the appearance of politics from above (however much they actually depend on and cater to the voters of the masses), while the populists value the appearance of popular participation (however elitist their actual policies may be). This is not, of course, meant as a systematic interpretation of Roman politics.

33. Other references to the *boni* with less paradigmatic application are at §§1, 9, 20, 29, 32, 35, and 71.

34. On "liteness" as a translation of *levitas* see chapter 3, note 69.

35. This question of state interest may relate to the explanation of Sulla's *ambitus* as *dignitatis . . . nimis magnam . . . cupiditatem* or even *fortuna . . . gravior* (§73). His motives were understandable, but his actions were misjudged (cf. §6).

36. The medical metaphor reappears at §§51 and 135. For examples elsewhere see *LA* 1.26; *Cat.* 2.11, 17, 4.2; *Red. Sen.* 9; *Red. Pop.* 15; *Sest.* 17; *Att.* 2.1.7, 4.3.3; Liv. 39.9.1, and Fantham 1972: 14–18, 128–29.

37. For the description of these circumstances see §§24, 33–35, 52, 69.

38. And more briefly at *Sest.* 86.

39. This condition is explicitly claimed in Sestius' case: *non modo nulla nova quaestio, sed etiam vetera iudicia sublata* (§85). Cicero may be referring particularly here to his assertion (§§40, 53, 73) that he was himself exiled without a legitimate criminal trial or accusation.

40. See chapter 2, section 3.

41. In fact Cicero generally introduces this distinction only to transcend *popularis* self-definition by narrowing it (*Off.* 1.85) or collapsing it into "optimate" (here and *LA* 2.6–10).

42. The definition of *popularis* at *Leg. Agr.* 2.9–10 (defending the interests, defined largely in terms of stability, of the people) is not at all complementary to this notion of optimate, nor does it correspond to this definition of *popularis*.

43. "Troubled at home" represents economic difficulties, but need not refer to the lower classes. In fact, the term is more likely to be applied among the elite, since only they are likely to be able to acquire significant debt.

44. See, among others, Wirszubski 1954 and Christes 1988, and their references, on *cum dignitate otium*; this vexed phrase does not bear directly on our discussion.

45. Just as Cicero can manipulate the value of Roscius' rusticity heavily once the fact has been asserted by the opposition. On the appropriation of opposing arguments see Riggsby 1995b.

46. *Sest.* 106: *Quae contio fuit per hos annos, quae quidem esset non conducta sed vera, in qua populi Romani consensus non perspici posset?*

47. *Sest.* 109: *Omitto eas quae feruntur ita vix ut quini, et ii ex aliena tribu, qui suffragium ferant reperiantur.*

48. But cf. §§75–85 for a few exceptions to the declaration.

49. Austin (1960:viii, note 2) and Craig (1989:316, note 6) show that (as usual) Cicero spoke last. See further note 52 below on the division of the defense.

50. Cicero's argument is somewhat ambivalent as to the relative importance of the external circumstances of Sestius' actions (which as a result made his actions beneficial to the state) or his motives (i.e. that he meant to do well by the state). In either case this is a matter of interpretation, unlike the question in Scamander's case (pp. 101–2)—did he realize what he was doing?

51. This speech has been extensively studied, and, I think, it is fairly well understood. See the commentary by Austin (1960); long studies by Heinze (1925), Geffcken (1973), and Stroh (1975:243–303); recent work by Gotoff (1986) and Craig (1989); for more bibliography see Stroh 1975:312–13) and Craig 1989 (his note 1).

52. The relative importance of these various issues in the prosecution's presentation is unknowable. The charges to which Crassus responded seem on the whole to be more relevant to a charge of *vis* than those discussed in Cicero's speech. On this point see Heinze 1925:200–202 and Craig 1989:315; the principle behind the *partitio* was first noted by Quintilian (4.2.27).

53. Cicero points out deficiency in a variety of standard rhetorical categories: speech (*Inv.* 1.36), place (1.38), time (1.39), argument, and witnesses.

54. *Pro Caelio* and *pro Roscio Comoedo* both use dilemma (as defined narrowly) eight times. For a full listing of dilemmas, see Craig (1993:212–13).

55. §78: *Non enim potest . . . esse in re publica civis turbulentus* reinforces that notion that *vis* involves a question of civic effect.

56. See Heinze 1925:203 on this point. Lintott (1968:119) reasonably suggests that Camurtius and Caesernius could have been tried in connection with the affairs of Catiline or Vettius and so might have been partially political. But his underlying interpretation of the passage—that Cicero here "admits" Camurtius and Caesernius "were not really liable under *vis* law"—is fundamentally mistaken. He wants them not to have been liable. See further below.

57. Note that *argumentum*, which is ancipital between "plot" and "argument," serves to link Cicero's rhetoric lecture (note 61 below) and the dramatic description here.

58. Literally the curtain is "raised" in this passage; at this period Roman curtains were apparently fixed at the bottom, not the top; see Austin 1960: *ad* §65.

59. In Axer's (1989) terms, comedy replaces conventional courtroom practice as the model for the communicative situation.

60. On the status of mime see Austin 1960: *ad* §65.21 and Sutton 1964:29–33, and note the diminutive *fabella* in §64.

61. We should note the lists of rhetorical terms at §§55 and 66 and compare the strategy of *in Caecilium*, where Cicero lectures his opposition and demonstrates proper rhetorical technique as a means of asserting superiority. In Axer's terms again the classroom becomes the model communicative situation.

62. Gotoff 1986 is a salutary warning on how far we may trust Cicero's version of events but is perhaps too radical. There were surely limits on what Cicero could say about an event (the prosecution speech), which the jurors had just witnessed themselves. See in general the discussion in section 2 of the introduction. The present argument does not, however, depend on how accurate Cicero's presentation was.

63. The account of the paragraph is based on the theories of Lakoff and Johnson (1980).

64. Asc. 36.5–13C. See Ruebel 1979 for chronology. The *lex Pompeia* established a *vis* court, with special procedural rules, specifically to deal with this and two other incidents.

65. See Asc. 41.24–42.4C. Asconius (42.2–4C) and Quintilian (9.2.54) appear to have had access to both versions of the speech. Clark (1895:xxvii) rightly plays down more dramatic versions of the story of Cicero's difficulties. See further note 80 below.

66. This is something of an oversimplification. In some instances the slaves, too, could be publicly punished; see Robinson 1981:214–22 on the slave as criminal.

67. The basic purpose of the clause was to allow recovery of property from which the rightful owner had been removed by force. Noxal surrender is not at issue here.

68. Lintott (1974:74–75) suggests a *dolo malo* clause to explain the prosecution's eagerness to show that Milo had actively plotted against Clodius (Asc. 41.17–18C; *Mil.* 46ff.). Stone (1980:91) objects that *dolus* never appears in Cicero's speech. However, the technical legal term is generally avoided in Cicero's oratory (once each in *Flacc.*, *Dom.*, and *II Verr.* 5; repeatedly in the highly technical *pro Tullio*). Stone also objects that the absence of such a clause would have allowed Cicero the accident defense. I take this up below. No clear resolution is possible.

69. Practically all praise of Milo is defined in terms of his opposition to Clodius and stands or falls, at least rhetorically, on one's feelings about the central conflict. Contrast this to the treatment of Sestius, who is placed in the contexts of the Catilinarian conspiracy, Cicero's exile, and the conflict with Clodius' gangs, as well as (briefly) provincial administration.

70. E.g., Clark 1895: *ad* 57.4.

71. Clark's (1895:l–lvii) analysis of the *dispositio* of the speech is very helpful here.

72. Clark (1895:lii–liii) says, "The rules laid down in the books as to the conduct of a *causa coniecturalis* are strictly followed." This is essentially true, but it does not take account of the fact that the *causa iuridicalis* has already been argued before it is explicitly advanced as the paradigm for this case.

73. As does Stone (1980:91–92).

74. Here I translate H's reading *ut ea cernamus quae non videmus* (apparently paraphrased by Quint. 9.2.41), rather than the OCT's *ut ea cernimus quae videmus* (after

ut ea cernamus quae videmus in BS). In his 1895 edition of *pro Milone* Clark preferred the former reading on the strength of its sharper point and especially the echo in Quintilian; in his OCT he switched, apparently based on his faith in what he had identified in the interim as the reading of the (lost) Cluniacensis 496. It is somewhat easier to explain the direction of corruption to the blander version. Nothing in the present interpretation depends on the choice of reading here.

75. Cf. May 1988:138.

76. Also: [Quint.] *Decl. Min.* 3, 3b; Val. Max. 6.1.12; Plut. *Mar.* 14.4–8.

77. *Cat.* 1.3, 4; *Dom.* 86, 91, 101; *Planc.* 88. There are also frequent references in the *philosophica* and *rhetorica*.

78. This strong view of self-defense is also supported by the parallel role of self-defense in civil actions under the *lex Aquilia* (Ulp. *D.* 9.2.5 pr). The argument at *Tull.* 47–52 based on the same passage of the Twelve Tables is certainly very different in spirit (Classen 1982:164–65) but not formally contradictory to the one here.

79. As when Cicero plays down the technical legal argument, at *Clu.* §§143ff. There Cicero uses the device to gloss over the questionable relevance of a logically and factually sound argument.

80. Cf. *SB* 112St. Quintilian (9.2.54) and the Bobbio scholiast (173St.) preserve a quotation from *pro Milone* which does not appear in the published text; presumably they still have (as Asconius claims to have) both texts. Settle (1962:237–60) wrongly believes that the well-attested ancient tradition of the two versions stands or falls with the more suspect (and largely modern) claim that the differences were in some way due to the disruptions of the original trial. Nor is the existence of a shorthand system at the period crucial to the two-version theory, especially if (again) we do not assume that the two versions differed because of the alleged problems in delivery. That said (and *contra* Settle [1962:244] and Marshall [1987:735]), shorthand can be dated so close to Cicero's lifetime (the early empire is granted) that the *argumentum ex silentio* for 52 is uncompelling.

81. *Planc.* 17 (discussed above). Cf. *Mur.* 58 to *Caec.* 69, and see Asc. 70.13–15C with Alexander 1993b; also Cicero's situational choice of the relative value of witnesses and arguments.

82. *Si se [Clodium] in turba ei [Miloni] iam obtulerit, occisum iri ab ipso Milone video (Att.* 4.3.5).

83. Lintott (1968:66) and Lakoff (1990:234–38) note the generality of the use of dehumanization to justify killing humans.

84. If the original *pro Milone* had had this argument incorporated in a more subtle fashion, as with the rhetoric of political alignment in *pro Sulla*, it might have escaped Asconius' mention. On the other hand the two arguments are well segregated in the published version, and Stone's (1980) theory of the additive composition (without substantial editing) of the later version seems plausible.

85. Cicero's argument on this subject (§15) is disingenuous and politically motivated, but contains a kernel of truth.

86. Weber (1968:54): "The term 'state' will be used to refer to an institutional enterprise of political character, when and insofar as its executive staff successfully claims a monopoly of the legitimate use of physical force in order to impose its regulations." He goes on to point out that this right originates with the state, but may, in some circumstances (e.g., self-defense), be delegated back to the people.

87. See Giddens 1987: chapters 1–3 for some of the potential criticisms.

88. This is not to say that the events of the 50's inevitably lead to the principate, but retrospectively we can see that, as it happened, the evolution was more-or-less continuous.

89. See Gellius *NA* 15.27.5; Lintott 1968:91; and Nippel 1995:80.

90. The main sources are Dio 55.26.5 for the *vigiles* and Suet. *Aug.* 49.1 for the cohorts. See also Dio 55.10.10 and 55.24.5–6. On the institutions see Reynolds 1926: chapter 1 and *RE* s.vv. *urbanae cohortes* (sup. 10.1125–40) and *praetoriae cohortes* (22.1607–34). On the conceptual issues, see Nippel 1995:16–26, 78–84, 90–98.

91. Lintott (1968:209–16) catalogs known major acts of violence.

92. Ti. Gracchus: Val. Max. 3.2.17. Gracchus: *Phil.* 8.14; Liv. *Ep.* 61; [Vict.] *Vir. Ill.* 65; App. *BC* 1.26. Saturninus: Val. Max. 3.2.18.

93. Aigner (1976:12) points to finds of swords in private contexts even in imperial Pompeii.

94. Other applications of *imperator* are rare under Augustus and last attested for Q. Iunius Blaesus in A.D. 22 (Tac. *Ann.* 3.74). No full triumphs were awarded outside the imperial family after Agrippa turned two down in 19 and 14 (Dio 54.24.10 and 54.11.6); cf. Mommsen 1887:135–36. See also Syme 1958 on the conversion of *Imperator* to a personal name. See Paterson 1985 on the use of lesser marks of status by still competitive aristocrats.

95. See Millar 1977:611–12, 617 on Pompey as forerunner of emperors in general.

96. For the wording of the resolution see Mendner 1966:263–64. On its legal force (if any) see the discussion and bibliography of Lintott (1968:149–74) and, subsequently, Mitchel (1971) and Duplá-Ansuategui (1990). I think the only clear conclusion that may be drawn on this point is that the legal force of the decree, if it had any, was as highly contested in antiquity as it is today. The practical effect is to encourage violence by the handpicked allies of the magistrates acting as posses.

97. For a specific case study (of Judea and Arabia) which confirms most of the conclusions below, see Isaac 1984.

98. Roman success seems to have been much greater against pirates (generally best understood as ship-borne bandits, not corsairs, in antiquity). During the Late Republic they periodically but temporarily suppressed pirate activity (Ormerod 1926:208–9, 235–40). These attempts failed in the long term because of their reliance on the cooperation of various local forces (much as with antibandit efforts), but with the establishment of a standing fleet, the first two centuries of the empire saw little pirate activity in the Mediterranean (Ormerod 1926:249, 256–57).

99. Opelt (1965:132–33). Opelt also notes (pp. 131–37) that *latro* is one of several

words used metaphorically (and more-or-less interchangeably) that all denote users of some kind of excessive or transgressive violence: *pirata, carnifex, parricida, proditor*.

100. Or, in the more nuanced formulation of Feldherr (1991:113–15), the claims of family and state are hierarchized in such a way that actions that do not look to the interests of the latter cannot truly be in the interests of the former.

101. The other attested cases of *perduellio* involve regal aspirations (338 B.C.; Liv. 6.20.12), military defeat in a battle fought despite ill omens (249; *SB* 27; Suet. *Tib.* 2; Liv. *Per.* 19), another military defeat (211; Liv. 26.2–3), interference with a tribune (169; Liv. 43.16.10–12), and the trial in 63 of Rabirius for the death in 100 of Saturninus (*Rab. Perd.*, Dio 37.27–28; Bauman 196:42–44). In the absence of statutes it is difficult to generalize from the meager evidence or even to tell whether there are generalizations to be drawn. Nonetheless, we should note that most of these offenses could (at some points in history) be tried as *maiestas* and that Claudius Pulcher was apparently convicted on that charge instead in 249 after his *perduellio* trial ended for technical reasons (Bauman 1967:27–28). Liou-Gille (1994:26–29) might conceivably be right to understand the original sense of *perduellio* as the extension of war into civilian space, but this clearly does not suffice for all the later cases; she rejects on procedural grounds all but the trials of Horatius and Rabirius. Brecht's distinction (1938) between internal *perduellio* and external *proditio* is plausible, but not demonstrably accurate. The same is true of Magdelain's theory (1973) of an evolution from "hostility to the plebs" (in the person of the tribunes) to "hostility to the state."

102. See Bauman 1969:26 and note 36, Magdelain 1973:409, and Ogilvie 1965: 114–15.

103. In Cicero's version (*Inv.* 2.78–79) the question before a court would have been "Given Horatia's disrespect of her brothers' deaths, her mourning of the enemies', and her failure to rejoice in the victory of her brother and of the Roman people, ought she have been killed uncondemned *(indamnatam)* by her brother?" This version, even from well before the period of increased violence discussed above, already suggests an attempt at extralegal justification of Horatius' act. However, it makes no mention of the father's role and, crucially, the accusation not of *parricidium* but of killing unjustly *(iniuria)*. Thus it is Horatia's right to a trial that is at stake here, not the state's right to try her.

104. For different views see Watson 1979 and Liou-Gille 1994. Watson (1979:442–43) rejects the above view of the basis of the charge in favor of the idea that offenses against one's private law superiors (patron and, as in Hortensius' case, *pater familias*) also constituted *perduellio*. Our knowledge of the law of the period is not good enough to discriminate well between theories, but I would point out that the one passage which he offers as an illustration of such a law (Dionysius 2.10.3) is not restricted to inferiors—it is in fact completely symmetrical. In any case, the crucial issue here is not the original judicial issue (the very historicity of which is far from certain), but Livy's interpretation. In his time, at least, the "private treason" explanation seems not to be available (Watson 1979:436). That usurpation of a state prerogative is a salient issue in

the Late Republic is confirmed by the prosecution of Rabirius on a charge of *perduellio* (rather than *de vi* or *de sicariis*).

105. Sources: *Dom.* 77, 84; Dion. Hal. 2.26.4; Papinian *Coll.* 4.8; *CT* 4.8.6 pr. Hadrian: Marc. *D.* 48.9.5. There may have been certain restrictions (e.g., just cause, taking the advice of a family council) from the beginning, but the evidence is unclear. In general on the *ius vitae ac necis* see also Sachers 1953:1084–89.

106. Similar conclusion already reached in Saller 1995:115–17.

107. Labruna (1971:241–48) would go back even further to the post-Hannibalic agricultural crisis and concurrent influx of imperial pelf. Against this background he sees the civil law on *vis* as a check on intra-elite struggles over property. The private and public law trends are at least parallel, but they may be no more.

108. For other examples see Appian *BC* 2.23, 25, 28; Plut., *Pomp.* 55, *Caes.* 28. Stone does not note the immediate history of the idea. Clark and Ruebel (1985:68, note 30) trace the idea of the sick state back to at least the time of Cato the Elder (cf. Plutarch *Cat. Mai.* 19.3), but the political connotations are not clear there.

CHAPTER 5

1. On *repetundae* in general, see Mommsen 1899:705–32; Zumpt 1868:6–54, 131–213; Pontenay de Fontette 1954; Serrao 1956; Venturini 1979; Lintott 1981, 1992:10–33; and Alexander 1984.

2. The fragments account for less than half of the text and so published versions depend heavily on conjectural reconstruction and humanist copies of two lost fragments. There are now full commentaries by Lintott (1992) and Crawford (1996:39–112), but the former presumes a reconstruction of the tablet of which even the author is now unsure. Even more fragmentary is the law of the *tabula Tarentina*, for which see the edition of Tibiletti (1953:39–55). Identification of this law is highly uncertain.

3. For a concise sense of the problems (in the context of *inventio*) see Preiswerk 1905:47.

4. Line 74: *ex lege quam L. Calpurnius L. f. tr. pl. rogavit exve lege, quam M. Iunius D. f. tr. pl. rogavit* confirms the reconstruction of the name Calpurnia in line 23.

5. See chapter 1, section 3 for the procedure involved.

6. For sources see *MRR* 1.518, but read "Diod. 34–35.25." All sources make the point of the law the transfer of the juries to the equestrians. Appian (*BC* 1.22) dates the measure to 122, while Velleius (2.6.3) seems to suggest 123; see Stockton (1979:234–35) on possible epigraphic evidence for 123.

7. *MRR* 1.519, note 4 points out a reference to a *lex Rubria* in line 22 of the inscribed law. This may put the law between 123 and 121. However, this depends crucially on a doubtful restoration of the inscription; see Stockton 1979:235.

8. On the historical inferences which can be drawn from this concern for procedure see Sherwin-White 1982.

9. On the length of lines see Lintott 1992:75–77; Mackay 1995; and Crawford 1996:45–49.

10. Venuleius Saturninus *D.* 48.11.6.2 gives an imperial limit as 100 aurei (10,000 sesterces at early imperial rates of exchange), which is quite low compared to the 40,000,000 sesterces Verres is supposed to have taken out of Sicily (*I Verr.* 56). Mommsen pointed out that awards of as little as 8,000 sesterces are attested (*II Verr.* 3.184, 4.22), which suggests a limit of no more than 4,000 sesterces (assuming a two-fold penalty).

11. The opening of the law is reconstructed by Mommsen (*CIL* I, p. 49) as [*Quoi soci(or)um no*]*minis Latini exterarumve nationum* . . . Some would prefer to read [*Quoi civei Romano socium no*]*minis Latini* . . . This has traditionally been rejected on the basis of Cicero's assertion (*Caec.* 18) that laws *de repetundis* were passed solely for the benefit of the allies, not citizens. See also Lintott 1981:178 and Sherwin-White 1972:94.

12. The list of magistracies appears to be the same as that in the clause of the *lex Cornelia de sicariis* cited at *Clu.* 148.

13. Successful prosecutors were also awarded Roman citizenship (lines 76–78).

14. Under the empire, even a slave could bring such an accusation *(deferentes)* on a charge of *maiestas* (Marc. *D.* 48.2.13 pr).

15. Lines 60 and 63 also specify that a prosecution may be brought "in the name of" *(nomine)* a foreign king or even an entire people.

16. For the sources for these laws see *MRR sub annis*. For possible redating of the tribunate of Glaucia see Ferrary 1979:101–5 and Lintott 1981:189.

17. It was also possible to use the *repetundae* procedure to recover from the heirs of an offender (line 29). This provision was retained (eventually with a one-year time limit) through imperial times (Scaevola *D.* 48.11.2).

18. Of course the *divinatio* only provides an obstacle to prosecution by noncitizens, not an absolute prohibition. *Balb.* 54 provides instances of prosecutions by Latins under the *lex Servilia Glauciae*. Levick (1967) is right to see that the words *acerbissima* and *passi sunt* show that this passage refers to Glaucia's law rather than Caepio's. Other objections to this identification (e.g., Serrao 1956:499) are based on the assumption, which Sherwin-White (1972:96–97) has shown to be unfounded, that this passage says anything at all about the granting of citizenship to non-Latins. For bibliography on the vexed question see Ferrary 1979:86, note 5 and Lintott 1981:187, note 97. Lintott (1981:188) argues that the antiprovincial bias is more in keeping with Caepio's reactionary bill than with Glaucia's program, which was otherwise supportive of noncitizens.

19. Lintott also points out (1981:196) that it is probably here that the process of *inquisitio* is first introduced. It is first attested in 93 (Asc. 2.20–231C); the surviving chapter of the *lex Acilia* (lines 30–32), which Mommsen entitled *de inquisitione facienda*, does not actually contain this language or any provision for subpoena of wit-

nesses. *Inquisitio* would only be necessary if the prosecutor did not necessarily have any connection with provincials who wished to bring a charge and so was probably introduced along with *divinatio*.

20. See *I Verr.* 38; Vel. Pat. 2.32.3; and Tac. *Ann.* 11.22. The latter two point out that all the courts were returned to the senate. Since Sulla was clearly revamping the *iudicia publica* in general, we cannot tell whether the change was effected by the individual laws (including the *lex de repetundis*) or by a general *lex iudicaria*.

21. The frequent repetition of very nearly these words (e.g., *ob rem iudicandam pecuniam accipere, II Verr.* 2.78, 3.206) in the *Verrines* would probably have sufficed to prove the point in the absence of direct testimony (Venturini 1979:365, 372). See also the reference at *I Verr.* 38 to the holding of a *litis aestimatio* on these grounds.

22. It has also been argued (e.g., Venturini 1979:84) that *Clu.* 116, *Scaevola condemnatus est . . . frequentissimis Apuliae testibus* shows that the normal recovery function was available to citizens. However, the ellipsed words are crucial—*aliis criminibus*. The connection of the Apulians (admittedly citizens in 72) to the formal charge of *repetundae* is not at all clear.

23. I omit here a discussion of a number of procedural changes such as the increase in the number of prosecution subpoenas (from 48 to 120) and the requirement that returning governors file their accounts on their return to Rome. For references on these provisions and on the *lex Iulia* in general, see Lintott 1981:202–4.

24. There is considerable discussion of raising money for a fleet at *Flacc.* 27–33; the trial was held in the same year as the passage of the *lex Iulia*. One might then wonder whether Flaccus was tried under the *lex Cornelia* or *lex Iulia*. Oost's (1956:20–22, 26–28) arguments for the former seem compelling, although some of his detailed reconstruction of the dating of the *lex Iulia* places too much faith in the literal truth of various Ciceronian texts. Presumably Flaccus was tried for extortion in the context of a legal act (raising fleet money), not for the act itself (as would shortly be outlawed).

25. See Lintott 1981:202 and note 153.

26. For broadly similar conclusions see Venturini 1979:321–61, esp. 360–61.

27. Fr. 97.1: ὡς δωροδωκή [σας] (adopting part of Boissevain's supplement).

28. The clause was almost certainly not part of the original *lex Calpurnia*. Tubero was tried before a *quaestio extraordinaria* in 142 because *cepit pecunias ob rem iudicandam* (*Fin.* 2.54). Had there been as standing court such a procedure would hardly have been necessary (Venturini 1979:383).

29. Marcianus (*D.* 48.11.1 pr) and Macer (*D.* 48.11.5 pr) assert that the *repetundae* laws apply to the *cohors/comites* of the officials also; the Cnidos law (3.15; see note 31 below) suggests that this was already true of the regulatory laws (however they were entitled) at the end of the second century. Assuming that Cicero is not making up or distorting this particular regulation, then it may have been poorly enforced. Otherwise the joke of Catullus 10.14–20 ("At least you could have gotten some litter-bearers") does not make much sense.

30. See also Lintott 1981:176.

31. The law is to be identified with the "piracy law" from Delphi (*Fouilles de Delphes* 3.37; Hassall et al. 1974:197–200); the subject matter in fact covers a number of foreign policy issues. For text, translation, and commentary see Hassall et al. 1974.

32. On the date see Hassall et al. 1974:218–19 and Lintott 1976a:66–69, 81.

33. Brunt (1988:526–30) and others have suggested that both groups were allowed actions for recovery (at least by the *lex Acilia*).

34. *Caec.* 17–18: *Quasi vero dubium sit quin tota lex de pecuniis repetundis sociorum causa constitua sit; nam civibus cum sunt ereptae pecuniae, civili fere actione et privato iure repetuntur. II Verr.* 2.15: *in hac quaestione de pecuniis repetundis, quae sociorum causa constituta est lege iudicioque sociali.*

35. For sources see Richardson 1987:1, note 6.

36. See Crook 1967:146, 153–54, 282.

37. On motivations see further Alexander 1984:526.

38. We might compare Roman practice to that of other "soft" colonial powers (i.e., ones which made no particular effort to displace indigenous peoples [as the British did in North America] or harness their labor to the conqueror's goals [as the Spanish did in Peru]). There were of course more brutal aspects of Roman colonialism as well, especially in Spain. In the Italian colony of Somalia (1911–41) disputes between Italians and Somalis were settled by regular Italian law (Hess 1966:110). Hence the indigenes were not specially protected; in fact, this kind of notional equality would have meant an advantage for the conquerors in the light of their greater familiarity with both legal procedure and language. A similar imposition of the colonial power's law on colonist/ indigene disputes is said to have produced precisely this actual inequality under British rule in India (Sanderson 1951:89, 250–51). For a broad range of colonial practice (generally much harsher than these two cases), see Carlton 1992.

39. Corporate entities had no standing to sue in Roman courts. There are also *actiones pro libertate* (on behalf of a slave) and *pro tutela. Inst.* 4.10 attributes these to the early period; later the scope of *actiones alieno nomine* was expanded even further to allow suits by (pro)curators. See Mercer 1983 and *Digest* 47.23.

40. Lintott (1976b:209), following notions of Klenze and Serrao and looking at *I Verr.* 56, suggests the form the *sacramentum* might take *aio te quadragintiens sestertium ex Silicia contra legem abstulisse.* Richardson (1987:5–6) objects that while this is formally possible, such a *sacramentum* would obviously not have the desired legal consequences such as restitution. But as Lintott points out, the judgment of the *sacramentum* would serve as a *praeiudicium* for a later assessment of specific damages as in the case of *provocare sponsione* (Crook 1976) or the *litis aestimatio* of later *leges de repetundis* (e.g., *lex Acilia*, lines 58–59). Gaius 4.95 specifically says that the *legis actio sacramento* is to be used as a *praeiudicium.*

41. Richardson's argument is actually that the prevention of usucapion (unless the property is first returned to the person from whom it came) itself implies that the orig-

inal holder was capable of Roman law ownership *(dominium)* and hence a citizen. This is not sound. For Gaius (4.43) the whole point of *usucapio* is acquisition of good title when doing business with nonowners. Buckland (1963:248–49) and Prichard (1961:201) show that the seller's citizenship is not at issue (and the purchaser may only have needed *commercium* to usucapt): the contract of sale (universally valid) would have provided the *iustus titulus* required for *usucapio*. The rule is simply intended to prevent the guilty official or his associates from acquiring legal ownership of illegally acquired merchandise (as in the rule forbidding the usucapion of items acquired by theft or *vis*, Gaius 2.45). The exception prevents this reasonable restriction from confusing title to the property should it be returned (for instance, after a suit *de repetundis*) to Roman hands by more conventional channels. The citizenship of the victim is never at issue.

42. On the decree see Sherwin-White 1973:279–87. For the possibility of a slightly later date, see most recently Rubin 1975.

43. This seems to have been a major function of the *patroni* assigned, *ad hoc*, to the Spaniards in 171 (Liv. 43.2; Serrao 1956:477).

44. The possibility of acting with no patron would have been reinforced by the preemptive exclusion of family and *sodales* of the accused and by a clause (line 11) rejecting those convicted under this statute (Serrao 1956:480–82).

45. Much of the same material is considered from a somewhat different point of view by Vasaly (1993:191–217).

46. Cf. *Font.* 3, 11, 34; *Flacc.* 23, 35; *ORF* 58.4.

47. Furthermore, the prosecution witnesses can always claim that a crime was committed when any given defense witness was not present. Since countertestimony will not always be available, arguments about credibility become more important.

48. He does so to the near total exclusion of arguments against witnesses *tout court*. The only such argument in these speeches is at *Scaur.* 15–16, and even there it is subordinated to a racial argument.

49. Cf. *Font.* 4: *Quae est igitur ista accusatio quae . . . libentius . . . utatur alienigenis quam domesticis testibus?*

50. For concern for *testimonium* as a particularly Roman concern cf. *Acad.* 2.146, Juvenal 8.79–82.

51. The relative rarity of such truly generic attacks may answer A. Kurke's (1989: 175) question as to why juries would listen to the more common *ad gentem* attacks (see below). The latter are merely racist generalizations, hardly rare in any society; the former, if readily admitted, would render the *quaestio* moot. There are, however, cases, such as *pro Flacco*, where there are witnesses, although not the plaintiffs themselves, who are citizens. They must be dealt with on an individual basis (or ignored amid the flow of the racial attacks). We will return to this topic.

52. Also at §§30–31 and 49.

53. Reports of human sacrifice among alien peoples are perhaps inherently suspect,

but the reports of Caesar (*BG* 6.16) and Strabo (4.4.5, if based on Posidonius) may ultimately derive from autopsy. In any case Graeco-Roman belief in the practice seems to have been pervasive; see Last 1949:3.

54. Cicero, following ordinary courtroom decorum, gives a purportedly Greek expression in Latin.

55. A. Kurke (1989:166, note 163, 183, note 221), following some suggestions of Du-Mesnil, points out that two of the four phrases do not, in their original context, bear on the Greeks' credibility, and the attack on the Lydians is, of course, exaggerated.

56. On mime cf. chapter 4, note 60.

57. Punic treachery really is proverbial: Livy 21.4.9: *perfidia plus quam Punica.* Consider also the ironic use of *Punica fides* (Sall. *BJ* 108.3; Livy 22.6.12; *OLD* s.v. *Punicus* [1b])

58. Discussion of witnesses is in general much less prominent in *pro Rabirio Postumo*. Vasaly (1993:193, 196, 203–4) notes some of the subdivisions but does not explain them (see, however, her remarks on the history of the division between European and Asian Greeks).

59. Collectively they are described as providing *fidelissima et gravissima auxilia* (§45).

60. Throughout the extant portions of the speech Cicero describes his adversaries, the descendants of the Phoenicians, as *Sardi*. If my interpretation of the passage of Pompeius is correct then Cicero is probably using the same tactics here as in *pro Flacco*: he uses one unmarked term (here *Sardi*, there *Graeci*) for everyone, except where he is making a point of the division. Another possibility is that Pompeius' *incolae* (of the *Sardi*) does not mean "autochthonous," when contrasted with *advenae* (as the *Sardinienses* are styled); the technical sense of *incola* is "resident alien." Compare Franko 1994 on the different forces of (unmarked) *Carthagines* and (negative) *Punici*. *Sardi* can be presented negatively; compare the proverb *Sardi venales, alius alio nequior* (*Fam* 7.24.2).

61. Contrast Vasaly (1993:191) who goes too far in the other direction, claiming that "no Roman orator ever came to grief overestimating his audience's prejudices towards ethnic minorities."

62. *TLRR* lists fifteen sure and seven other possible trials under the *lex Cornelia* between 81 and 50.

63. Cf. Richlin 1992:100–102. At *Scaur.* 20 and fr. g Clark (= Severianus 357.11H) and *Flacc.* 9 Cicero explains the need to paint the opposition with fairly broad strokes.

64. For similar sentiments about the Greeks, cf. *Q. fr.* 1.1.19, 27–28; 1.2.4; Verg. *Aen.* 2.49.

65. For avoidance of other overly generic arguments, see Riggsby (forthcoming).

66. There is one partial exception. One of the witnesses against Scaurus was Valerius, a Sardinian by birth, who had been granted citizenship by the father of Scaurus' prosecutor (*Scaur.* 29).

67. On Greek dress as a topic of invective, see Richlin 1992:92–93.

68. The *exemplum* of Rutilius Rufus (*TLRR* 94) is the last and longest of the three. It is perhaps not coincidental that Cicero chooses to dwell on a person "wrongly" convicted of *repetundae*. Scipio was wrongly (in Livy's eyes) convicted of something like *peculatus*, although there is no standing court in 187, for his actions in Asia (Livy 38.54–60, esp. 55.4–5). For more on both these *exempla*, see section 5.

69. Cf. Vasaly 1993:212–13 on how Cicero similarly de-Romanizes Verres himself.

70. *Avaritia* is a recurring theme of this speech (§§7, 41, 83, 85, 89, 98) but is surprisingly rare in the other orations *de repetundis*.

71. Presumably, given the context, he was *triumvir monetalis*, one of the annually elected junior magistrates in charge of minting coins.

72. The issue in *pro Rabirio Postumo* is, as Cicero constructs it, purely legal, hence there is little room for this kind of argument. He does try in a general way to establish Rabirius as nice but not particularly bright. One might have expected more discussion of ethos in *pro Scauro*, but that speech is the most fragmentary. Particularly problematic is the loss of both the beginning and the end of the speech.

73. Webster (1931: *ad loc.*) suggests something along the lines of *praescribere ut reliqua vita Flacci neglecta magistratus unum annum animadvertas* to complete the broken sentence. Though he has little else to say, this seems to anticipate the core of Kurke's argument.

74. In discussing the bad example that would be set by convicting Flaccus despite what the jurors knew of his character, Cicero says: *Multa enim sunt eius modi, iudices, ut, etiam si in homine ipso de quo agitur neglegenda sint, tamen in condicione atque in exemplo pertimescenda videantur* (*Flacc.* 24). This may echo the use of *condicio* Kurke perceives in §5.

75. For the former reconstruction see Jouanique 1960:111; for the latter Jouanique 1960:107. He prefers the first; I incline toward the second, though one might well question the extent of debts owed by the Roman state at this period.

76. *Font.* 40: *Frugi igitur hominem, iudices, frugi, inquam, et in omnibus vitae partibus moderatum ac temperantem, plenum pudoris, plenum offici, plenum religionis videtis positum in vestra fide ac potestate, atque ita ut commissus sit fidei, permissus potestati.*

77. Dessau (1911:613) records everything known with certainty about Rabirius; the rest of the article is interesting but highly speculative.

78. For Gabinius' trial see *TLRR* 303 and Fantham 1975.

79. This account is not contradicted by anything in the story of M. Servilius (*TLRR* 337) who was also tried under the clause *quo ea pecunia pervenerit*. See *Fam.* 8.8.2–3 and Shackleton Bailey, *ad loc.* There is no particular reason to doubt either of Cicero's accounts. For a possible reconstruction of the whole text of this part of the law, see Lintott 1981:190. The only other known possible trials under this clause are those of C. Manilius (*TLRR* 205; see Ramsey 1980a) and the anonymous series of trials cited at *Clu.* 116: *cotidie fieri videmus ut reo damnato de pecuniis repetundis, ad quos pervenisse pecunias in litibus aestimandis statutum sit, eos idem iudices absolvant.* This

incidentally supports the position Cicero adopts in *pro Rabirio*, that this clause was normally used against persons who had come up in the *litis aestimatio*.

80. See Daube 1956:73–77 for the form of the criminal judgment. Note that *redigam* implies neither the "careful inquiry" nor the "detachment" that Daube identifies in the form of the normal verdict. Cf. also *Acad.* 2.146.

81. Contrast the Loeb translation of *quo ea* (at *Fam.* 8.8.2, note b) as "for receiving money with intent to defraud." Such intent is neither required nor relevant.

82. The case was heard by the senate, and Pliny never uses the word *repetundae*, but the case was as *causa publica* (§1) which was allowed to stand posthumously (§6, as was allowed under the *lex Iulia de repetundis* [Scaevola *D.* 48.11.2 pr]) for despoiling provincials (§§1, 17). Special provision was made that Classicus' daughter would receive the property he had held before his governorship (§17).

83. The pathetic rhetoric of *Rab. Post.* 48 does not justify the claim that the *lex Iulia* imposed *infamia* on those subject to this clause. See Klodt 1992; the amounts of money at stake in the Gabinius affair could easily have driven Rabirius (or almost anyone else) into bankruptcy and disgrace.

84. Thus at Caes. *BG* 7.65.5: *a tribunis militum reliquisque equitibus Romanis*, *BG* 3.7.3–4 + 9.3 + 10.2 (where the identity of the referents in the three passages is not immediately clear to the reader unless it is assumed that *tribuni militum* are knights); Polybius 6.19. For complete detail on the social background of the *tribuni* see Suohlati 1955:52–145, esp. 52–57, 140–45.

85. And as Sherwin-White (1972:89) and Hopkins (1983:111–16) point out, many of these military tribunes and sons of senators would never become senators themselves. The two groups (tribunes and sons) probably overlapped considerably (Polybius 6.19; Livy 44.12).

86. In both cases (as well as *Flacc.* 4) Cicero also conflates the equestrians and the *tribuni aerarii*. This is also an oversimplification, but it does not seem to be as disingenuous as the other. Mommsen (1899:3.1.192, note 4), Wiseman (1970), Brunt (1988:146, 210–11), and others have used this frequent rhetorical conflation (also *Font.* 36; *Planc.* 41; *Clu.* 121, 130; *Flacc.* 96) to argue that the *tribuni aerarii* were actually men of equestrian census, but without the public horse. The Bobbio scholiast (94.24–26St.) reached the same conclusion: *eiusdem scilicet ordinis viri* (explaining *Flacc.* 4). *Scilicet* indicates it is his inference from the text. However, incidental uses of the term normally refer clearly to the original treasury function (e.g., Varro *LL* 5.181, *D.* 4.6.32 pr., Florus *Epit.* 2.13) or to the jurors (e.g., Suet. *JC* 41.2, *Q. fr.* 6.16.3, *Planc.* 21). If the phrase really referred to *equites* in the broad sense, one would expect clear attestation in some other context. Cicero does twice refer to the *tribuni aerarii* as an order in listing the groups that came together against revolutionaries (*Cat.* 4.15, *Rab. Perd.* 27).

87. Also referred to more briefly at *Clu.* 153.

88. On the sense of "conservative" used here, see chapter 4, note 32.

89. Kurke (1989:113–14) is presumably right to see this whole line of attack as a

swipe at the Triumvirate, especially given the reference to Pompey's backing of Laelius (§14).

90. Cf. also §37: *Quod si in turpi reo patiendum non esset ut quicquam isti se minis profecisse arbitrarentur, quid faciendum vobis in M. Fonteio arbitramini?*

91. Cf. also §49 (the final words of the speech): *Postremo prospicite, iudices, id quod ad dignitatem populi Romani maxime pertinet, ut plus apud vos preces virginis Vestalis quam minae Gallorum valuisse videantur.*

92. On this line of argument, see further Riggsby (forthcoming).

93. E.g., *tum in re militari cum summi consili et maximi animi, tum vero usu quoque bellorum gerendorum in primis eorum hominum qui nunc sunt exercitatus* (§41).

94. Actually, if we look at the known cases of trials for provincial misconduct between Sulla and Verres' trial (*TLRR* 131, 135, 139, 140, 144–158, 172, 174), we find four convictions and three acquittals. Doubtless Cicero would have argued that these four unfortunates did not have the cash to escape, as he does at *I Verr.* 46 for the one senator convicted since the recent "restoration" of the tribunate.

95. As it happened the senate did lose its control of the juries later that year (despite Verres' exile) when the *lex Aurelia* introduced the tripartite division of the jurors (one-third each senators, equestrians, and *tribuni aerarii*) which held for most of the Ciceronian period.

96. Similarly, the claims of Cluentius' innocence and his protection by *praeiudicia* are extrinsically connected. The telling of the same stories progressively indicates the prior judgments and Cluentius' lack of motive for murder.

97. The *tituli* at the end of *Font.* 20 indicate the omission of much further substantive argument from that speech. In *pro Scauro* Cicero postpones the factual matters to the end, now lost (§22).

CHAPTER 6

1. Gruen (1974:222–23).

2. Assuming that its motives were largely practical in the first place. In addition to the actual legislation, there were also a *senatus consultum* (on *divisores*) and a proposed law to fine candidates for their use of bribery in 61 (*Att.* 1.16.12–13).

3. There is no general connection drawn. It is true that the series of *praeiudicia* are also used to show that Cluentius had no motive for one of his alleged crimes.

4. The character of the offenses does differ in that *repetundae* (but not *ambitus*) involves abuse of power, but the evidentiary symmetry is nonetheless precise.

5. In essence what I offer here is a "model," or rather an interlocking set of models, in the sense of Finley 1985:60–66. Some are comparatively based (e.g., the exchange-oriented interpretation of *ambitus*), and others (e.g., the "duality" of the criminal courts discussed below) are more *ad hoc*. While they cannot be deduced (in the strict sense) from the ancient evidence, they do account for a lot of data in a reasonably

efficient and self-consistent way. Given the limits of the evidence for this period, deductive certainty on virtually any matter seems uncertain. Instead, internal consistency and explanatory breadth should be our criteria.

6. This is even aside from admitted legal questions which do not happen to come up in the surviving speeches.

7. Williamson 1990 and Nicolet 1980:250–58, 270–77, 281–85.

8. One might ask how, if the jurors actually held such a conception of their role, the defense could ever make the claim that any prosecution charges were irrelevant. There are two responses. One is that such claims are not particularly common. The second is that the citizen who is dangerous for some reason can normally be convicted by the appropriate court (especially given the existence of broadly defined crimes such as *maiestas*), so there is no real harm in observing procedural safeguards. In contrast, claims by the defense as to overall benefit to the society must prevail in any court; otherwise, they mean nothing.

9. For a list of these courts see Macer, *D.* 48.1.1. For a contrasting view of the coherence of the system of *quaestiones* see Jones 1991:759; her observation that the courts had overlapping jurisdiction is undoubtedly sound.

10. Contrast the civil action for *iniuria*, which involves (among other things) intentional physical injury (Gaius 3.220, 223–25).

11. *Peculatus* is specifically defined by Labeo as theft *(furtum)* of public or sacred funds (Paul. *D.* 48.13.11.2 and Ulp. *D.* 48.13.8). It need not involve funds the defendant is officially in charge of (Ulp. *D.* 48.13.13), and in fact Labeo's definition specifically excludes this case. Hence the usual translation of "embezzlement" is misleading.

12. Declamations involving poison (cf. below) highlight the slipperiness of the charge (it is often claimed by one side that the poison was thought to be medicine) and the pervasiveness of the danger (it is often said to be administered by women [see note 23 below for citations] and/or those with an inheritance as a motive: i.e., persons from whom one would not normally protect oneself).

13. In the context of other Augustan legislation designed to encourage marriage (Suet. *Aug.* 34.1; Dio. 54.16.3–4), it might be argued that the goal of the adultery law was also to encourage marriage by discouraging an alternative form of sexual behavior; this is described as an effect of the law by some later authors (Treggiari 1991:296, note 203). But the other laws rewarded not just any marriage or children, but socially acceptable marriages (e.g., senators cannot marry freedwomen) and legitimate children of such couples; thus even they emphasize having the "right" children. Cf. Hor. *Car.* 4.5.23: *laudantur simili prole puerperae*, in the context of an unnamed Augustan *lex*.

14. As Fascione (1984:18) says of *ambitus*, "the central axis of the offense is in fact the injury to the interest of the collectivity in the free formation of a majority."

15. Since creation of a legal institution of any sort demonstrates state interest, this claim, as usually framed, is nearly tautologous (e.g., Mommsen 1899:180, note 2; Tellegen-Couperus 1993:52; Wolff 1951:53; Nicolet 1980:334; Santalucia 1989:76);

Jones (1972:46–47) notes the problem. Kaser (1986:50) seems to hedge between this interpretation and the idea (cf. note 30 below) that courts are *publicus* because of the system of popular accusation. If we instead advance the penal character of the judgments as a criterion for "being of interest to the state" then the claim is false. Punishment of some delicts by double and quadruple damages (rather than simple restitution) would count as state interest by this criterion (cf. Alexander 1984:528), yet they are not tried by *iudicia publica*.

16. As the case of the political arguments of the first *Verrine* showed, it is also an ambiguity that can be used by both sides.

17. Note that Kunkel (1962:137) himself calls the entire civil/criminal distinction into question. Cf. also Alexander 1984:536–39.

18. Livy 4.51.2; for other early examples see Kunkel 1962:57, note 216.

19. Kunkel (1962:14, 60) notes that the very phrase *nomen deferre*, "offer a name" (which predates the standing *quaestiones*), seems to imply a stage at which the prosecutor and the person bringing the indictment were distinct.

20. Perhaps better, according to the persuasive arguments of Garnsey (1966:177–80), the *consilium* formed a mandatory but nonbinding advisory panel. Cf. Lintott 1992:14 on the influence of civil recuperatoral procedure on the *repetundae* court.

21. The legal force of such senate authorization is technically suspect, even before the *lex Sempronia*, but in practice seems often to have sufficed.

22. One crucial aspect is that the *repetundae* courts probably did not have *nominis delatio* (free public accusation) until the *lex Acilia* of 123–22; see Kunkel 1962:61–62, 96.

23. The particular example is the Bacchanalia incident of 186. He also gives somewhat vague reasons for the inquiries into the rash of poisonings in the first half of the second century (184: Liv. 39.41.5; 180: Liv. 40.37.4, 43.2; 150: Liv. *Per.* 48), and the Silian wood incident of 138 (*Brut.* 85). The general explanation of *veneficium* given above applies to the former; the latter is a perfect example of what Cloud (1969) showed was the original sense of what a *sicarius* did.

24. Kunkel (1962:94) also speaks of the "obvious" advantages of a *quaestio* over a private trial by *sacramentum*. Yet for the public process to completely displace the private, the advantages would have to be entirely for the prosecution; such asymmetrical advantage is not obvious.

25. The matter is somewhat controversial, but it seems that impeachment must precede the ordinary criminal prosecution.

26. This view seems to be the norm among those not personally involved in the impeachment proceedings. Specifically, I follow here the account of Berger (1973:53–102); cf. also Gerhardt 1996:103–11 and Impeachment Inquiry Staff n.d.:38–44. It is occasionally argued, generally by those facing impeachment themselves, that an impeachable offense must have a criminally indictable offense as its substrate; see St. Clair et al. n.d.:59–61. If this view were widely held, it would make the American system rather more similar to the Roman *iudicia publica*.

27. Though the phrase itself is vague, there are considerable common-law restrictions on its scope; see Berger 1973:69–71, 86–90.

28. The murder trial of Scamander is the clearest example, but in this context the trials of apolitical equestrians (e.g., Rabirius Postumus, Cluentius) are also relevant. Cloud (1994:523) offers some more circumstantial but interesting arguments that the social reach of the homicide court went much lower than that of the other courts.

29. See Watson 1995.

30. Kunkel (1963:723–25), Jones (1972:47), and Pugliese (1982:727) tie the term to "public" accusation, i.e., *nominis delatio*, all apparently following Justinian (*Inst.* 4.18.1). However, there are *iudicia publica* with restricted accusation *(repetundae)* and private actions that are open to any citizen; see Kaser 1986:51. Kaser himself (1966: 117–18) suggests that *iudicium publicum* has no systematic meaning, at least at this period. The use of *criminalia* to designate these courts (or at least their original area of jurisdiction) seems to date to the very late second century A.D. (Wolff 1951:70, note 15]).

31. Cf. chapter 3, note 30 on words for "offense."

32. On the history and prehistory of academic criminology, see Leps 1992:17–43; for the detective story, which has a rather more complicated origin, see Leps 1992:136, note 4.

33. In much the same sense that Foucault (1978:105–14) suggests that not sex or sexual acts but "sexuality" (an object of discourse and formant of identity) is a localized historical construct.

34. Alexander (1993a) shows that on another criterion, intensity of usage, at least within the upper classes, they were a much more robust institution.

35. In that year we know of several apparently independent *ambitus* prosecutions, which suggests the existence of a standing court by then (Plut. *Mar.* 5.3–5; Val. Max. 6.9.14; *Brut.* 113). For possible dates for the various courts see Kunkel 1962:62–64; Gruen 1968:29, 167, 261; and Cloud 1994:505–24.

36. On this process see Kunkel 1963:776–79; the *maiestas* and *repetundae* courts are superseded almost immediately under the empire; adultery is the last to be replaced, though the timing is disputed. See Garnsey 1967 and Bauman 1968.

37. On *cognitio* in criminal cases see Pugliese 1982. In this respect true *cognitio* and senatorial processes are not significantly different.

38. This generally holds for senatorial trials (only allowed for senatorial defendants) on selected charges during the early empire (Pugliese 1982:747, note 48, 749, note 53, 770).

39. On Gaius' chronology see Honoré 1962:46–96.

40. This is despite (or because of?) the decline in imperial times of distinct institutions to try public offenses.

41. There are also scattered references to possibly related topics, primarily the legal consequences of exile; see *D.* 48.22.3. This may perhaps better be read in the more ex-

tensively attested context of capture in war. A number of jurists discuss the question of who counts as a member of the community, i.e., who is a citizen under what conditions (especially but not always in connection with *postliminium*). This starts no later than P. Mucius Scaevola (cos. 133; *D.* 50.7.8) and M. Iunius Brutus (probably praetor around 150; *D.* 49.15.2). Many other, slightly later jurists are cited in the Digest and (collectively) at *de Or.* 1.181.

42. For the date see Tac. *Ann.* 3.75; Pomp. *D.* 1.2.2.47. On the (entirely imperial) history of juristic works *de iudiciis publicis*, see Bauman 1975.

43. There is a technical difficulty in the text here. The book on the public courts is also referred to as book 9 by the manuscripts of Gellius. Strzelecki (1958) shows that it is paleographically easy (and perhaps even preferable) to read the book number for the book on the senate as IIII. Unfortunately, this solution requires the same error and emendation in both 14.7.9 and 14.8.2. Thus I would lean toward the solution of Schoppe and Hertz to emend 4.14.7 from VIIII to VIII instead.

44. For the title of Tuditanus' work see Macrob. *Sat.* 1.13.21; for Gracchanus' see Ulp. *D.* 1.13.1 pr and cf. *Leg.* 3.47–48.

45. Cf. Kaser 1986 : 49–52.

46. Of course, we often have only general titles like *Digesta* and *Coniectanea*, so it is hard to tell.

47. See *Inv.* 1.10–19, *Her.* 1.18–25, and Kennedy 1972 : 620–25.

48. I do not mean to claim that all of these arguments would necessarily be equally successful in an actual trial. The point is merely that status is not logically restricted to criminal cases.

49. It is true, as Heath (1994 : 121, 122) shows, that a few systems attempted to add some further levels of analysis to the determination of status. However, as he also shows, these systems either fall into self-contradiction (121, 122) or collapse back into a single level (122–28). Furthermore, and most important to the present argument, even while the extended analyses give the orator more specific options, the choice between them remains ultimately intuitive.

50. See, for instance, *Her.* 2.9, 12.

51. Furthermore, while the legal texts use the verbs *praebere* and *praestare*, declamation uses *esse* instead. Hence, arguments developed in one sphere would be open to criticism in the other by interpreting a difference in meaning of the verbs.

52. Certainly by the time of Celsus (Ulp. *D.* 9.2.7.6). For Labeo, see *D.* 9.2.9 pr, where Ulpian appears to supply the phrase in question, but it seems to be required in any case to support the distinction between true Aquilian actions and *actiones in factum* that Labeo is making. Furthermore, Watson (1965 : 241–43) points out that even Republican jurists seem already to have extended the scope of the *lex Aquilia* in a similar direction by interpretation, rather than resort to *in factum* actions (see Alfenus *D.* 9.2.52.2). Thus they may well have introduced the *causa mortis* terminology already.

53. For the common formula "actio sit" see Bonner 1949:85, and even this would not have been the correct edictal formulation. For the public offenses see *quaestio* in the *lex Acilia* (4) and *quaerito* in the *lex Cornelia* (*Clu.* 148).

54. E.g., the Budé introduction of G. DePlinval (1959:liii–liv) and the introduction of A. DuMesnil (1879:9). *Leg.* 3.47 suggests probably further discussion of *iudicia*, but nothing suggests these are other than *iudicia privata*.

55. This section also roughly reproduces the Gracchan law *ne quis iudicio circumveniretur*, but no other part of the *lex Cornelia de sicariis et veneficiis* into which the Gracchan law was eventually assimilated.

56. Cicero's commentary on this bit of legislation is *Sequitur de captis pecuniis et de ambitu. Quae cum magis iudiciis quam uerbis sancienda sint, adiungitur: "noxiae poena par esto" ut in suo uitio quisque plectatur, uis capite, auaritia multa, honoris cupiditas ignominia sanciatur (Leg.* 3.46).

57. In separate parts of the list of the duties of the minor magistrates we find *capitalia vindicanto*, but *litis contractas iudicanto* (*Leg.* 3.6).

58. And also before the broad expansion of "criminal" jurisdiction, discussed above in the context of Kunkel's reconstruction of the pre-Sullan court system.

59. E.g., *ad Her.* 2.5. The one clear exception is Rabirius Postumus (who made foolish errors). Cicero also hints at youthful indiscretions by Caelius but admits little.

60. Cloud 1994:528.

61. For the expansive theory see Kunkel 1962:71–79 and Cloud 1994:500–501. For strong arguments against, see Nippel 1984; 1995:16–26.

APPENDIXES

1. It is also worthwhile to note that the audience of Cicero's published speeches had a similar make-up to that of the jury members of the original audiences; the former differs from the latter largely in the self-consciousness in its members of their role as jurors. For the significance of this self-consciousness see Lakoff 1990:90. The published speeches may also have a more senatorial audience.

2. On this issue see, for instance, Humbert 1925, Heinze 1925:239–45, Laurand 1928, Settle 1962, Stroh 1975:31–54, Classen 1985:2–13, Marshall 1987, and Kirby 1990:163–70.

3. It has been suggested to me that Nepos found the event noteworthy precisely because he was surprised by the correspondence of the two versions. I would suggest that what was unusual was simply the author's presence at a narrated event *(se praesente)*.

4. For the *Verrines* see Alexander 1976; for the second *Philippic* see *Att.* 15.13.2, 16.11.1.

5. There has, however, been some tendency to overestimate the extent of the disruption; see Clark 1895:xxvii and Stone 1980. See above, chapter 4, section 6, for extensive discussion of the two versions.

6. It is true, as Cicero recognized, that style can have political implications (see *Brut.* 289–90 [and Douglas' commentary] and *OGO* on "Atticism," and cf. Riggsby 1995a). However, the differences of style in question usually involve a conscious difference in object, and not merely in the degree to which that object is achieved. Furthermore, the "politics" at issue are (at this period) fairly abstract, cultural ones, rather than the partisan kind of politics that are explicitly associated with the judgment of individual cases.

7. Cf. note 13 below for the fact that Cicero did not normally have a written text to work from. Marshall (1987) goes too far in denying the possibility of transcripts, but there is not good evidence for their routine use.

8. It is not clear whether "more Attic," ἀττικώτερα is literal and so refers to a Greek speech (and hence an epideictic work) or is used to contrast to an Asiatic style, or whether it is solely a joke on Atticus' cognomen (and it must be at least partly this). The pun is more explicit at *Att.* 14.1a.2. The first speech referred to is completely unknown (and may never have been delivered at all). The second was probably that delivered in January 62 after Q. Metellus Nepos attacked Cicero in a *contio* on 3 Jan. (*Fam.* 5.2.6, 8).

9. The exact sense of the verb *putaram* is not clear. I have not found it used elsewhere of editing, though it is commonly used of balancing accounts.

10. Cf. Kennedy 1972:177 and Cape 1991:11, 19–22 on the *Catilinarians*. More generally see Stroh 1975:40–50, esp. 50, note 84.

11. This *titulus* is preserved only in a supplement of a single manuscript. Austin (1960:*ad loc.*) rightly points out that the speech has a difficult but not incomprehensible transition between §§19 and 20. Hence it is quite likely that the *titulus* was mistakenly added by a reader of the speech.

12. Further on this letter see Riggsby 1995a.

13. *Brut.* 91 and *TD* 4.55 probably relate the normal state of affairs. When speeches are described as being given from a prepared text *(de scripto)* it seems to be treated as something extraordinary (*Mur.* 28; *Planc.* 74; *Phil.* 10.5; *Att.* 4.3.3).

14. Note that we know of a number of speeches which were apparently never published at all. See Crawford 1984.

15. We might compare *Att.* 15.1a.2, where Cicero says that he did not make changes in a speech Brutus had given him for comment, because it was already perfect given Brutus' choice of a spare style. Brutus' object was apparently an idealization of his original, not a general rewrite.

16. In the former case, he refused to add some remarks about the family, in the latter he wanted to remove the name of a person who was dead and so not only was not but could not have been present at the time.

17. See Kennedy 1969:64, 73 and Yavetz 1984:19 and note.

18. Similarly Stroh 1975:53.

19. Mommsen (1899:399, note 1) suggests a trial *de iniuriis*; this, or some other, noncriminal charge seems likely.

20. See also chapter 4, note 56.

21. Asc. 60.9–15C, *SB* 119St.; *MRR* 2.157–58.

22. Dio 38.10.3, Quintilian 4.2.123–24; and Gruen (1973:308–9).

23. If Cicero does imply that Antonius' Catilinarian associations were central to the charge, then Antonius' trial is presumably yet another example of a conspirator being tried under the *lex Plautia de vi*.

24. Such a charge would have precedent such as the trial of Q. Servilius Caepio in 103 (*TLRR* 66; *Brut.* 135, *ad Her.* 1.24). Cf. *D.* 48.4.4.

25. For the charge see *SB* 94St. Gruen's (1973: note 40) article anticipates and counters Alexander's (1990: *ad loc.* note 3) prosopographical objection to acceptance of the scholiast's word.

Bibliography

Adamietz, J. 1986. "Ciceros Verfahren in den Ambitus-Prozessen gegen Murena und Plancius," *Gymnasium* 93.102–17.

——. 1989. *Marcus Tullius Cicero* pro Murena (Texte zur Forschung 55). Darmstadt: Wissenschaftliche Buchgesellschaft.

Afzelius, A. 1942. "Zwei Episoden aus dem Leben Ciceros," *Classica et Medievalia* 5.209–17.

Aigner, H. 1976. "Zur Wichtigkeit der Waffenbeschaffung in der späten römischen Republik," *GB* 5.1–24.

von Albrecht, M. 1992. *Geschichte der römischen Literatur.* Bern: K. G. Saur.

Alexander, M. 1976. "Hortenius' Speech in Defense of Verres," *Phoenix* 30.46–53.

——. 1982. "Repetition of Prosecution, and the Scope of Prosecutions, in the Standing Criminal Courts of the Late Republic," *CA* 1.141–66.

——. 1984. "Compensation in a Roman Criminal Law," *University of Illinois Law Review* 1984.521–39.

——. 1985. "Praemia in the Quaestiones of the Late Republic," *CP* 80.20–32.

——. 1990. *Trials in the Late Roman Republic, 149 B.C. to 50 B.C.* Toronto: University of Toronto Press (= *TLRR*).

——. 1993a. "How Many Roman Senators Were Ever Prosecuted? The Evidence from the Late Republic," *Phoenix* 47.238–55.

——. 1993b. "Forensic Oratory in the Late Republic: Audience and Politics" (MS, University of Illinois, Chicago).

Allan, K. 1986. *Linguistic Meaning.* London: Routledge & Kegan Paul.

Appadurai, A. 1986a. *The Social Life of Things: Commodities in Cultural Perspective.* Cambridge: Cambridge University Press.

——. 1986b. "Commodities and the Politics of Value," pp. 3–63 in Appadurai 1986a.

von Arnim, H. 1903–5. *Stoicorum Veterum Fragmenta*, 3 vols. Leipzig: Teubner (= *SVF*).

Astin, A. 1967. *Scipio Aemilianus.* Oxford: Oxford University Press.

——. 1988. "Regimen Morum," *JRS* 78.14–34.

Atkins, E. 1990. "'Domina et Regina Virtutum': Justice and Societas in *de Officiis*," *Phronesis* 35.258–89.

Austin, R., ed. 1960. *M. Tulli Ciceronis* pro M. Caelio Oratio³. Oxford: Oxford University Press.

Axer, J. 1978. "*Condemnatio Postumi*: A Comment on M. T. Cicero's 'pro C. Rabirio Postumo' 46," *Eos* 66.227–30.

———. 1979. *The Style and the Composition of Cicero's Speech "Pro Q. Roscio Comoedo": Origin and Function* (Studia Antiqua 3). Warsaw: Wydawnictwa Uniwersytetu Warszawskiego.

———. 1989. "Tribunal-Stage-Arena: Modeling of the Communication Situation in M. Tullius Cicero's Judicial Speeches," *Rhetorica* 7.299–311.

Balsdon, J. 1963. "The *Commentariolum Petitionis*," *CQ* 57.242–50.

Bauman, R. 1967. *The* Crimen Maiestatis *in the Roman Republic and Augustan Principate.* Johannesburg: Witwatersrand University Press.

———. 1968. "Some Remarks on the Structure and Survival of the *Quaestio de adulteriis*," *Antichthon* 2.68–93.

———. 1969. *The Duumviri in the Roman Criminal Law and in the Horatius Legend* (Historia Einzelschriften 12). Wiesbaden: F. Steiner.

———. 1975. "I libri 'de iudiciis publicis,'" *Index* 5.39–48.

———. 1996. *Crime and Punishment in Ancient Rome.* New York: Routledge.

Beard, M. 1986. "Cicero and Divination: The Formation of a Latin Discourse," *JRS* 76.33–46.

Beard, M., and M. Crawford. 1985. *Rome in the Late Republic.* Ithaca: Cornell University Press.

Benner, H. 1987. *Die Politik des P. Clodius Pulcher: Untersuchungen zur Denaturierung des Clientelwesens in der ausgehenden römischen Republik (Historia Einzelschriften 50).* Stuttgart: Steiner-Verlag-Wiesbaden.

Berger, R. 1973. *Impeachment: The Constitutional Problems.* Cambridge, Mass.: Harvard University Press.

Berry, D., ed. 1996a. *Cicero: pro P. Sulla Oratio.* Cambridge: Cambridge University Press.

———. 1996b. [omnibus review of books on Cicero] *JRS* 86.201–7.

Bonner, S. 1949. *Roman Declamation in the Late Republic and Early Empire.* Liverpool: University Press of Liverpool.

———. 1977. *Education in Ancient Rome from the Elder Cato to the Younger Pliny.* Berkeley: University of California Press.

Bourdieu, P. 1977. *Outline of a Theory of Practice*, trans. R. Nice. Cambridge: Cambridge University Press.

Bradley, K. 1987. *Slaves and Masters in the Roman Empire: A Study in Social Control.* Oxford: Oxford University Press.

Brecht, Ch. 1938. *Perduellio.* Munich.

Bremer, F. 1896. *Iurisprudentiae Antehadrianae Quae Supersunt*, 2 vols. Leipzig: Teubner.

Broughton, T. 1951–60. *The Magistrates of the Roman Republic.* New York: American Philological Association (= *MRR*).

Brunt, P. 1965. "Amicitia in the Late Roman Republic," *PCPS* 11.1–20.

———. 1988. *The Fall of the Roman Republic.* Oxford: Oxford University Press.

Buckland, W. 1963. *A Text-Book of Roman Law from Augustus to Justinian*[3], rev. P. Stein. Cambridge: Cambridge University Press.

Bürge, A. 1974. *Die Juristenkomik in Ciceros Rede pro Murena.* Zurich: Juris.

Cape, R. 1991. *On Reading Cicero's Catilinarian Orations* (diss. UCLA).

Carlton, E. 1992. *Occupation: The Policies and Practices of Military Conquerors.* London: Routledge.

Champlin, E. 1991. *Final Judgments: Duty and Emotion in Roman Wills, 200 B.C.–A.D. 250.* Berkeley: University of California Press.

Chenoll Alfaro, R. 1984. *Soborno y elecciones en la Republica Romana*. Málaga: Universidad de Málaga.

Christes, J. 1988. "Cum dignitate otium (Cic. Sest. 98) eine Nachbereitung," *Gymnasium* 95.303–15.

Clark, A. 1895. *Pro T. Annio Milone: ad Iudices Oratio*. Oxford: Oxford University Press.

Clark, M., and J. Ruebel. 1985. "Philosophy and Rhetoric in Cicero's *pro Milone*," *RhM* 128.57–72.

Classen, C. 1972. "Die Anklage gegen Cluentius," *ZSS* 89.1–17.

———. 1978. "Cicero, the Laws, and the Law-Courts," *Latomus* 37.597–619.

———. 1982. "Ciceros Kunst der Überredung," pp. 149–84 in Ludwig 1982.

———. 1985. *Recht, Rhetorik, Politik: Untersuchungen zu Ciceros Rhetorischer Strategie*. Darmstadt: Wissenschaftliche Buchgesellschaft.

Cloud, J. D. 1968. "How Did Sulla Style His Law *de Sicariis*?," *CR* 18.140–43.

———. 1969. "The Primary Purpose of the *lex Cornelia de Sicariis*," *ZSS* 86.258–86.

———. 1971. "Parricidium: From the *lex Numae* to the *lex Pompeia de parricidis*," *ZSS* 101.1–66.

———. 1988. "*Lex Iulia de Vi*: Part 1," *Athenaeum* 76.579–95.

———. 1989. "*Lex Iulia de Vi*: Part 2," *Athenaeum* 77.427–65.

———. 1994. "The Constitution and Public Criminal Law," pp. 491–530 in *CAH*[2] IX.

Cody, J. 1973. "The Use of Libero-Damno and Absolvo-Condemno in the Judicial Proceedings of the Late Republic," *CP* 68.205–8.

Cohen, D. 1991. *Law, Sexuality, and Society: The Enforcement of Morals in Classical Athens*. Cambridge: Cambridge University Press.

Conley, J., and W. O'Barr. 1990. *Rules vs. Relationships: The Ethnography of Legal Discourse*. Chicago: University of Chicago Press.

Corbeill, A. 1996. *Controlling Laughter: Political Humor in the Late Roman Republic*. Princeton: Princeton University Press.

Craig, C. 1979. *The Role of Rational Argumentation in Selected Judicial Speeches of Cicero* (diss. Chapel Hill).

———. 1985. "The Structural Pedigree of Cicero's Speeches *pro Archia*, *pro Milone*, and *pro Quinctio*," *CP* 80.136–37.

———. 1986. "Cato's Stoicism and the Understanding of Cicero's Speech for Murena," *TAPA* 116.229–39.

———. 1989. "Reason, Resonance, and Dilemma in Cicero's Speech for Caelius," *Rhetorica* 7.313–28.

———. 1990. "Cicero's Strategy of Embarrassment in the Speech for Plancius," *AJP* 111.75–81.

———. 1993. *Form as Argument in Cicero's Speeches: A Study of Dilemma*. Atlanta: Scholars Press.

Crawford, J. 1984. *M. Tullius Cicero: The Lost and Unpublished Orations* (*Hypomnemata* 80). Göttingen: Vandenhoeck & Ruprecht.

———. 1994. *M. Tullius Cicero: The Fragmentary Speeches*[2]. Atlanta: Scholars Press.

Crawford, M. 1982. *The Roman Republic*. Cambridge, Mass.: Harvard University Press.

———, ed. 1996. *Roman Statutes* (*BICS* Supplement 64). London: Institute of Classical Studies, School of Advanced Study, University of London.

Crook, J. 1967. *Law and Life of Rome*. London: Thames & Hudson.

———. 1976. "*Sponsione Provocare*: Its Place in Roman Litigation," *JRS* 66.132–38.

———. 1995. *Legal Advocacy in the Roman World*. Ithaca: Cornell University Press.

Daube, D. 1956. *Forms of Roman Legislation*. Oxford: Oxford University Press.

David, J.-M. 1992. *Le patronat judiciaire au dernier siècle de la république romaine* (*BEFAR* 277). Rome: École française de Rome.

———, et al. 1973. "Le 'Commentariolum Petitionis' de Quintus Cicéron: État de la question et étude prosopographique," *ANRW* 1.3.239–77.

Deniaux, E. 1987. "De l'ambitio a l'ambitus: Les lieux de la propagande et de la corruption electorale a la fin de la Republique," *Coll. Ec. Fr. Rome* 98.279–304 (= *L'Urbs Espace urbain et histoire*).

DeRobertis, F. 1938. *Il diritto associativo romano*[16]. Bari: Laterza.

———. 1971. *Storia delle corporazioni e del Regime Associativo nel mondo romano I*. Bari: Laterza.

Derrida, J. 1992. *Given Time: I. Counterfeit Money*, trans. P. Kamuf. Chicago: University of Chicago Press.

Dessau, H. 1911. "Gaius Rabirius Postumus," *Hermes* 46.613–20.

Dixon, S. 1993. "The Meaning of Gift and Debt in the Roman Elite," *CV* 37.451–64.

Dunbabin, K., and M. Dickie. 1983. "*Invidia Rumpantur Pectora*: The Iconography of Phthonos/Invidia in Graeco-Roman Art," *JAC* 26.7–37.

Duplá-Ansuategui, A. 1990. "El Senatus consultum ultimum: Medida de salvación pública o práctica de depurción política?," *Latomus* 49.75–80.

Dyer, R. 1990. "Rhetoric and Intention in Cicero's *pro Marcello*," *JRS* 80.17–30.

Earl, D. 1960. "Political Terminology in Plautus," *Historia* 9.235–43.

———. 1967. *The Moral and Political Tradition of Rome*. Ithaca: Cornell University Press.

Egan, T. 1995. "One Juror Smiled: Then They Knew," *New York Times* 145 (Oct. 4, 1995) A11, national edition.

Enos, R. 1984. "Heuristic Structures of Dispositio in Oral and Written Rhetorical Composition: An Addendum to Och's Analysis of the Verrine Orations," *CSSJ* 35.77–83.

———. 1988. *The Literate Mode of Cicero's Legal Rhetoric*. Carbondale: Southern Illinois University Press.

Epstein, D. 1987. *Personal Enmity in Roman Politics, 218–43 B.C.* London: Croom Helm.

Ewins, U. 1960. "Ne Quis Iudicio Circumveniatur," *JRS* 50.94–107.

Fantham, E. 1972. *Comparative Studies in Republican Latin Imagery*. Toronto: University of Toronto Press.

———. 1975. "The Trials of Gabinius in 54 B.C.," *Historia* 24.425–43.

Fascione, L. 1984. *Crimen e quaestio ambitus nell'età repubblicana*. Milan: A. Giuffrè.

Fausset, W., ed. 1887. *M. Tulli Ciceronis pro A. Cluentio Oratio* London: Rivingtons.

Fedeli, P., ed. 1987. *Manualetto di campagna elettorale*. Rome: Salerno editrice.

Feldherr, A. 1991. *Spectacle and Society in Livy's History* (diss. University of California, Berkeley).

Ferguson, J. 1989. "Cultural Exchange: New Developments in the Anthropology of Commodities" (review of Appadurai 1986a), *Cultural Anthropology* 3.488–513.

Ferrary, J.-L. 1979. "Recherches sur la legislation de Saturninus et de Glaucia, II: La loi de iudiciis repetundarum de C. Servilius Glaucia," *MEFRA* 91.85–134.

———. 1991. "Lex Cornelia de Sicariis et Veneficis," *Athenaeum* 79.417–34.

Finley, M. 1985. *Ancient History: Evidence and Models*. London: Chatto & Windus.

Fornara, C. 1983. *The Nature of History in Ancient Greece and Rome*. Berkeley: University of California Press.

Foucault, M. 1977. *Discipline and Punish: The Birth of the Prison*, trans. A. Sheridan. New York: Pantheon Books.

———. 1978. *The History of Sexuality*, volume I: *An Introduction*, trans. R. Hurley. New York: Pantheon Books.

Franklin, J. 1980. *Pompeii: The Electoral Programmata, Campaigns, and Politics*, A.D. 71–79 (*Papers and Monographs of the American Academy in Rome* 28). Rome: American Academy in Rome.

Franko, G. 1994. "The Use of Poenus and Carthaginiensis in Early Latin Literature," *CP* 89.153–58.

Frier, B. 1980. *Landlords and Tenants in Imperial Rome*. Princeton: Princeton University Press.

———. 1985. *The Rise of the Roman Jurists: Studies in Cicero's* pro Caecina. Princeton: Princeton University Press.

Garnsey, P. 1966. "The *lex Iulia* and Appeal under the Empire," *JRS* 56.167–89.

———. 1967. "Adultery Trials and the Survival of the Quaestiones in the Severan Age," *JRS* 57.56–60.

———. 1970. *Social Status and Legal Privilege in the Roman Empire*. Oxford: Oxford University Press.

Geffcken, K. 1973. *Comedy in the* pro Caelio, *with an Appendix on the* in Clodium et Curionem (*Mnemosyne* Supplement 30). Leiden: Brill.

Gerhardt, M. 1996. *The Federal Impeachment Process: A Historical and Constitutional Analysis*. Princeton: Princeton University Press.

Giddens, A. 1984. *The Constitution of Society*. Berkeley: University of California Press.

———. 1987. *The Nation-State and Violence*. Berkeley: University of California Press.

Girard, C. 1913. "Les leges Iuliae iudicorum publicorum et privatorum," *ZSS* 34.295–372.

Gordon, A. 1983. *Illustrated Introduction to Latin Epigraphy*. Berkeley: University of California Press.

Gotoff, H. 1986. "Cicero's Analysis of the Prosecution Speeches in the *pro Caelio*: An Exercise in Practical Criticism," *CP* 81.122–32.

———. 1993. "Oratory: The Art of Illusion," *HSCP* 95.289–313.

Greenidge, A. 1901. *The Legal Procedure of Cicero's Time*. Oxford: Oxford University Press.

Gregory, C. 1982. *Gifts and Commodities*. New York: Academic Press.

Gruen, E. 1965. "The *Lex Varia*," *JRS* 55.59–73.

———. 1968. *Roman Politics and the Criminal Courts, 149–78 B.C.* Cambridge, Mass.: Harvard University Press.

———. 1969. "Notes on the 'First Catilinarian Conspiracy,'" *CP* 64.20–24.

———. 1973. "The Trial of C. Antonius," *Latomus* 32.301–10.

———. 1974. *The Last Generation of the Roman Republic*. Berkeley: University of California Press.

———. 1991. "The Exercise of Power in the Roman Republic," in A. Molho, K. Raaflaub, and J. Emlen, eds., *City States in Classical Antiquity and Medieval Italy*, pp. 251–67. Ann Arbor: University of Michigan Press.

Halm, C., ed. 1983. *Rhetores Latini Minores*. Leipzig: Teubner.

Harris, W. 1986. "The Roman Father's Power of Life and Death," in R. Bagnall and W. Harris, eds., *Studies in Roman Law in Memory of A. Arthur Schiller*, pp. 81–95. Leiden: Brill.

———. 1990. "On Defining the Political Culture of the Roman Republic: Some Comments on Rosenstein, Williamson, and North," *CP* 85.288–94.

Hassall, M., M. Crawford, and J. Reynolds. 1974. "Rome and the Eastern Provinces at the End of the Second Century B.C.," *JRS* 64.195–220.

Heath, M. 1994. "The Substructure of Stasis-Theory from Hermagoras to Hermogenes," *CQ* 44.114–29.

Heinze, R. 1925. "Ciceros Rede pro Caelio," *Hermes* 60.193–258.

Hellegouarc'h, J. 1972. *Le vocabulaire latin des relations et des partis politiques sous la republique*[2]. Paris: Les Belles Lettres.

Henderson, M. 1950. "De Commentariolo Petitionis," *JRS* 40.8–21.

Hendrickson, G. 1933. "The Memoirs of Rutilius Rufus," *CP* 28.153–75.

Hess, R. 1966. *Italian Colonialism in Somalia*. Chicago: University of Chicago Press.

Hoenigswald, G. 1962. "The Murder Charges in Cicero's *pro Cluentio*," *TAPA* 93.109–23.

Honoré, A. 1962. *Gaius*. Oxford: Oxford University Press.

Hopkins, K. 1983. *Death and Renewal (Sociological Studies in Roman History* 2). Cambridge: Cambridge University Press.

Hough, J. 1930. "The *lex Lutatia* and the *lex Plautia de Vi*," *AJP* 51.135–47.

Humbert, J. 1925. *Les plaidoyers ecrits et les plaidoires realles de Cicéron*. Paris: Presses universitaires de France.

———. 1938. "Comment Cicéron mystifia les juges de Cluentius," *RÉL* 16.275–96.

Huschke, P., E. Seckel, and B. Kuebler, eds. 1908. *Iurisprudentiae Anteiustinianae Reliquiae*[6]. Leipzig: Teubner.

Impeachment Inquiry Staff, Committee on the Judiciary of the U.S. House of Representatives. n.d. "Constitutional Grounds for Presidential Impeachment." Washington, D.C.

Isaac, B. 1984. "Bandits in Judea and Arabia," *HSCP* 88.172–203.

Jackendoff, R. 1983. *Semantics and Cognition*. Cambridge, Mass.: MIT Press.

Jones, A. 1972. *The Criminal Courts of the Roman Republic and Principate*. Totowa, N.J.: Rowman and Littlefield.

Jones, H. 1992. "L'ordre penal de la Rome antique: Contexture et limites," *Latomus* 51.753–61.

Jongman, W. 1988. *The Economy and Society of Pompeii*. Amsterdam: J. C. Gieben.

Jouanique, P. 1960. "Sur l'interpretation du pro Fonteio 1.1–2," *RÉL* 38.107–12.

Kallet-Marx, R. 1990. "The Trial of Rutilius Rufus," *Phoenix* 44.122–39.

Kaser, M. 1966. *Das römische Zivilprozessrecht*. Munich: C. H. Beck.

———. 1986. "'Ius publicum' und 'ius privatum,'" *ZSS* 103.1–101.

Kelly, J. 1966. *Roman Litigation*. Oxford: Oxford University Press.

Kennedy, G. 1968. "The Rhetoric of Advocacy in Greece and Rome," *AJP* 89.419–36.

———. 1969. *Quintilian (Twayne's World Authors* 59). New York: Twayne Publishers.

———. 1972. *The Art of Rhetoric in the Roman World, 300 B.C.–A.D. 300*. Princeton: Princeton University Press.

Kent, R. 1946. *The Forms of Latin: A Descriptive and Historical Morphology*. Baltimore: Linguistic Society of America.

Kinsey, T. 1975. "Cicero's Speech for Roscius of Ameria," *So* 50.91–104.

———. 1980. "Cicero's Case against Magnus, Capito, and Chrysogonus in the *pro Sex. Roscio Amerino* and Its Use for the Historian," *AntCl* 49.173–90.

Kirby, J. 1990. *The Rhetoric of Cicero's pro Cluentio*. Amsterdam: J. C. Gieben.

Klodt, C. 1992. *Ciceros Rede Pro Rabirio Postumo*. Stuttgart: Teubner.

Kroll, W. 1937. "Ciceros Rede für Plancius," *RhM* 86.127–39.

Kroon, C. 1989. "Causal Connectors in Latin: The Discourse Functions of Nam, Enim, Igitur, and Ergo," *Cahiers de l'institut de linguistique de Louvain* 15.231–43.

Kunkel, W. 1962. *Untersuchungen zur Entwicklung des romischen Kriminalverfahrens in vorsullanscher Zeit (Bayerische Akademie der Wissenschaften, Abhandlungen, Philosophische-Historische Klasse*, NF 65).

———. 1963. "Quaestio," *RE* 24.720–96.

———. 1967. *Herkunft und soziale Stellung der römischen Juristen* [2] *(Forschungen zum römischen Recht* 4). Graz: Böhlau.

———. 1973. *An Introduction to Roman Legal and Constitutional History* [2], trans. J. Kelly. Oxford: Oxford University Press.

Kurke, A. 1989. *Theme and Adversarial Presentation in Cicero's* pro Flacco (diss. University of Michigan, Ann Arbor).

Kurke, L. 1989. "{ΚΑΠΗΛΕΙΑ} and Deceit: Theognis 59–60," *AJP* 110.535–44.

———. 1990. "Counterfeit Friends: Alkaian Invective and the Origin of Coinage" (MS, University of California, Berkeley). *Helios*.

———. 1991. *The Traffic in Praise: Pindar and the Poetics of Social Economy*. Ithaca: Cornell University Press.

Labruna, L. 1971. *Vim fieri veto: alle radici di una ideologia*. Naples: Jovene.

———. 1975. *Il console 'sovversivo.'* Naples: Jovene.

Lakoff, G. 1987. *Women, Fire, and Dangerous Things*. Chicago: University of Chicago Press.

Lakoff, G., and M. Johnson. 1980. *Metaphors We Live By*. Chicago: University of Chicago Press.

Lakoff, R. 1990. *Talking Power: The Politics of Language*. New York: Basic Books.

Landgraf, G. 1914. *Kommentar zu Ciceros Rede Pro Sex. Roscio Amerino* [2]. Leipzig: Teubner.

Last, H. 1949. "Rome and the Druids: A Note," *JRS* 39.1–5.

Laughton, E. 1942. "The Learner and the Latin Period," *GR* 11.84–91.

Laurand, L. 1928–31. *Études sur le style des discours de Ciceron* [3], 3 vols. Paris: Les Belles Lettres.

LeBenniec, H., and G. Vallet, eds. 1980. *Melanges de litterature et d'epigraphie latines, d'histoire ancienne et d'archeologie: Hommage á la memoire de Pierre Wuilleumier (Collection d'etudes latines, serie scientifique* 35). Paris: Les Belles Lettres.

Leeman, A. 1982. "The Technique of Persuasion in Cicero's *pro Murena*," pp. 193–228 (236) in Ludwig 1982.

Lemosse, M. 1944. *Cognitio: Étude sur le role du juge dans l'instruction du procès civil antique (Studia Iuridica* 63). Paris: A. Lesot.

Leps, M.-C. 1992. *Apprehending the Criminal: The Production of Deviance in Nineteenth Century Discourse*. Durham: Duke University Press.

Levick, B. 1967. "Acerbissima Lex Servilia," *CR* 71.256–58.

Liebs, D. 1989. "Römische Jurisprudenz in Afrika," *ZSS* 160.210–47.

Linderski, J. 1961. "Ciceros Rede pro Caelio und die Ambitus- und Vereinsgesetzgebung der ausgehenden Republik," *Hermes* 89.106–19.

———. 1985. "Buying the Vote: Electoral Corruption in the Late Republic," *AW* 11.87–94.

Lintott, A. 1968. *Violence in Republican Rome*. Oxford: Oxford University Press.

———. 1974. "Cicero and Milo," *JRS* 64.61–78.

———. 1976a. "Notes on the Roman Law Inscribed at Delphi and Cnidos," *ZPE* 20.66–82.

———. 1976b. "The Procedure under the *Leges Calpurnia* and *Iunia de Repetundis* and the *Actio per Sponsionem*," *ZPE* 22.207–14.

———. 1981. "The *Leges de Repetundis* and Associate Measures under the Republic," *ZSS* 98.162–212.

———. 1990. "Electoral Bribery in the Roman Republic," *JRS* 80.1–16.

———. 1992. *Judicial Reform and Land Reform in the Roman Republic*. Cambridge: Cambridge University Press.

Liou-Gille, B. 1994. "La perduellio: Les procès d'Horace et de Rabirius," *Latomus* 58.3–38.

Longo, G. 1960. "L'onere della prova nel processo civile romano," *Iura* 11.149–82.

Ludwig, W., ed. 1982. *Eloquence et rhetorique chez Cicéron (Entretiens sur l'Antiquite Classique* 28). Geneva: Fondation Hardt.

Mackay, C. 1995. Review of Lintott 1992, *BMCR* 95-4–15.

MacMullen, R. 1974. *Roman Social Relations*. New Haven: Yale University Press.

Magdelain, A. 1973. "Remarques sur la perduellio," *Historia* 22.405–22.

———. 1984. "Paricidas," pp. 549–70 in *Du châtiment dans la cité (Collection de l'école française de Rome* 79).

Marshall, B. 1987. "*Excepta Oratio*, the Other *pro Milone*, and the Question of Shorthand," *Latomus* 46.730–36.

Massengil, R. 1994. *Portrait of a Racist*. New York: St. Martin's Press.

May, J. 1988. *Trials of Character: The Eloquence of Ciceronian Ethos*. Chapel Hill: University of North Carolina Press.

Mendner, S. 1966. "Videant Consules," *Philologus* 110.258–66.

Mercer, P. 1983. "The Citizen's Right to Sue in the Public Interest: The Roman *Actio Popularis* Revisited," *University of Western Ontario Law Review* 21.89–103.

Michel, A. 1960. *Rhetorique et philosophie chez Cicéron: Essai sur les fondemonts philosophiques de l'art de persuader*. Paris: Presses universitaires de France.

Millar, F. 1977, afterword 1992. *The Emperor in the Roman World (31 B.C.–A.D. 337)*. Ithaca: Cornell University Press.

Minyard, J. 1985. *Lucretius and the Late Republic: An Essay in Roman Intellectual History (Mnemosyne* Supplement 90). Leiden: Brill.

Mitchel, T. 1971. "Cicero and the Senatus Consultum Ultimum," *Historia* 20.41–61.

Mitchell, R. 1990. *Patricians and Plebians: The Origin of the Roman State*. Ithaca: Cornell University Press.

Mommsen, T. 1887. *Romisches Staatsrecht*[3]. Leipzig: S. Hirzel.

———. 1899. *Romisches Strafrecht*. Leipzig: Duncker & Humblot.

Morgan, M. 1993. Review of Woodman 1988, *Plutarchos* 9.34–37.

Morris, I. 1986. "Gift and Commodity in Archaic Greece," *Man* 21.1–17.

———. 1992. "The Early Polis as City and State," in J. Rich and A. Wallace-Hadrill, eds., *City and Country in the Ancient World*, pp. 25–57. London: Routledge.

Nardo, D. 1970. *Il "Commentariolum Petitionis": La propaganda elettorale nella "ars" di Quinto Cicerone*. Padua: Liviana.

Nicholas, B. 1962. *An Introduction to Roman Law*. Oxford: Oxford University Press.

Nicholson, J. 1994. "The Delivery and Confidentiality of Cicero's Letters," *CJ* 90.33–63.

Nicolet, C. 1966. *L'ordre equestre a l'epoque republicaine (312–43 av. J.-C.) (BEFAR* 207). Paris: E. de Boccard.

———. 1980. *The World of the Citizen in Republican Rome*, trans. P. S. Falla. Berkeley: University of California Press.

Nippel, W. 1984. "Policing Rome," *JRS* 74.20–29.

———. 1988. *Aufruhr und "Polizei" in der römischen Republik*. Stuttgart: Klett-Cotta.

———. 1995. *Public Order in Ancient Rome*. Cambridge: Cambridge University Press.

Nisbet, R. 1961. "The *Commentariolum Petitionis*: Some Arguments against Authenticity," *JRS* 51.84–87.

Nörr, D. 1986. *Causa Mortis (Münchener Beiträge zur Papyrusforschung und antiken Rechtsgeschichte* 80). Munich: C. H. Beck.

North, J. 1990. "Politics and Aristocracy in the Roman Republic," *CP* 85.277–87.

Nossiter, A. 1994. *Of Long Memory: Mississippi and the Murder of Medgar Evers*. Reading, Mass.: Addison-Wesley.

Ochs, E. 1982. "Rhetorical Detailing in Cicero's Verrine Orations," *CSSJ* 33.310–18.

Ogilvie, R. 1965. *Commentary on Livy, Books 1–5*. Oxford: Oxford University Press.

Oost, S. 1956. "The Date of the *lex Iulia de Repetundis*," *AJP* 77.19–28.

Opelt, I. 1965. *Die lateinischen Schimpfwörter und verwandte sprachliche Erscheinungen*. Heidelberg: C. Winter.

Ormerod, H. 1924. *Piracy in the Ancient World*. Liverpool: The University Press of Liverpool Ltd.

Parry, J., and M. Bloch, eds. 1989. *Money and the Morality of Exchange*. Cambridge: Cambridge University Press.

Paterson, J. 1985. "Politics in the Late Republic," pp. 21–43 in Wiseman 1985.

Perelli, L. 1994. *La corruzione politica nell'antica Roma*. Milan: Rizzoli.

Perelman, C., and L. Olbrechts-Tyteca. 1958. *La nouvelle rhetorique: Traite de l'argumentation*. Paris: Presses universitaires de France.

Philips, E. 1970. "Cicero and the Prosecution of C. Manilius," *Latomus* 29.595–607.

Pontenay de Fontette, F. 1954. *Leges Repetundarum*. Paris: Librairie générale de droit et de jurisprudence.

Pöschl, V. 1961. "'Invidia' in Reden Ciceros," pp. 11–16 in V. Pöschl and W.-L. Liebermann, eds., *Literatur und geschichtliche Wirklichkeit* (Heidelberg, C. Winter) = *Bibliothek der klassischen Altertumswissenschaften*, NF, 2R, 74, 1983.

Preiswerk, R. 1905. *De Inventione Orationum Ciceronianarum* (diss. Basel).

Prichard, A. 1961. *Leage's Roman Private Law* [3]. London: Macmillan.

Pugliese, G. 1956. "L'onere della prova nel processo romano per formulas," *RIDA* 3.349–422.

———. 1960. "La prova nel processo romano classico," *Ius* 11.386–424.

———. 1982. "Linee generali dell'evoluzione del diritto penale publico durante il principato," *ANRW* 2.14.722–89.

Radin, M. 1920. "The *lex Pompeia* and the *Poena Cullei*," *JRS* 10.119–30.

Rambaud, M. 1980. "Le pro Fonteio et l'assimilation des Gaulois de la Transalpine," pp. 301–16 in LeBenniec and Vallet 1980.

Ramsey, J. 1980a. "The Prosecution of C. Manilius in 66 B.C. and Cicero's *pro Manilio*," *Phoenix* 34.323–36.

———. 1980b. "A Reconstruction of Q. Gallius' Trial for Ambitus," *Historia* 29.402–21.

Reynolds, P. 1926. *The Vigiles of Imperial Rome*. London: Oxford University Press.

Riccobono, R., J. Baviera, C. Ferrini, J. Furlani, and V. Arangio-Ruiz, eds. 1940. *Fontes Iuris Romani Anteiustiniani*, 3 vols. Florence: S. a. G. Barbèra (= *FIRA*).

Richardson, J. 1971. "The *Commentariolum Petitionis*," *Historia* 20.436–42.

——. 1987. "The Purpose of the *Lex Calpurnia de Repetundis*," *JRS* 77.1–12.

Richlin, A. 1992. *The Garden of Priapus: Sexuality and Aggression in Roman Humor*[2]. New York: Oxford University Press.

Riggsby, A. 1995a. "Self-Fashioning in the Public Eye: Pliny on Cicero and Oratory," *AJP* 116.123–35.

——. 1995b. "Appropriation and Reversal as a Basis for Oratorical Proof," *CP* 90.245–56.

——. 1997. "Did the Romans Believe in Their Verdicts?," *Rhetorica* 15.235–51.

——. Forthcoming. "Iulius Victor and Cicero's Defenses *de repetundis*," *RhM*.

Robinson, O. 1981. "Slaves and the Criminal Law," *ZSS* 98.213–54.

——. 1995. *The Criminal Law of Ancient Rome*. Baltimore: Johns Hopkins University Press.

——. 1997. *The Sources of Roman Law*. London: Routledge.

Rohde, F. 1903. *Cicero Quae de Inventione Praecepit Quatenus Secutus Sit in Orationibus Generis Iudicalis* (diss. Koenigsburg).

Rosch, E., et al. 1975. *Basic Objects in Natural Categories* (*Language Behavior Research Lab Working Paper* 43). Berkeley: University of California, Language Behavior Research Laboratory.

Rose, P. 1995. "Cicero and the Rhetoric of Imperialism: Putting the Politics Back into Political Rhetoric," *Rhetorica* 13.359–99.

Rosenstein, N. 1990. Imperatores Victi: *Military Defeat and Aristocratic Competition in the Middle and Late Republic*. Berkeley: University of California Press.

Rotondi, G. 1912. *Leges Publicae Populi Romani*. Milan: Società editrice libraria.

Rubin, Z. 1975. "Further to the Dating of the *Constitutio Antoniniana*," *Latomus* 34.430–36.

Ruebel, J. 1979. "The Trial of Milo in 52 B.C.: A Chronological Study," *TAPA* 109.231–49.

Sachers, E. 1953. "Potestas Patria," *RE* 22.1046–175.

Sahlins, M. 1972. *Stone Age Economics*. Chicago: Aldine-Atherton.

St. Clair, J., et al. n.d. "An Analysis of the Constitutional Standard for Presidential Impeachment." Washington, D.C.

Saller, R. 1995. *Patriarchy, Property, and Death in the Roman Family*. Cambridge: Cambridge University Press.

Sanderson, G. 1951. *India and British Imperialism*. New York: Bookman Associates.

Santalucia, B. 1989. *Diritto e processo penale nell'antica Roma*. Milan: Giuffrè.

Scheppele, K. 1991. "Facing Facts in Legal Interpretation," in R. Post, ed., *Law and the Order of Culture*, pp. 42–77. Berkeley: University of California Press.

Schulz, F. 1946. *History of Roman Legal Science*. Oxford: Oxford University Press.

Scott, J. 1990. *Domination and the Arts of Resistance: Hidden Transcripts*. New Haven: Yale University Press.

Seager, R. 1964. "The First Catilinarian Conspiracy," *Historia* 13.338–47.

Serrao, F. 1956. "Appunti sui 'patroni' e sulla legittimazione all'accusa nei processi 'repetundarum,'" in *Studi in onore di Pietro de Francisci*, vol. 2, pp. 471–511. Milan: Giuffrè.

Settle, J. 1962. *The Publication of Cicero's Orations* (diss. Chapel Hill).

Shaw, B. 1975. "Debt in Sallust," *Latomus* 34.187–96.

——. 1984. "Bandits in the Roman Empire," *Past and Present* 105.3–52.

Sherwin-White, A. 1972. "The Date of the *Lex Repetundarum* and Its Consequences," *JRS* 62.83–99.

——. 1973. *The Roman Citizenship*[2]. Oxford: Oxford University Press.

———. 1982. "The *Lex Repetundarum* and the Political Ideas of Gaius Gracchus," *JRS* 72.18–31.

Stockton, D. 1979. *The Gracchi*. Oxford: Oxford University Press.

Stone, A. 1980. "*Pro Milone*: Cicero's Second Thoughts," *Antichthon* 14.88–111.

Stowers, S. 1986. *Letter Writing in Greco-Roman Antiquity*. Philadelphia: Westminster Press.

Strachan-Davison, L. 1912. *Problems of the Roman Criminal Law*, vol. 2. Oxford: Clarendon.

Strathern, M. 1987. "Out of Context: The Persuasive Fictions of Anthropology," *Current Anthropology* 28.251–81.

Stroh, W. 1975. *Taxis und Taktik: Ciceros Gerichtsreden*. Stuttgart: Teubner.

Strzelecki, W. 1958. "Über die Coniectanea des Ateius Capito," *Hermes* 86.246–50.

Suohlati, J. 1955. *The Junior Officers of the Roman Army in the Republican Period* (*Annales Academiae Scientiarum Fennicae* B97). Helsinki: Suomalainen Tiedeakatemia.

Sutton, D. 1964. "Cicero on Minor Dramatic Forms," *SO* 59.29–36.

Swarney, P. 1993. "Social Status and Social Behaviour as Criteria in Judicial Proceedings in the Late Republic," in B. Halpern and D. Hobson, eds., *Law, Politics, and Society in the Ancient Mediterranean World*, pp. 137–55. Sheffield: Sheffield Academic Press.

Syme, R. 1958. "*Imperator Caesar*: A Study in Nomenclature," *Historia* 7.172–88.

Taylor, L. 1949. *Party Politics in the Age of Caesar* (*Sather Classical Lectures* 22). Berkeley: University of California Press.

Tellegen-Couperus, O. 1993. *A Short History of Roman Law*. London: Routledge.

Thomas, Y. 1981. "Parricidium I: Le pere, la famille, et la cite," *MEFRA* 93.643–715.

Tibiletti, G. 1953. "Le leggi de iudiciis repetundarum fino alla guerra sociale," *Athenaeum* 31.5–100.

Treggiari, S. 1969. *Roman Freedmen during the Late Republic*. Oxford: Oxford University Press.

———. 1991. *Roman Marriage*. Oxford: Oxford University Press.

Usener, H. 1901. "Italische Volksjustiz," *RhM* 56.1–21.

Vasaly, A. 1985. "The Masks of Rhetoric: Cicero's *pro Roscio Amerino*," *Rhetorica* 2.1–20.

———. 1993. *Representations: Images of the World in Ciceronian Oratory*. Berkeley: University of California Press.

Vaughn, J. 1985. "Law and Rhetoric in the *Causa Curiana*," *CA* 4.208–22.

Venturini, C. 1979. *Studi sul "Crimen Repetundarum" nell'età Repubblicana* (*Pubblicazioni della Facoltà di Giurisprudenza della Università di Pisa* 69). Milan: Giuffrè.

Vitzthum, W. 1966. *Untersuchungen zum materiallen Inhalt der Lex Plautia und Lex Iulia de vi* (diss. Munich).

Wagenvoort, H. 1947. *Roman Dynamism: Studies in Ancient Roman Thought, Language, and Custom*. Oxford: Blackwell.

Watson, A. 1965. *The Law of Obligations in the Later Roman Republic*. Oxford: Oxford University Press.

———. 1968. *Law of Property in the Later Roman Republic*. Oxford: Oxford University Press.

———. 1974. *Law Making in the Later Roman Republic*. Oxford: Oxford University Press.

———. 1979. "The Death of Horatia," *CQ* 29.436–47.

———. 1985. *The Evolution of Law*. Baltimore: Johns Hopkins University Press.

———. 1995. *The Spirit of Roman Law*. Athens, Ga.: University of Georgia Press.

Weber, M., G. Roth, and C. Wittich, eds. 1978. *Economy and Society*. Berkeley: University of California Press.

Webster, T., ed. 1931. *M. Tulli Ciceronis: pro L. Flacco Oratio*. Oxford: Clarendon Press.

Welsch, R. 1991. "How to Bear Gifts," *Natural History* 100/12.63–66.

White, H. 1973. *Metahistory: The Historical Imagination in Nineteenth Century Europe*. Baltimore: Johns Hopkins University Press.

———. 1978. *Tropics of Discourse: Essays in Cultural Criticism*. Baltimore: Johns Hopkins University Press.

———. 1987. *The Content of the Form: Narrative Discourse and Historical Representation*. Baltimore: Johns Hopkins University Press.

Williamson, C. 1990. "The Roman Aristocracy and Positive Law," *CP* 85.226–76.

Wirszubski, C. 1954. "Cicero's *cum Dignitate Otium*: A Reconsideration," *JRS* 44.1–13.

———. 1961. "*Audaces*: A Study in Political Phraseology," *JRS* 51.12–22.

Wiseman, T. 1967. "T. Cloelius of Tarracina," *CR* 81.263–64.

———. 1970. "The Definition of 'Equus Romanus,'" *Historia* 19.67–83.

———, ed. 1985. *Roman Political Life, 90 B.C.–A.D. 69* (*Exeter Studies in History* 7). Exeter: University of Exeter.

Wolff, H. 1951. *Roman Law: An Historical Introduction*. Norman: University of Oklahoma Press.

Wood, N. 1988. *Cicero's Social and Political Thought*. Berkeley: University of California Press.

Woodman, A. 1988. *Rhetoric in Classical Historiography*. London: Croom Helm.

Yakobson, A. 1992. "*Petitio et Largito*: Popular Participation in the Centuriate Assembly of the Late Republic," *JRS* 82.32–52.

Yavetz, Z. 1984. "The Res Gestae and Augustus' Public Image," pp. 1–36 in Millar and Segal 1984.

Zarefsky, D. 1987. "Argument as Hypothesis-Testing," in D. Thomas and J. Hart, eds., *Advanced Debate: Readings in Theory, Practice, and Teaching*[3], pp. 205–15. Lincolnwood: National Textbook Co.

Zetzel, J. 1993. Review of Craig 1993, *BMCR* 4.446–51.

Ziegenmueller, J., and C. Dause. 1990. *Argumentation: Inquiry and Advocacy*. Englewood Cliffs: Prentice Hall.

Zumpt, A. 1868–69. *Das Criminalrecht der Romischen Republik*, zweiter band (erste abtheilung [1868], zweite abtheilung [1869]). Berlin: F. Dümmler.

General Index

NOTE: *The general index is followed by an* index locorum. *Romans are listed under the conventional English forms of their names if such exist, otherwise under their* nomina. *In the general index, primary discussions of a topic are noted in* **bold face**, *and references to all laws may be found under the heading* leges. *In the* index locorum, *only passages individually quoted or interpreted are listed.*

adultery, 158, 224, 226
ambitus, 7, 12–13, 18, 21–49, 151–152, 158,
    162, 168, 173, 203, 204, 226
  and *sodalicia*, 22–23, 46, 199
  vs. other offenses, 61, 64, 75–76, 88, 100,
    139, 150, 153–156
  arguments
    from character, 29, 37–38, 56–61, 68,
      70–71, 78, 84–89, 136–139, 153, 169,
      197–198
    from motive, 57–59, 70, 77, 202
    from opportunity, 59, 77, 85
    from place, 60, 63, 85, 107, 190, 210
    from time, 107, 210
audience, 3, 10, 112, 118–119, 189, 205
authority of texts, 25, 47

bandits (*latrones*), 51, 116–117, 200, 213–
  214
beneficium. See exchange
boni, 64–65, 87–89, 92–93, 145, 154, 167,
  209
burden of proof,
  legal, 15, 191
  rhetorical, 28, 31, 41, 56, 59, 66–67, 69,
    84, 99, 103, 196

Caelius Rufus, Marcus, 10
Cassius Longinus Ravilla, Lucius, 16
Catiline, Lucius Sergius, 9, 79–80, 84–85,
  89, 144, 186, 208, 210

Cato, Marcus Porcius (pr. 54), 12, 35, 36,
  38–39
causa mortis, 166–167, 201, 227
Chrysogonus, 60, 65, 137, 204
Cicero, Marcus Tullius (selected references
  only), 3, 5, 12, 84, 111, 116, 182–183
Clodius Pulcher, Publius, 23, 92, 95, 105–
  112, 118, 188, 191, 195
cognitio, 164
collusion, 5–9
constitutio. See status
contentio dignitatis, 29–30, 38, 41–42, 198
contra rem publicam, 80–83, 89, 92, 97, 100,
  102–103, 112, 153–154, 158, 208
Cornelius, Gaius (tr. pl. 67), 81, 84, 178, 185,
  194
crime, 5, 163–171
  words for, 163, 202

debt, 86, 203, 209, 210
declamation, 166–167, 224
decuratio, 22–23, 30
dilemma, 63–64, 70, 99, 103
Dio (murder victim), 80, 97, 102
dolus. See intent
double jeopardy, 54, 139

equites, 17–18, 30, 226
  vs. senators, 7, 53–54, 121, 140–143,
    149–150
  vs. *tribuni aerarii*, 222

Index Locorum